THE
FORTUNATE FEW

IVS VOLUNTEERS
From Asia To The Andes

THE FORTUNATE FEW

IVS VOLUNTEERS
From Asia To The Andes

Thierry J. Sagnier

NCNM Press
Portland, Oregon

Photographs provided by IVS volunteers
Back cover photo:
Frank Bewetz helps build a school in Kengkok, Laos, 1966

For permission to reproduce selections from this book, write to:

NCNM Press
National College of Natural Medicine
049 SW Porter Street
Portland, Oregon 97201
www.ncnm.edu

ISBN: 10-digit number 0-9771435-7-0
13-digit number paperback 978-0-9771435-7-3

Library of Congress Control Number: 2015909683

Production by Fourth Lloyd Productions, LLC
Cover and book design by Richard Stodart

Printed in the USA

This book is dedicated to the eleven IVS volunteers
who lost their lives during hostile actions.

Fred Cheydleur
Martin J. Clish
Chandler Scott Edwards
David L. Gitelson
Peter M. Hunting
Dennis L. Mummert
Michael Murphy
Alexander D. Shimkin
Max Sinkler
Richard M. Sisk
Arthur Stillman

TABLE OF CONTENTS

FOREWORD

This is a story about people, generally young people, motivated to leave their homes, to venture to distant lands, to do good. They lived within cultures radically different from their own, observing, learning, sharing and helping others undertake the business of life. They interacted; they dug and built and sowed and reaped and taught. Some perished.

Theirs was the legacy of a group of individuals who had grown up early in the 20th century, before the WWII era, and who believed there was a role to play for young, idealistic volunteers living and working within traditional societies. This concept took form and grew and ultimately became known as the International Voluntary Services, IVS, to all who helped found and serve the organization.

Finances came from various sources, but predominantly from the U.S. Operations Mission within the U.S. Department of State.

This, then, was the post-WWII period when many countries were rebuilding from devastating conflicts, where the rule of colonial powers was already ebbing amidst a global awakening of nationalism. The U.S., victorious both economically and politically, could not overlook the glaring gaps of opportunity around the world, and this concern motivated IVS founders to initiate change and make a difference. Thus, in 1953, IVS was created. Under the guidance of a board of visionaries and led by Dr. John Noffsinger, whose original volunteer experiences as a Thomasite in 1910 heralded back to the Philippines.

This book is a collection of first-person voices, the voices of the volunteers, the ones who were eager to better lives on unfamiliar grounds.

Beyond the introduction, the book is divided into five decades of activities involving more than thirty countries. The first two decades were the most active and included initial projects in the Middle East, Iraq and Egypt, Nepal, and South Asia.

In 1956, three years after IVS opened its doors, Southeast Asian projects began to take form amidst the flow of refugees from North to South Vietnam that followed the Geneva Accords of 1954. Development projects in Laos began at about the same time.

Volunteers' stories from Southeast Asia inevitably include the experiences of men and women whose assignments became perilous as major conflicts began to emerge. With greater risk, lives often developed newer and greater meaning; close personal relationships were a necessity when situations heated up. Not unexpectedly, areas of conflict often determined where volunteers would be working.

In other areas such as Bangladesh or Algeria, newly acquired nationhood spawned equally daunting issues caused by new bureaucracies, unprepared personnel, and purposes often ill-defined. Each area produced its own circumstances. Here were opportunities to meet challenging problems, to accomplish, to develop new and lasting relationships, to fail, and to learn. Volunteers gained understanding and delivered solutions, even as the responsibilities faced in-country were often much greater than those a person of similar age might encounter in his or her own society.

IVS bridged a period when volunteerism within international development was very limited, if recognized at all, to a time when it became institutionalized with the 1961 establishment of the Peace Corps under the Kennedy administration. The years of experience IVS had already accumulated served the launching of the Peace Corps well. When retiring IVS Director Dr. John Noffsinger became a senior consultant in the establishment of the Peace Corps, he relied heavily on the IVS operational procedures that had already proven workable both within host countries and the U.S. government.

There are hundreds of IVS alums around the world today, many in positions of consequence. Those of us who experienced IVS first-hand feel the opportunities given by service have contributed monumentally to better understanding of a greater world.

This book offers in the volunteers' own words insights gathered during their activities in faraway lands.

And subsequently, one could speculate: How might their earlier undertakings and unique experiences have reshaped the world? That's a story yet to be told.

Mike Chilton
Vietnam 1960-65
President of IVS Alumni Association

Preface

Anne Shirk, the last Executive Director of IVS, approached me in 2012 and asked whether I'd be interested in putting together a collection of brief articles written by former IVS volunteers. At the time, I did not know what IVS was and had never heard of the organization. I wish I had. Some forty years ago, like many IVSers, I was a conscientious objector (CO) during the Vietnam War, and many COs became IVS volunteers.

I thought the project might take a few weeks at most. It took almost three years from start to finish. What began as a book for former volunteers became a history of their voices, their ambitions, their fears, and their accomplishments. As the work progressed, so did the sense of being involved in the creation of something both special and necessary.

I had to do some judicious editing. It should be noted here that what is in print does not come from a necessarily representative group of volunteers. Less than five percent of those who served with IVS contributed to this volume, and their opinions and experiences varied widely. While there simply was not enough space in this book to include everyone's every word, I made it a point not to alter opinions or criticisms, and I trust that after a dozen drafts and months of reviews, re-reads, and rewrites, this work remains true to the memories of the volunteers who were kind enough to send in their stories.

It's been three years well spent.

Thierry J. Sagnier

"I claim without exaggeration that of all my experiences, the time I spent in Laos with IVS has had the greatest impact on my life. I became who I am because of it."

—Alex McIntosh

IVS/Laos, 1967-70

"IVS has been the model for countless non-government organizations (NGOs) doing education and development work in host countries. The impact of IVS is everywhere."

—June Pulcini

IVS/Cambodia, 1963; IVS/Vietnam, 1964-65;

IVS/Laos, 1965-70

"How much did my time in Vietnam with IVS change my life? I continued to be a teacher all my life. Surely the many hardships, adventures, successes, and friendships with the Vietnamese taught me self-reliance."

—Forest Gerdes

IVS/Vietnam, 1962-64

Acknowledgements

This book could not have been produced without the assistance of the former IVS volunteers who patiently gave of their time to write and talk about their experiences far from home.

Specifically, the author would like to thank the International Volunteer Services Alumni Association Board of Directors and volunteer alumni at the Estes Park, Colorado, and St. Paul, Minnesota, reunions, who encouraged this endeavor.

Particular thanks go to Gary Alex, William Betts, Mike Chilton, and Anne Shirk who shepherded the project from beginning to end.

Linda Worthington and Carlie Numi were particularly helpful and supportive throughout the entire period.

Some stories were excerpted from *The IVS Experience— From Algeria to Vietnam,* edited by Stuart Rawlings.

We are grateful for the efforts of Frank Huffman, John Mellor, Rufus Phillips, and Paul Rodell who read the final draft of this book and offered wise advice.

The Mennonite Church USA Archives held in Goshen, Indiana, on the Goshen College campus, maintains the International Voluntary Services Inc. records and reports archives. These are made available to researchers and have been extremely helpful in researching specific questions and making materials available for the preparation of the book.

And lastly, our thanks to everyone who helped us search for and provide the photographs shown in these pages.

INTRODUCTION

Organizations come, organizations go. Many leave little behind save acronym-laden reports and sheaves of papers in dusty archives. Their accomplishments are forgotten, and the men and women who devoted years of their lives to achieving the organizations' missions are forgotten as well.

Other groups, such as the International Voluntary Services, make history. They quietly change lives for the better. Their achievements and successes are worth recording, remembering, and emulating not only for work well accomplished, but for lessons learned and passed on.

The strength of IVS, its triumphs and its accomplishments great and small, from 1953 in Egypt to 2002 in Bolivia, have everything to do with its volunteers. Without them much good would have been left undone.

This, then, is not the story of an organization; it is the story of the people who made the organization effective, the often unheralded workers, the fortunate few who went abroad not to sway opinions or conquer but to spread knowledge and better lives—theirs and those of others—in less privileged societies.

CHRISTIAN PACIFISM

IVS was created in 1953, its roots firmly embedded in the Christian pacifism of Mennonites, Quakers, and Brethren organizations, the latter descendants of the Anabaptists who flourished during the Protestant Reformation. From its inception, IVS was the work of a community of organizers whose primary advocates were *Dr. Dale Clark* and *Dr. John Noffsinger*.

Clark was a State Department employee and a seasoned Washington hand. After a stint aiding the Arab Development Society to set up a dairy program in Jordan, Clark approached Mennonite and Brethren representatives with a proposal: Would they be interested in setting up a voluntary organization employing Marshall Plan funds to help other Middle-Eastern nations?

A series of meetings to discuss staffing, personnel, financial and administrative matters followed, and IVS was born and named.

In *The New Partnership in International Development*, a paper written in July 1954, Clark cited IVS's background. He wrote: "International Voluntary Services, Inc., grew out of a desire on the part of private persons and organizations to support the technical assistance program, an effort in which they sincerely believed. Also, it met a need in our foreign technical assistance operations–the need for a technique to align the government effort more closely and systematically with the energy, experience and altruistic motivations of private voluntary agencies.

"The pattern is basically this: Several private organizations, some of them church connected, which possess spirit for foreign technical assistance work, have united to support a non-profit, non-denominational corporation under direction of a board of experienced and public-spirited Americans. Volunteer workers are recruited, trained and assigned to foreign village projects. Volunteers receive a nominal payment of $60 per month plus costs for tools, transportation and living expenses."

Clark's $60 a month probably came from his belief that volunteers should be paid the same stipend as Americans recruited in the U.S. armed forces.

Clark was soon introduced to Dr. John S. Noffsinger, a Brethren who as a young college graduate had already worked under the aegis of the U.S. government as a teacher with a volunteer organization in the Philippines. A former college president, Noffsinger was highly respected for his work with various academic and educational councils. Clark and Noffsinger met and the search for an IVS executive director ended there and then. Times were simpler then; no hearings, no committees, no lengthy interviews. No other candidates were considered; Noffsinger, according to Clark, "was perfect, and that's all there was to it."

APOLITICAL

IVS, from the very start, was non-denominational, completely apolitical, and free of government influence. The aim of this up-start organization was to promote people-to-people cooperation in poorer countries, to raise living standards and productivity. According to its original mission statement, IVS saw itself as "a mechanism for uniting the energies of individuals and private organizations."

Unlike other groups already in the field, IVS never sought to proselytize. It remained adamantly independent throughout its almost fifty years of existence, sending "young people without guns," in the words of one volunteer, to remote parts of the planet with the sole aim of improving the lot of fellow humans.

The first IVSers were two young American men, one Brethren and one Mennonite, who arrived in southern Egypt to help farmers in a village called Asyut increase their dairy and poultry produc-tions. Shortly after this an IVS office opened in Iraq, where teams improved village sanitation, agriculture, home construction, and nursing. Within a few years, there was a school in Nepal to train local community workers, while in Liberia, teams of instructors began teaching elementary grades. Projects were also set up in Ghana, Cambodia, Laos, and Jordan. In Vietnam the concern was resettlement and agriculture.

VOLUNTEERS IN COLD WAR CONFLICT

Vietnam, a nation that had endured decades of colonization and war, became one of the main focuses of IVS' second decade of operations. By 1972, 800 volunteers had served there, working both in rural and urban settings. It was a time of controversy and of great progress tempered by equally great loss. Eleven volun-teers died in Vietnam and Laos, and three were captured and held prisoner by North Vietnamese armed forces. The IVS Vietnam country director and three senior volunteers resigned in protest of the United States' actions there. By 1975, IVS had ended its operations and left mainland Southeast Asia altogether.

The end of the organization's "Indochina" efforts led to an expansion of IVS energies in other regions, and Bangladesh became a focal point. Initiatives there ran the gamut: agriculture, health and family planning, forestry and horticulture. IVS for the first time found itself involved in disaster relief to assist a recently formed nation plagued by typhoons, earthquakes and floods. Madagascar, meanwhile, benefited from a clean water project. Offices opened in Latin America and Africa, and work began in Papua New Guinea and Indonesia.

L<small>OCAL</small> V<small>OLUNTEERS</small>

From 1983 to 1992, the fourth decade of IVS's existence, the organization shifted its focus from sending young North Americans to host countries and began employing a smaller number of seasoned professionals. In some regions, local volunteers were recruited and trained to work in projects. In others, IVS sought and found skilled and educated volunteers and staff both from the host countries and internationally. IVS also for the first time began HIV/AIDS education programs in Thailand and Cambodia.

The International Voluntary Services' last ten years witnessed a winding down both of funds and programs as IVS allied itself with other private voluntary and non-governmental organizations. Inevitably, financial concerns forced IVS to shut its doors, and the remaining programs in Bangladesh, Bolivia and Ecuador were granted national NGO (Non-government Organization) status.

By the end of IVS's existence, approximately 3,000 American and international IVS volunteers had served to improve the lives of poorer nations worldwide, changing their own lives in the process.

From its inception, IVS was mostly young people, often right out of college, adventuresome, idealistic, and eager. They wanted to see parts of the world tourists rarely visited and to immerse themselves in cultures radically different from what they knew. Their work so impressed the powers back home that it helped prompt President John F. Kennedy to mandate the creation of the

Peace Corps. In a 1961 speech on the House floor, Rep. Henry Reuss of Wisconsin, supporting President Kennedy's aspirations, said, "In carrying out the Peace Corps program, we are fortunately able to draw on the experience of ... the International Voluntary Services [that] has done a superlative job in its limited but thoroughgoing overseas ventures."

IVS is no longer sending young men and women to help others, but its successes still echo brightly, and its achievements will always be seen as models of the generosity and courage needed to change a world for the better of all concerned.

THE FIRST DECADE
1953–1962

EGYPT · JORDAN · IRAQ · NEPAL · LAOS
VIETNAM · GHANA · LIBERIA

IVS's FIRST TEN YEARS would set the tone for the following four decades. A small and essentially modest project in Egypt was established to assist farmers with dairy and poultry production. The first two official volunteers became the vanguard of what would, over the years, be more than 2,000 young men and women—the few and the fortunate, in the words of one—sent to carry the IVS banner and philosophy.

This philosophy, though, took time to evolve. Volunteerism did not spring fully formed—its evolution from concept to reality took time to develop and, in the United States, involved a cast of diverse and colorful players.

Among the first were the Thomasites, named not after a person but after a ship.

In answer to President McKinley's desire to create educational programs for the newly-colonized Philippines, 509 American teachers, many of whom were women, arrived in Manila aboard the U.S. Army Transport ship, the *Thomas* on August 23, 1901, to work in schools previously built by the American military. They had three responsibilities: to teach citizens democracy; to ensure schools were open to all classes of society; and for these schools to create an English-speaking culture of people who could read and write.

Among these teachers was John S. Noffsinger, who would years later become the first director of the International Voluntary Services, bringing to the post the Thomasite experience. But much was needed to happen behind the scene before Noffsinger's stewardship could begin.

Volunteerism funded by the U.S. government flourished during the 20th Century. A classic example was the Civilian Public Service Program (CPS). CPS was founded at the onset of World War II by conscientious objectors who chose to volunteer for projects of national importance as an alternative to military service. The CPSers dug irrigation ditches, planted ground cover, and built dams and watering systems. In time, some found their way to working in mental hospitals and their involvement helped spark major changes in the care of the mentally ill in the United States. Though service in CPS was mostly male, a number of women served as well. No women were drafted during World War II and as such, those who served in CPS did so voluntarily. At first, they served as nurses, dieticians, and matrons, but when work in mental hospitals began, women also served as attendants there.

MARSHALL PLAN

The Marshall Plan, established in April, 1948, gave economic support for the rebuilding of European economies after World War II. A few months later, on January 20, 1949, President Harry S. Truman called for a "bold new program for making the benefits of our scientific advances and industrial progress available for the improvement and growth of underdeveloped nations." Though not openly presented as such, what came to be known as the Point Four Program (PFP) was part and parcel of the country's decision to limit the influence of the Soviet Union overseas.

The program offered scores of U.S. experts and millions of dollars in technical and scientific expertise to nations in Asia, the Middle East, Latin America, and Africa. Such assistance, Truman believed, would foster economic development, which in turn would benefit trade with the United States.

In October 1950, the Technical Cooperation Administration (now USAID—the United States Agency for International Development) was established within the Department of State to administer the Point Four Program.

Following President Truman's lead and wanting to further his predecessor's basic foreign affairs policies, President Dwight D. Eisenhower abolished what was then called the Office of Foreign Agricultural Relations in March, 1953, and saw to the creation of the Foreign Agricultural Services (FAS) as a natural follow-through to the Marshall Plan, which by then had contributed $13 billion to the reconstruction of war-torn European nations. The FAS was charged with, among other assignments, helping other countries become better customers through technical assistance and foreign investment.

A short time later, Secretary of State John Foster Dulles said in a speech that U.S. foreign policy could benefit from the experience of American institutions that already had decades of familiarity with working for development overseas. He cited the American Friends Service Committee, the Mennonites and Amish, as well as other missionary-backed groups.

Enter *Dale Clark*, a Mormon and consummate Washington civil servant who had worked for the Department of Agriculture and served with the Military Government in post-war Germany. Shuttling between Washington and Berlin, Clark came to believe "that German citizens should form a voluntary corps to repair some of the havoc they had visited on other nations." When that particular plan proved impractical, he embraced the PFP and became one of its first hundred supporters. Clark, in a 1988 interview, said he "had always taken a liking to the private voluntary agency side of it and that was virtually nonexistent."

GRASS-ROOT INITIATIVES

Clark had witnessed the 1951 Iran crisis when that country's revolutionary leader, Mohammed Mossadegh had moved to nationalize his nation's oil reserves. Working for the Point Four Program, Clark soon became head of its Iran Office. With Stanley Andrews, a former chief of the Office of Foreign Agricultural Relations, he formulated a plan that would allow private groups to mount voluntary, grass-root initiatives in Iran under the aegis of the Point Four Program. At the time, the Point Four Program in Iran was staffed largely by Mormon personnel from Brigham Young University, Utah State and the University of Utah.

The initial effort would assist Musa Bey Alami, a charismatic figure and former civil servant in Jerusalem, to establish an orphanage, which he was having a difficult time launching.

Clark and Andrews both believed that "the beginnings of a movement could be built around him." Brethren and Mennonite organizations seconded workers to this Point Four Program, and in time, more than 6,000 orphans would benefit from the orphanage.

FIRST OFFICIAL VENTURE

From these roots sprang the idea for the International Voluntary Services. It was endorsed by the Point Four Program, Mennonites, Quakers, Brethren, and other groups experienced in placing young volunteers in overseas projects. They met to discuss staffing, financing and fund-raising, organization and workforce, and launched the newly named IVS's first official venture, the Musa Alami Project in Jericho, which included a poultry farm and a dairy.

Concurrently, an opportunity arose to cosponsor a project with World Neighbors, a non-profit international development organization founded in 1951. Two young Americans arrived in Asyut, **Egypt**, seconded from the Brethren Volunteer Services, to work with farmers and cattlemen. They were the first official IVS volunteers, to be followed by two more and the new wife of a member of the first team.

Clark, in the 1998 interview, recalled that, "One Mennonite young man and another from the Church of the Brethren, Otis Rowe, were recruited for the project. They were the first to actually arrive. The reason it took a little longer to get the Jericho, **Jordan**, thing off the ground was the fact that Musa Alami came to America. He wanted to start with a poultry project. We arranged a trip for him down to Broadway, Virginia, where the Mennonites are strong in the poultry business."

Mennonite Leaders

"He came back the most delighted person I think I've ever seen. He said he sat there with those Mennonite leaders and one of them picked up the phone and made a rapid fire series of telephone calls. He oversubscribed the 5,000 chicks that he was after in just a matter of minutes. Then Musa quoted the Mennonite organizer as saying, 'Well, you see, we're oversubscribed. Now I won't have to contribute any of my own chicks.'

"So the chicks were sent and that was the first project undertaken by IVS."

Originally a six-month project, it was carried out by a team of two, and later three, volunteers for two years. Riots in the area eventually destroyed most of the buildings and equipment, which were later replaced.

IVS phased out the project in 1956 for lack of funding, and control of the project passed to Alami's Arab Development Society.

In **Iraq**, a team of demonstration workers in agriculture, village sanitation, nursing, home construction and home economics arrived early in 1954 and an office was opened in Baghdad. These volunteers worked with the Kurds in the northern part of Iraq and were the largest IVS group in country during the early years.

Conscientious Objector

Among this group was *Carl Jantzen*, a young conscientious

objector to the Korean War. Jantzen joined IVS as a member of one of the first groups to combine volunteers of the Church of the Brethren, Quakers, and Mennonites to work in the Middle East. In December 1953, he joined *Martha Rupel*, a nurse, and *Everett Jenne*, an agriculturalist, in Iraq to work with the Point Four Program.

This project was located in and near Shaqlawa, a town of about 3,000 people comprising roughly two-thirds Sunni Muslims and one-third Chaldean Catholic Christians. All were Kurdish speakers; some also spoke Iraqi Arabic and a few spoke English. The three IVSers quickly engaged in local projects, working with Kurds in visitation and clinic development in local villages and fixing local houses for IVS use. Jantzen visited Kurdish villages and showed villagers movies, which they'd never seen before.

One of the first major projects was the introduction of American New Hampshire Red chickens into the local chicken populations. Jenne and Jantzen worked with villagers to build a chicken house in Shaqlawa with a combination of Kurdish and American ideas. Soon they could distribute eggs and roosters to regional villages. Two American trailer houses meant to be used for housing instead served as a demonstration and working area for villages in the region. In November 1954, two new IVS team members brought twenty head of Jersey and Brown Swiss cattle—mainly bulls for use in introducing an artificial insemination project for villages in the region.

Cherie (Woodcock) Mitchell, a home economist, became the second woman IVSer and began a cooking/sewing school for girls in a small town further into Kurdistan in northeastern Iraq.

She remembers her time in Shaqlawa. "We women home economists and nurses ran the well-baby clinics and taught in the girls' schools. When I first arrived, I knew no Kurdish. The Kurds were a little more liberal about having men interpreters but it was obvious that we had to learn Kurdish very quickly. We were soon running the clinics, distributing UNICEF-funded milk and vitamins. I haven't had much chance to practice my

Kurdish lately but I will never forget the phrases for 'my baby has a fever or headache,' or 'my baby has diarrhea'."

DEFICIENCY DISEASES

"I had never seen deficiency diseases except in textbooks and here we were seeing scurvy and mild forms of other deficiencies. One case I encountered that still haunts me was a young mother who was nursing two babies. When we arrived in the village she was brought to me as she had an ulcerated breast and she wanted me to treat her. The women there assumed all Western women must be doctors. Oh, how I wished I was. I tried to talk her into going with me into Erbil to the nearest doctor but because they were all men doctors she wouldn't go."

Mitchell met her soon-to-be-husband, Don, and they were married in Baghdad in 1957. Don was originally assigned as the poultry husbandry specialist in Shaqlawa.

He recalls that, "It immediately became evident that poultry production was only a small part of my duties. Prior to my arrival, the team leader had ordered about twenty kerosene incubators from Germany that were to be sent to villages for hatching chicks. These dome-shaped monsters were poorly designed and it took great persistence to hatch even a few chicks; needless to say none were ever sent to a village. One of my early assignments was to go to Baghdad to receive an air shipment of 1,000 chicks and share a compartment with them on the overnight train ride to Erbil.

"We built a chicken house to raise chicks to four to six weeks of age, when they would no longer need a brooder. They were vaccinated and distributed to the villages where workers would see they were well fed and cared for with the expectation that the White Rock and New Hampshire Reds would mate with local chickens to produce a larger more productive flock. This was great in theory, but the mortality rate was very high not only from endemic diseases, because these well-fed American chickens had to compete with the local flock. And then the sheik happened to have visitors and needed a nice plump rooster for dinner..."

The IVS program in Iraq also purchased several European seed cleaners, tractors, and threshers. Carl Jantzen taught Kurds how to run a seed cleaner to help clean over 250 metric tons of seed wheat and barley in a business near Sulaymania. Several IVS workers also led groups in various areas to drill water wells. These projects made clear that what worked best were interactions with people who valued what was being done for them.

In 1954, *Peter Barwick* was given the opportunity to do his alternative service when IVS Director Noffsinger approached him to go to northern Iraq.

LONG HISTORY OF VOLUNTEERISM

Barwick's family had a long history of volunteerism. His father worked with the International YMCA, running programs in a camp for German POWs. By the time Barwick joined IVS, he had already worked in Beirut with Palestinian refugees and was packing clothing for refugees in New Windsor, MD. "Of course, I jumped at the chance, especially as my parents were then living in Jerusalem."

The program involved taking cattle, chickens and rabbits on a freighter from New York to Beirut. Heavy seas washed through the pens, which were built on the stern, only six feet above the waterline. The rabbits got loose. "We lost count as they multiplied, but we had a great time coping.

"From Beirut we were loaded with the animals in cattle cars onto a train going up through Syria and Turkey. When we arrived in Mosul, we were put onto trucks to Shaqlawa.

"This was a lovely village in northern Kurdistan near the Iranian border north of Erbil. It had many trees and gardens fed by five springs flowing into the valley. We initially stayed in a small, stone hotel, built by the British who were the administrators of post-Ottoman Iraq. Incredibly, there was an ancient Chaldean church high above the village and half of the population was a community of Christians, founded in the first century by St. Thomas on his way to India! Moslems and Christians lived happily together in those days and we hired both equally to run the farm."

The staff included Mennonites, Brethren and Quakers, as well as two ex-military men and four civilian women, drawn to such foreign aid programs as a career. The men had agricultural training; the women were nurses and home economics majors. "The work was run by a Christian school teacher, the most valuable of our assets, along with a Moslem master stone mason who built the most beautiful barn I ever saw using labor much the same way as those in the Middle Ages. Our housing was two comfortable thirty-foot trailers."

Although most of the program involved the introduction of improved agricultural techniques and crops, the team had a very successful artificial insemination program using Jersey bulls. It was run by a young Quaker from Ohio and was unfortunately terminated when the man came down with polio and barely survived his return to the States. "Gamma globulin flown in to protect the rest of us was intercepted by the embassy staff in Baghdad, who panicked and used all of it, even though none of them were exposed, since they were 160 miles away."

OTTOMAN RULE

"Our chicken program was equally successful in upgrading the local stock," says Barwick. "As it grew, however, more and more of the new birds were to be found in the local sheikh's care. His brother had been placed on our payroll doing nothing and skimming off whatever he felt his family deserved. When we tried to change this arrangement, our farm manager was told to report for duty in the Iraqi army the same day. We gave in.

"My job, apart from teaching English and math to the farm workers, was the village well program. This was much needed to improve their filthy open wells and was quite successful. I imagine it would have continued after our departure, since we used only hand-operated equipment.

"Our nurses made weekly rounds of the nearby villages, dispensing shots and health education via cartoon films imported from Egypt. The Home Ec team was probably the most enduring of all our projects and Shaqlawa still has a thriving honey and jam industry. Nothing else survived destruction of the village by Saddam Hussein."

In Nepalgunj, **Nepal,** a four-man team became advisors in a training school for community development workers. At the end of two years, this program was transferred to local administrators when the original contract with the U.S. government ran out.

IVS' initial program in what was then Indochina began in 1954 when the first of several hundred volunteers sent to **Laos** arrived to assist with community development, agricultural and education projects. These men and women often worked in conjunction with U.S. government rural development programs and among the people displaced by the growing conflicts.

Frank Huffman, who arrived in Laos in 1956, remembers. "In 1955, when IVS Director Dr. John Noffsinger sought to recruit a 'down-to-earth dirt farmer who could speak French' to serve as an interpreter for a project in Laos, I jumped at the chance to have an adventure and to fulfill the requirements of the draft. So I went to the IVS office in Washington to be tested in French by Noffsinger's daughter, who was a professor of French at the University of Toronto. I passed the test and was promised the job, pending finalization of the contract between IVS, the U.S. Aid Mission in Vientiane, and the Royal Government of Laos."

BRETHREN VOLUNTEER SERVICE

"In the meantime, it was agreed that I would join the Brethren Volunteer Service for work and training at their relief clothing processing center in Maryland. There I met *Carl Coppock,* another prospective member of the IVS/Laos team. Carl had just finished an MS in Animal Husbandry at Texas A&M.

"Finally word came that the IVS contract had been signed, and we were to leave for Laos on February 19, 1956. The Chief-of-Party, *Wendell Ralston,* was a retired Iowa farmer, and was already in Laos making advance preparations for the arrival of the team. His wife Frances was to meet Carl and me in San Francisco and accompany us to post."

Ralston met Coppock and Huffman in Bangkok, and after the two spent several days of acclimatization, accompanied them to Vientiane, the sleepy little administrative capital. Laos, a mountainous, land-locked country about the size of New York and Pennsylvania combined, was at the time involved in a communist insurgency similar to the on-going war in Vietnam, with the Royal Lao Army (RLA) fighting the Pathet Lao (PL), who had occupied two provinces in the North.

"That was why the USOM (the U.S. Operations Mission) to Laos was financing our relatively small-scale IVS community development project. It was part of their overall objective of 'winning hearts and minds' and preventing Laos from falling into the hands of the communists," recalled Huffman.

MUDDY STREETS

Headquarters was the little town of Phon Savanh (Heavenly Hill) in Xieng Khouang Province on the Plain of Jars, named for thousands of stone jars reputedly used as burial urns by an earlier civilization. Phon Savanh consisted of a muddy street lined on both sides with one-story shops and houses. The most impressive building in town was the new post office, built of woven bamboo and mud stucco; since there seemed to be very little mail arriving in Phon Savanh, it was agreed to let the volunteers use it as a base and dormitory. They built a mess hall and garage in the compound, using lumber purchased from local sawyers.

In May of 1956 the team was expanded by the arrival of *Clyde Searl*, an entomologist from California, and *Martha Rupel*, a public health nurse who had previously served on an IVS team in Iraq. *Wallace Brown*, an industrial arts specialist from Warrensburg, Missouri, arrived five months later.

Huffman and Coppok began to offer English classes several evenings a week in response to popular demand, and to show movies. "It was one of the most popular things we did. We projected the films through the window of the mess hall onto a sheet tacked up on two four-by-four poles. We usually showed the films on Saturday evenings, and crowds of children and adults would show up in the compound waiting for the show to start. Sometimes we simply showed the previous week's films over again; it didn't seem to make much difference to the crowd. They were starved for entertainment.

"I started a library and reading room, with materials in six languages—English, French, Lao, Thai, Chinese, and Vietnamese—provided by the U.S. Information Service in Vientiane. I hired and trained a young girl as librarian; she was not terribly diligent, and a significant number of books and magazines tended to disappear while she flirted with various male admirers."

CHILD CARE CLINICS

With the arrival of Nurse Martha Rupel, the volunteers began to offer child care clinics in surrounding villages. "As word of our clinics spread, King Touby of the Hmong, asked us to expand our clinics to various Hmong villages in the surrounding mountains, so that eventually we were holding clinics in ten to twelve villages within twenty or thirty miles of the base. I became the Jeep driver, interpreter and general assistant for the program. A crowd of some forty to sixty mothers and children would be lined up outside the house used for the clinic. Since most of the Hmong women didn't speak Lao, I had to learn a certain amount of Hmong medical vocabulary to determine the baby's problem, whether fever, cough, diarrhea, etc. The villagers inevitably assumed that I was the doctor, since I would pass the information on to the nurse, who would then administer the required treatment."

Huffman recalled that, "Our flagship livestock improvement project was to be the importation of Brahma bulls from Texas, as it was thought that the Plain of Jars had great potential for the production of beef cattle. Carl Coppock and I had built miles of three-strand barbed wire fence to contain the bulls.

"When the bulls arrived in Bangkok, they must have realized they were coming to the land of their origin, as they jumped overboard and swam ashore. The entire project had to be abandoned in the 1960s when the Plain of Jars again became a battleground between the communists and the royal government.

"There was very little demand for my official role as a French interpreter, since most of the villagers we worked with spoke no French, so to be at all effective I had to learn as much Lao as possible. I did have the opportunity to interpret when we were visited by the provincial governor and by Prime Minister Souvanna Phouma, who showed a genuine interest in our activities."

After IVS, Huffman obtained a PhD from Cornell in 1967, taught Southeast Asian linguistics at Yale and Cornell, and served as a diplomat in London, Burma, Morocco, Paris, Cambodia, and New Zealand. "The influence of IVS on my life has been total: a fascination with Asian languages and cultures that determined the course of my academic and diplomatic careers over the next half-century."

Dayton L. Maxwell, who graduated with an engineering degree from Iowa State College (now University) in 1958, wanted to work overseas. He says, "My mother was a French, Greek and Latin teacher very much interested in world affairs. I'm a strong, believing Christian who feels it is our duty to provide assistance to those not born with our privileges and opportunities. Finally, President Hoover was born ten miles from my birthplace in Tipton, Iowa. He became an engineer and spent his early career overseas. I applied to IVS, and they contacted me several months later to offer me a job in Laos. I was still single, just paid off my student loans, and it didn't take long to decide to go, even though I'd never heard of Laos before."

TEACHERS' TRAINING SCHOOL

Maxwell's Education Team was the first one to begin work establishing a new Teachers' Training School in the jungle outside Vientiane, Laos. "We had a sixty-something retired farmer and his wife as a team leader, two agriculturists, a nurse, a generalist and two home economics team members. My job as electrician (not really as an engineer) was to install the school generators and electrical system and train locals to maintain them The pythons had to be moved away and a tiger badly frightened the night staff one evening. We learned all about the *phis* (spirits—the Lao have quite a range and number of spirits they believe in) during this construction period."

The Teachers' Training School, run by the French, was moving from a facility in town to this new location. The IVS Team and a University of Michigan team created an English language section, and the students there went on to get scholarships to the U.S. and return to start the first comprehensive High School in Laos years later.

The school hired some electrician graduates to supervise the electrical installations at the time of the king of Laos' death. "One of my most memorable Lao cultural events was to attend and take photographs at this funeral, where I saw the Cambodian King Norodom Sihanouk.

"Our most striking experience was a *coup d'état* by a paratrooper captain. Kong Le overthrew the rightist government and installed a neutralist government. Then in early 1961 a full civil war broke out in Vientiane. I happened to be in town when the first shots fell. I couldn't go back home for a few days. During a break in the fighting, I was asked to drive out to instruct our team to prepare to evacuate and come right back to town. I was recruited to be part of USAID's evacuation staff."

EVACUATION

Following the evacuation, Maxwell was in Thailand preparing to return to Vientiane as part of the U.S. mission's residual staff. He was standing by the Mekong, watching the waning air bursts in the evening light after the rightist military had driven Kong Le out of town. "A voice behind me asked if I were going back to Vientiane. It was a beautiful, young Vietnamese girl, a receptionist at USAID. We took her and her sister back to Vientiane the next morning, and that was the beginning of a lasting friendship.

We were married at the end of my tour and have two children and three grandchildren."

After returning to the U.S., Maxwell was immediately recruited to work as a field representative by the Peace Corps to assist in recruiting efforts. "Those studying the requirements for launching the Peace Corps ransacked the IVS headquarters office for information. One official performing the study wrote a book which contained fragments of my letters home as examples of the life of a volunteer."

Meanwhile, the aftermath of the Kong Le *coup* led to a much more prevalent presence of Pathet Lao in Laos. "It became a priority for U.S. national interest to mitigate that presence. The VARDA program–I think it stood for Voluntary Assistance for Rural Development Activities–was established to assign IVS rural development teams to rural areas of Laos. It gradually evolved into a 'village cluster' (*mu ban samaki*) program, stationing IVSers in the forward areas bordering the Pathet Lao areas, with the intention of winning rural populations over to support the Lao government," Maxwell continued.

Team Leader

IVS offered Maxwell another job as Team Leader under the VARDA program in early 1962. He opened the IVS office in Sayaboury, Laos. The team there consisted of two agriculturists, a nurse and a generalist. "My wife had our first child in Vientiane and joined me in Sayaboury. USAID asked me to serve as its representative until they assigned an officer there; we helped resettle a Hmong village away from the Pathet Lao threat, and a visit by the Crown Prince became a major elephant ceremony and festival."

The VARDA program was growing rapidly, placing teams in Pakse, Savannakhet and Luang Prabang. Maxwell became a deputy to the VARDA Chief of Party in Vientiane in 1963. "As the Village Cluster program was initiated, we placed small teams and individuals in several locations. These were risky locations, and the two-person team in Phone Hong experienced what we would call today an IED explosion on the road in front of their house."

At the end of this assignment, Maxwell was awarded a Fellowship at the East-West Center at the University of Hawaii to get a Master's Degree focusing on development assistance. His career path was set. "My technical orientation and my IVS experience resulted in USAID offering me a job as a technical training advisor in Laos in early 1967. That USAID career lasted until 2008."

He now believes that, "One simple conclusion about our contribution to Laos is that we achieved virtually nothing given the turn of events there, when the Pathet Lao ejected us from the country in 1975. All the institution-building activities achieved during our time were not supported after our departure. Most of the Laos officials associated with the assistance activities went into exile or were imprisoned. That's a conclusion that isn't encouraging to spend time thinking about.

"I'd like to think our presence did leave a lasting impression on the lives of the people we met and worked with. Perhaps their lives were improved; we can offer no evidence but anecdotes abound. In 1992, I led an OFDA (Office of U.S. Foreign Disaster Assistance) team in response to a humanitarian emergency in southern Laos. *Win McKeithen*, a former IVSer working for USAID Public Health, was a member of our team." There was an end-of-visit party during which McKeithen was asked by a middle-age woman whether he had lived two doors from a merchant's house when he was serving as an IVS volunteer in a remote Pakse region. "The woman was the merchant's daughter and retained vivid memories of Win's presence there."

BRANCH OUT

Maxwell believes, "All IVSers can be proud that we were the vanguard of international volunteer work that was popularized by the Peace Corps. But we can wonder why IVS did not adjust to the international needs as they evolved over time. In 1991, when I was the OFDA Deputy Director, I remember talking to *Don Luce*, the IVS Director, about possibilities for IVS to branch out and provide general humanitarian assistance, which was the growth industry among NGOs at the time. He was not responsive to my question about IVS branching out but thought IVS should maintain its 'niche' as an NGO."

ARZELLA AND DUONG (DOOLEY) BUI, VIETNAM 1956

Dooley Bui worked as an English translator and Assistant Editor for the National Radio Broadcasting Service in North Vietnam prior to joining IVS in late 1956. His first work with IVS was in Cai San, the largest Refugee Resettlement Center in the Mekong Delta, as an interpreter/language teacher to newly arriving volunteers. He married Arzella, an IVS volunteer, and later they and their daughter Kim settled in Southern California. He says, "IVS gave me a stepping stone to many opportunities I have had in my adopted country. IVS turned me into a considerate and caring person. Lastly, the most precious gift was knowing the many volunteers I worked with in Vietnam."

Arzella Bui joined IVS as a volunteer in 1956 after graduating from the University of Iowa with a public health registered nurse degree. She chose Vietnam as her first assignment. She was stationed with other IVS volunteers in Ban Me Thuot in the Highlands of South Vietnam. She remembered that, "A few months later, the station was closed and most of the other volunteers went back to the U.S. I volunteered to work in Cai San, the largest refugee resettlement center in the Mekong Delta. I provided health care to refugees and their children. When the communist insurgents began operating in the region, I was sent to Saigon for my safety. In Saigon, I helped out at An Lac orphanage."

A year later, Dooley and Arzella moved to Monterey, CA, where Dooley taught at the Defense Language Institute, a division of the Department of Defense. During thirty-nine years at the Institute, he held various academic positions, the last as Chairman of the Vietnamese Department. He retired in 2006 and currently is still doing Vietnamese language Oral Proficiency Testing for International Language Testing Company in New York City.

"IVS volunteers who worked at Ban Me Thuot, Cai San and other places in South Vietnam imparted their humanitarian dedication to many Vietnamese people who fled the communist regime when the country was divided in half at the 17th parallel," said Dooley Bui.

After war's end, many Vietnamese nationals who worked for IVS returned to their old work places in South Vietnam. They met their Vietnamese counterparts from agriculture to animal husbandry. Their reminiscences were the beginning of capturing the IVS history in Vietnam. "Several former Cai San refugee families settled in Germany and in Orange County, California," said Bui.

"In 1975, I assisted U.S. Immigration Service as an interpreter in Los Altos. While filling out paper work, several Vietnamese women told me they had worked for An Lac orphanage in Saigon, where they knew an American nurse who used to take care of them when they themselves were orphans at An Lac. A few months later, I went to Camp Pendleton in Oceanside, California, to look for a Vietnamese family for a church to sponsor. Guess what? The first interview was a family of five from Cai San. They talked about the American nurse and how caring she was, and remembered other IVS members. The church sponsored this family. This is one of Arzella's legacy."

VOLUNTEER SAFETY

From the very start there was doubt among the IVS leadership as to the wisdom of sending volunteers to an already embattled country. In his paper, *International Voluntary Services in Vietnam: War and the Birth of Activism, 1958-1967,* Paul Rodell writes that, "Initially, IVS was cool to the idea of sending volunteers to the former French colony of Vietnam. In June and December 1954, Director John S. Noffsinger visited the U.S. Overseas Mission, but at first he was not receptive to USOM proposals. He was concerned about volunteer safety and the possibility that the government's primary objectives were more politically motivated than they were concerned with development." IVS thinking shifted by mid-1955 when a proposal to work with Catholic refugees from the north met with Noffsinger's approval and subsequent visits by IVS board members from the Church of the Brethren and Roman Catholic Monsignor L.G. Ligutti confirmed the possibility of working in Vietnam. A contract with ICA (the predecessor of USOM) was signed in late fall of 1956 and the first batch of volunteers arrived shortly.

Ray Borton, who wasn't inclined to stay on his family farm in Michigan, arrived in 1958. After getting a scholarship to Cornell, spending a year abroad—where he first heard of IVS—and two years in the military, he volunteered.

"My two years in the U.S. Army Quartermaster Corps as a Food Service Officer gave me good training for my Dalat, Vietnam, assignment. In addition to our work at a horticultural experiment station, we operated an IVS team guest house in a French villa provided by the USAID program."

CHOUFLEUR XIN

"Dalat has delightful spring weather year-round and at the station we added to the list of crops that could be grown and marketed there. Onions were the most visible addition, since the varieties we introduced made bulbs rather than just great big green onions; broccoli was new to the Vietnamese growers and they dubbed it 'choufleur xin,' green cauliflower. Iceberg head lettuce was marketable to members of the American community in Saigon who had grown up without knowing the joys of delectable French butterhead lettuce.

"Some things did not work: our potatoes were leveled by blight and the soybeans we planted as a cover crop for plowing under were harvested for edible seeds instead.

"Everybody wanted us to teach English and we did in various kinds of groups and classes. Our contacts with the American military were limited to two American West Point graduates and their families that were assigned to teach at the Military Academy located in Dalat."

Another volunteer, *David Nuttle*, arrived in Vietnam in 1959. "I had a personal services contract with International Voluntary Services to provide agricultural and community development services in South Vietnam. IVS volunteers assisted in resettling refugees from North Vietnam as well as general agricultural development and extension education. We also assisted the Vietnamese in starting and developing ten diverse agricultural experiment stations scattered over the entire country. My Tho Station concentrated on rice; Hung Loc, Nha Ho, and Phan Rang were dual purpose crops and livestock stations; Bao Loc and Di Linh focused on lacquer, oil palm, and cacao production; Dalat was into vegetables; M' Drak was an experimental ranching operation; and Ban Me Thuot was a combination of fiber crops, upland rice, livestock, and vegetables. Most of these stations had training centers dedicated to teaching Vietnamese technicians improved agricultural methods. Tan Son Nhut was a livestock station on the outskirts of Saigon near the airport. This was also the location of IVS's South Vietnam headquarters."

TRYING CIRCUMSTANCES

Nuttle was amazed by the things IVS had accomplished under trying circumstances. He was now assigned to the Ban Me Thuot Station and concentrating his efforts on several projects in Montagnard tribal villages in Darlac Province. Two other IVSers at the station were working on refugee resettlement programs as well as training, experiments, and development projects. The actual station name was Ea Kmat. "Mr. Trach was the Vietnamese Station Manager," Nuttle wrote. "The station staff included nine Vietnamese graduates of the relatively new National College of Agriculture at Bao Loc.

"We were all proud of the accomplishments at Ea Kmat. The station had started from zero, and in a year had produced 120 hectares of kenaf seed."

This and prior seed production would bring Vietnam into third place in the world production of fiber. The station was also starting to propagate ramie as a fiber crop. IVS had helped initiate other programs including field crops, vegetables, tree crops, and livestock improvement.

"It seemed unbelievable, but we had convinced some of the Vietnamese to start helping the Montagnard tribes." This, it turned out, was a feat, considering the mutual distrust and dislike between the parties, but it reflected a common theme in the work of IVS volunteers who were often drawn to serving the disadvantaged. This included refugees, orphans, street kids, and ethnic minorities. In Indochina, many volunteers in rural development worked with tribal hill peoples, who had long faced discrimination by the dominant ethnic groups. As the hill tribe groups were caught up in the larger war in Indochina, the results were often tragic.

"I was confident the local Rhade villagers would not disclose my presence or plans to the Viet Cong (VC)," Nuttle says. "For over a year, I had tried to better their lives with improved agricultural practices. I traveled from village to village by jeep or by motorcycle."

At one point, he remembers, "The Montagnards had warned me of VC threats against my life. Only a few weeks before, a government inspection team planned to visit an agricultural project in a village southeast of Ban Me Thuot. I was scheduled to accompany the group. I'd been advised not to go under any circumstances. I made an excuse for not being able to attend." The inspection team departed as planned, but the officials never reached their destination. A well-concealed 'spider-hole' ambush changed their plans.

"All thirty-six ARVN (Army of the Republic of Vietnam) security guards were killed, as well as seven of eight GVN (Government of Vietnam) officials. The lone survivor was a lesser official and former military sergeant under the French."

VIETNAMESE WILDLIFE

"My first experience with wild animals involved a rogue elephant that attempted to pull me and *Don Sumner*, another IVSer, out of a makeshift tree stand. When the huge animal couldn't grab hold of two shivering IVSers (Don said he could feel the hot breath from his trunk) he attacked our Jeep and managed to rip off the cloth top, bang in the hood and bend in the tailgate. Don said this was his first big game hunt in Vietnam, and it would definitely be his last!"

And then there was the tiger in the Highlands near Ban Me Thout. A Vietnamese military officer had shot and wounded a tiger but was too scared to track the bleeding animal. Nuttle and *Burr Frutchey*, another IVSer, agreed to help track down the tiger as they didn't want any of their Montagnard friends to be attacked.

"We tracked it to a bamboo thicket some 200 meters in width. After a discussion between two inexperienced tiger hunters, we decided that I would fire into the thicket with my .375 magnum rifle, hoping to chase the tiger out so we could get a shot to dispose of him. Immediately after the shot, a loud and angry growl broke the stillness. Then we saw the grass parting; the tiger was less than twenty-five meters away! He was leaping and running towards us with his mouth open!" Burr shot first with his .12 gauge shotgun. The tiger kept coming. The Vietnamese guards began firing with their submachine guns. Nuttle fired and the tiger faltered and fell a few feet in front of them.

REFUGEES

Nuttle also assisted in the relocation of refugees. "IVS provided some help: seeds, a few tools, and demonstration projects. We had to scrounge things from USOM, Hung Loc Station, and from American welfare organizations like CARE (Cooperative for American Remittances to Europe)."

Richard J. Peters, who would serve as IVS Executive Director from 1971 to 1973, began his IVS career with a stint in Vietnam, following two years in Germany with the U.S. Army. "I was at the University of California, Davis, to pursue a degree in Soil Science when I was told about IVS. I immediately applied. IVS accepted me and assigned me to Vietnam. I had to look up Vietnam to learn that it was a part of Indochina." He graduated from UCD in 1959 and worked on his father's farm before leaving for Saigon in September. "My first exposure to other IVS people was on the plane to Vietnam. *C. Francis Lay* and *Cowles Clevenger* were on the same plane as we departed for Honolulu. That was before jets, so it took quite a while. We'd had two days in Honolulu, then flew on to Tokyo for another two days and finally, two more days in Hong Kong before arriving in Saigon."

In Vietnam, they were sent by Land Rover to Ban Me Thuot and the Ea Kmat Station. "*Clyde Eastman* was the resident IVSer at Ea Kmat, and he quickly took us in charge to begin our orientation. We started a crash course in Vietnamese, three hours per day of class time. We then spent time visiting markets to hear the use of Vietnamese in that situation. We also took on a variety of projects. I recall that one of my projects was a disastrous wiring of the IVS house at Ea Kmat. My knowledge of electricity was minimal, based on having installed electric lights in two of my Dad's barns."

After three weeks in Ban Me Thuot, Peters was assigned to Nha Ho, a few kilometers north of Phan Rang along the road to Dalat. Much of the work was devoted to the preparation of ten-by-ten meter irrigated plots where they planted a variety of crops they thought would grow in the area, including corn. "Much of our seed was acquired through family and friends. While crops were growing, I soon became involved in an effort to survey the interests and needs of farmers in the area. One of my more interesting results was a serendipitous discovery in the nearby village of Phu Thanh. An earlier USOM program had given this village three turbine pumps and engines. I found them still in their packing crates.

"My work in Vietnam included short assignments at the Dalat Station. I also did a short assignment at the Hung Loc Station to help identify subterranean water flows and requisite drainage."

FIRST LANDINGS

In 1961 Peters was asked to join *Harvey Neese* as an assistant to the Chief of Party, *Don Luce*. At the time, IVS had volunteers in the Delta, as well as in Hung Loc, Dalat, Phan Rang, M'drak, Ban Me Thuot and, farther north in Quang Ngai. "I decided to learn how to fly a small airplane in order to visit some of these stations. I enrolled in a training program at Tan Son Nhut. I still recall those first landings! Later, I concluded that only major airports were open, and I dropped the whole idea."

IVSers were given one month each year for vacation. "My first vacation was with Don Luce. We went to Bangkok, then to Singapore by train. Onward to Sarawak, Brunei and North Borneo, and then by ship to Hong Kong and back to Saigon by air. One of my favorite adventures was the chance to climb Kina Balu in North Borneo. Don was a reluctant climber because all he had was a pair of dress shoes, and they were soon torn up by the arduous two-day climb. My second vacation was solo to the Philippines and Japan."

Peters' entire career was in international agriculture. Following IVS/Vietnam, he obtained an MS Degree at Cornell in Soil Microbiology. IVS then asked him to go to Algeria and work with the Soils Conservation project as well as the project with orphanages. He then joined *Cliff Doke* as his assistant program officer at headquarters in Washington, D.C.

"In 1971 I was asked to become the Executive Director to replace Arthur Z. Gardiner."

PERENNIAL SECRETARY

As a frail kid from a small farm in Northern Maine, *Richard Keirstead* was encouraged but told not to expect to accomplish too much. In high school, "I seemed to be perennial Future Farmer secretary at local and district level while taking honors at state judging contests." A stint in the U.S. Army, stationed in Italy, had whetted his appetite for travel and adventure. "Yes," he remembers, "I joined IVS for the adventure and to trade the cold of Maine for the warmth of Vietnam. My mother was onto me for she knew I didn't have an altruistic bone in my body. Those bones slowly developed as time went on."

Two days after graduating from the University of Maine in 1959, he was on a plane bound for Vietnam. Many days later he was greeted by "a throng of IVS volunteers and interpreters. At Hung Loc Cattle Station, a teacher tried his best to pound Vietnamese language into my head. For me he was but marginally successful, but I know what he accomplished saved my life later."

In Dalat, Keirstead worked with Ray Borton and Burr Frutchey, then moved to Ea Kmat, near Ban Me Thuot to replace Don Luce when Luce was promoted to assistant team leader. "This was a wild wonderland. Wildlife from wild chickens to deer to leopards, tigers and elephants. And work to do. Other stations were under the Ministry of Agriculture. Ban Me Thuot was under the Commissariat General for Land Development. This was big. We were testing and propagating every kind of plant we thought would grow."

Not long after getting settled into the IVS house, an old man appeared riding bareback on a white horse and accompanied by two loincloth-clad spear carriers. "This was the welcoming committee from the nearby Rhade village, a tribe included by the French in the category of Montagnard, with an invitation to come to a weekend celebration. I still wonder if the celebration was just to see what these foreigners would do when tanked up on the homemade rice wine.

"Most memorable was *Harvey Neese*'s desire to shoot the tiger that was taking our cattle. Short of it was, at night, I was alone up in a tree over the cattle on a bamboo platform when I heard the tiger. It was under me. I waited. After many hours of no sound, I gave it up, climbed down, and headed back to the house. Halfway there, the flashlight bulb burnt out. Well, I did say I went for the adventure, didn't I?"

KICKED UPSTAIRS

"I'll lay it to my failure to perform that got me kicked upstairs." Keirstead was asked to be interim USAID/Agriculture Program Officer in an air-conditioned office in Saigon where he spent his final six months with IVS.

"With me and perhaps with others, I think a major contribution was personal contacts with the Vietnamese people. We worked hand in glove with people who remember us not so much for what we did but for what we were, friends.

"In 1988 I joined a tour of Vietnam led by Don Luce. On the first full day in Hanoi, where I had never been before, I walked into a shop in the central market area where I think the bamboo telegraph must have been in action. As I spoke in English to the proprietor, he said, 'You speak Vietnamese. You were in Vietnam before and you helped the Vietnamese people.' What can you say after that?"

EXPERTISE

"When I graduated in 1959 from Kansas State University with a BS in Agricultural Education," recalls *Donald Sumner*, "there was a surplus of wheat in the USA and I didn't feel that my services were needed in U.S. agriculture. I read an advertisement from IVS about positions for agricultural technicians in South Vietnam and I thought I could use my expertise there."

When Sumner arrived in Saigon, he and other new volunteers were placed in a six-week Vietnamese language course, and Sumner was sent to Hung Loc to work on a new crops research station about forty miles north of Saigon. The station was adjacent to an existing livestock station and the jungle was still being cleared when he got there.

After fourteen months at Hung Loc, Sumner was transferred to the two-year National College of Agriculture at Bao Loc in the highlands of central South Vietnam. "I stayed with *Robert Knoernschild*, an IVSer already there working on horticultural crops at an experiment station near Bao Loc, and *Richard Koegel*, an agricultural engineer who was a former IVSer working with the Vietnamese government. Sumner's work involved helping school personnel set up research programs in field and forage crops, as well as planting observation plots of many crops.

TRENCH SILO

"The college had cattle but they had difficulty finding enough feed for them during the dry season. I showed them how to dig and fill a small trench silo, the first in the area. It was opened in a few months and provided high quality feed for the cattle during the dry season. I helped the college animal husbandry staff set up a small forage nursery that would eventually contain most of the grasses and legumes grown in the tropics. Also, in my spare time, I would teach English to high school students."

Sumner left Bao Loc in May after serving nine months there. "I don't know what the long term effects of my work were because the war became widespread a few years after I left. I do not know if the stations and the college survived the war."

Larry Laverentz recalls that, "Dr. C.W. Mullen, Assistant Dean of Agriculture at Kansas State, read a brief announcement that International Voluntary Services was recruiting agricultural volunteers to go to Laos. This was in late 1959. My roommate and I copied the announcement information and after some research, determined that Laos had formerly been a part of Indochina." They both submitted applications to IVS and were approved to go to Laos in August of 1960. When skirmishes broke out in Laos their assignments were put on hold, and Laverentz spent the fall and part of the winter on his family's farm. He received a call from IVS in May asking if he would go to Vietnam in June and left Kansas City on June 23, 1961.

"There were five of us recruits who met Dr. Noffsinger in San Francisco for two days of orientation, but I remember only two pieces of his advice. He said to be successful you had to have three things, patience, more patience and more patience yet."

After a month of language study and some orientation in Thap Cham, he was assigned to Qui Nhon to work with cattle in the four provinces from Phu Yen to Quang Nam. "I was the first IVS volunteer in Vietnam to work solely in extension, as opposed to working on an experiment station. It was an ill-conceived concept for several reasons and thus never got off the ground. The Animal Husbandry Chief in Binh Dinh never really bought into the idea. Any arable land was used for crops, and cattle fed mostly on grass along roadsides, in cemeteries, and on rice straw. Mr. Loc, the Agricultural Affairs Chief, must have viewed me as a resource. Early on he grabbed me and during the time I spent in Qui Nhon we became good friends and worked and traveled together a lot. I soon discovered Mr. Loc did not need my limited knowledge of tropical agriculture. I decided my best role was to support his work as well as be a liaison with USOM technicians in Saigon."

RAT POISON

"Early on I went with my interpreter to hamlets to talk to farmers. With sincerity and naiveté, I would ask something like, 'How can I help you?' or 'What do you need?' The early answers were almost always the same. They wanted rat poison because they were overrun by the creatures. I passed this information on to the USOM folks in Saigon. Rat hunts were organized. Mr. Loc and I visited a rice paddy area where farmers were digging rats out of holes in the dikes. Down the road past An Nhon on the front steps of a village office was a pile of probably 300 to 400 dead rats.

"After the rat poison arrived, Mr. Loc was responsible for

organizing the dispensing of the poison. Cadres from each hamlet were trained on how to use the poison and determine the results, and were responsible for cutting the tails off dead rats to count the kill. I had no way of knowing or verifying this figure, but Mr. Loc said in Binh Dinh Province more than 900,000 tails were collected."

USOM and IVS decided a long-term solution to the production of rat poison within the borders of Vietnam was needed. *Ted Lingren* of IVS was designated to start some seedbeds and begin growing the raw plants for producing rat poison. "I was asked to go to watch the creation of the seed bed at the nursery in An Nhon District. There were two young girls who probably weighed less than one-hundred pounds each carrying soil from a nearby rice paddy to the seedbed in the nursery.

"I decided that the gentlemanly thing would be to offer to carry a load of dirt. I filled the two baskets and lifted the pole off the ground. Twice I slipped off the dike into the paddy. When I got to the bank leading up to the higher ground of the nursery, I fell down. One of the baskets was crushed beyond repair. Once I tumbled down the bank strewing dirt along the ground. There was no hiding the girls' amusement."

After Laverentz had been in Qui Nhon for a while, he learned the price of meat had gotten higher. "I thought, why not peanut butter since peanuts were plentifully grown, the Vietnamese liked them, and there was this supply of good French style bread?"

He bought a meat grinder in the Saigon market, purchased some local peanuts and ran these through the grinder a couple of times and added some salt. "I bought several loaves of bread and invited twenty or so kids from the neighborhood to try bread and peanut butter. Although some were hesitant in the beginning, they all ate what I had dispensed and said it was *ngon* (delicious). A second time doing this got the same results."

Peanut Butter

Next, Laverentz made a good sized batch of peanut butter and got the owner of a mobile sandwich cart to peddle bread and peanut butter on the street. "About a week later, I asked him about the results of selling peanut butter. He said customers liked it but they were not willing to pay. Because I had sanctimoniously concluded that I was being ripped off, I stopped the peanut butter project. It was a good example of impatience and the imposition of my value system."

Laverentz taught English in the evenings to high school students, merchants and government officials. "For several months at the end of class, my response to '*Ong manh gioi khong?*' (How are you) when translated to English, meant 'I have syphilis today.' One of the male students eventually told me the true meaning of the words I had been provided by either my interpreter or driver.

"I learned more than I taught and received more than I gave while with IVS. The Vietnamese were friendly, patient and gracious, to the point of not telling me things they should have. I eventually realized that the values and wants of most were not too different from those I had learned growing up. I learned to recognize that most persons have reasons for acting or not acting the way they do, which is often contrary to what is wanted or expected by myself and other Americans."

IVS AND RURAL AFFAIRS

TOM LUCHE

USOM's Office of Rural Affairs was started in 1962 by Rufus Phillips and Bert Fraleigh, and drew staff from many sources including military and Foreign Service officers. We were a diverse gang with a taste for direct action, helping the Vietnamese, and contesting communism.

In this group of inspired activists, one early input was IVS volunteers, who were already in the field. They were used to living modestly in remote locations. Many were fluent in Vietnamese and involved with their communities. Thanks to an arrangement with Don Luce, the IVS chief-of-party in Vietnam, many IVS volunteers were seconded to Rural Affairs to serve as provincial representatives. Many were later hired by USOM.

The original work sites were in villages of refugees, the million or so who made it down from North Vietnam. Most were Catholic and ended up around Ban Me Thuot, the Highlands, Bien Hoa and the Mekong Delta. We were to provide technical assistance in animal husbandry, surveying crops and crop protection, and marketing. We learned far more than we taught.

IVS became a willing and able part of the Rural Affairs team. Our mutual objective was to help the Vietnamese have a chance for a richer and more rewarding life.

I was on the first IVS team in Vietnam. The first volunteer was *Paul Worthington*, in December of 1956. The rest of us landed in January of 1957.

We were a diverse lot:

> Paul Worthington, a second lieutenant in the Air Force who served in Japan, an ag extensionist
>
> Art King, an African American who had been an M.P. in Korea, an animal husbandry man
>
> Dick Koegel, a brilliant ag and mechanical engineer
>
> Bob Yates, an animal husbandry man from Tennessee
>
> Gordon and Shirley Brockmueller, a Mennonite farming couple from South Dakota, and
>
> Gene Meyer, an ag extentionist from Missouri "Swampeast."

I have probably forgotten some names after spending about thirty years in the tropical sun. I may be what the French in Africa called "bien cuit"—well done. ❧

No Politics

IVS's philosophy of non-involvement in politics or intelligence work was made clear to each and every volunteer at the out- set of their assignment. In Southeast Asia, however, where the intelligence agencies of a dozen nations thrived, battled and sought primacy, being uninvolved had its difficulties. Nuttle remembers that when he wanted to help shield the Montagnards from the fighting that had already overtaken the country, "I looked to Saigon for help. I counted on the hard-nosed chief of the MAAG (Military Assistance Advisory Group) Combined Studies Division, which was connected with intelligence work in Vietnam. We discussed the Montagnard problem and a variety of possible solutions." (See Appendix I for more on IVS and the Montagnards.)

AFRICA

Work had begun in Africa. In 1959, a small team spent a year in **Ghana** under the auspices of the Rockefeller Brothers Fund demonstrating a simple machine that made bricks from earth and cement. In 1960, a much larger team of teachers was sent to **Liberia** to teach at the elementary level in village and rural schools under funding from USAID.

John Hughes remembers being interviewed by Noffsinger, "who called me to his office in the Woodner Hotel and told me I had been accepted for an assignment in Liberia."

"Well, Hughes," he said, "I don't know a thing about you, but I think you'll do just fine."

Soon afterward, Hughes boarded a jet destined for Africa. "We were squeezed like sardines into six seats abreast as the plane rolled suddenly forward and then skyward with a great whooshing of engines.

"We arrived at 2 a.m. at a very hot airport near Dakar, Senegal. Dressed in scratchy wool clothes and hiding my wallet in my underwear, I awoke in the dim dawn in the midst of tall black-skinned figures in long white robes, red fez hats, and bare feet."

THATCH-ROOFED MUD HUTS

Two days later Hughes had traveled by plane and truck to the village of Sucromo, Liberia, some 180 miles into the interior. Sucromo was a group of thatch-roofed mud huts with fires burning inside, and the people there spoke Kpelle. "My home for the first few months was a large white-washed building with a galvanized iron roof, kitchen, bath, and several small sleeping rooms. My English teaching was done in an old mud-thatch structure nearby."

Americans starting a life abroad in cultures very different from their own are warned about culture shock and cautioned that virtually no one can escape it, "yet some warm-hearted individuals expect that their good will and love for mankind will enable them to avoid it," Hughes remembered. "That was my expectation upon arrival in Africa. Riding up and down the motor road in our shiny green Jeep, I smiled and waved at the people walking along the road, filled with warm feelings about how I was going to help them live more fulfilled lives.

"As time passed, I had an uneasy feeling that the Africans around me were joking among themselves at these obviously green, foolish Americans who had traveled a long way from home to make a dent in their lives."

It took three to six months for Hughes to learn to accept matters as they were. "During this time I became quite friendly with people at the Lutheran Mission Hospital. I turned to them in the early days to see how they had dealt with this strange land. They also gave me access to their radio and occasionally to their airplane."

FIRST SCHOOLS

Two years earlier, the dirt path had been replaced by a road and with its completion had come the first schools. Now in the school's third year of operation, "the desire to 'learn book' was so great that our classes included youth of all ages, including many young men in their twenties."

Hughes traveled extensively in West Africa during his two-and-a-half years in **Liberia**, but had misgivings upon leaving.

"I had achieved the building of a school, the writing of a teacher's handbook, and two years' instruction of both African students and teachers. I had also helped to break in the IVS program in Liberia. But it was disappointing to find that, after barely two years in this country, the IVS program was being phased out and replaced by the Peace Corps, as the State Department had a policy of not having two U.S. programs competing in the same area."

Not all who served with IVS did so in developing countries. *Galen Beery* worked with Dr. Noffsinger in Washington, D.C., from 1959 to 1962 before heading off to Laos, where he stayed until 1967. In a 2014 memoir, he wrote: "My experience with International Voluntary Services was somewhat different from that of other IVSers. I first served with IVS's headquarters office in Washington, D.C., doing alternative service, continued on for a third year, then spent five years with IVS in Laos on the Rural Development Division (RDD) headquarters team.

"In 1959 I graduated from La Verne College in La Verne, California, and drove east to enter Brethren Voluntary Service (BVS). I had to register for the military draft, the norm for men in those days, but elected to request alternative service. I believed I could not with any conscience enter the armed forces of the U.S. I had been a member of the Church of the Brethren all my life and received a student deferment while attending college. The Brethren were one of the three historic peace denominations, the others being the Mennonites and the Quakers. My father was a minister. My mother's parents had been missionaries of some fame, initiating the church's mission field in India and serving there for twenty-five years.

"At this point it wasn't necessary to take a physical, but I had the chance to get one courtesy of the government and drove into a military recruiting center in Los Angeles. A hundred or so men aged seventeen and eighteen were there, for a cursory exam *en masse*. We stripped to boxer shorts and briefs and lined up for a doctor's examination holding our papers. Mine were the only ones stamped with a red 'I-AO', which intrigued other inductees in line, and I explained my choice."

ROLES IN LIFE

"Late that August six of us from La Verne drove to New Windsor, Maryland, for a six-week training period in the 44th BVS unit. This group had sixty men and women from all over the U.S. The Brethren Service Center had been built as a college, with dormitories, a cafeteria, and classrooms. We had small classes designed to make each of us aware of what we could do as volunteers, with discussion about goals and roles in life."

During this period the staff evaluated the group and looked over possible assignments. Beery was told there was a position in a small office in Washington, D.C., with a group known as International Voluntary Services, Inc. It was the first time he had heard of IVS. He would replace another man as recruiting secretary. "I felt a bit odd about the role as it was a white collar office job. The other BVSers in the group would be in what I thought of as real service."

THE CREATION OF THE PEACE CORPS

GALEN BEERY

"Quite a myth has grown around the beginning of the Peace Corps, that it was the dream of John F. Kennedy. Being with IVS in Washington gave me a deeper perspective.

In 1960, three members of Congress made a fact-finding trip to Southeast Asia. The most famous was progressive Sen. Hubert Humphrey, accompanied by representatives Reuss and Neuberger. Their goal was to check out whatever had inspired the writing of a book, *The Ugly American*, which fictionalized American aid programs in the country of 'Sarkan,' based on some rather ill-administered programs in Laos, Vietnam, and Cambodia. Americans were aghast, and the State Department took steps to correct problems.

During the few weeks while the three were in Vietnam and Laos, they were quite impressed by the IVSers. On flights back to the U.S. the delegation became excited about the idea of developing some sort of IVS group at the national level and when the three landed at National Airport, they immediately headed to telephones and contacted their offices to outline the concept.

The idea had merit, and soon a rather sharp assistant from (Senator) Humphrey's office showed up quite punctually for appointments. We'd talk a bit, and then after a few minutes Dr. Noffsinger would welcome him into his office. The two would discuss principles and programs for an hour. Each time Humphrey's man left, Dr. Noffsinger would close the door, turn and comment that "things seem to be moving quite well." And several days later *The Washington Post* would carry some of Noffsinger's ideas in an article on Sen. Humphrey's latest concept in what was being called the "Point Four Youth Corps."

Humphrey was running for President on the Democratic ticket, but although he had a following, he did not draw the attention given to young, charismatic Sen. John F. Kennedy. A Board member familiar with the race stated that when Humphrey decided to bow out, he passed on to Kennedy the idea of the "Point Four Youth Corps." His office received more mail and questions from the public on this than all other issues combined. Realizing a sure thing when he saw it, Kennedy and his advisors discussed the idea. His campaign took him to the steps of the University of Michigan in Ann Arbor, where he spoke of setting up a "Peace Corps." Students and supporters seized upon the concept, Kennedy was elected president, and the Peace Corps came into being.

Rather than having emerged like Minerva from the brain of Zeus, the Peace Corps was derived from the IVS experience. Or it goes back to Dr. Noffsinger and the arrival of the ship of teachers in the Philippines forty years earlier. Or, perhaps, even back to St. Paul and the Biblical plea, "Come over to Macedonia and help us!" ⁓

"The IVS office was then in Washington, D.C., in a large one-bedroom apartment. I was cordially greeted by *Frank*

Brainard, whom I was replacing, and shown around the main room. It had three desks, several filing cabinets and two typewriters. A mimeograph machine sat on the kitchen counter.

"After a short wait Dr. Noffsinger came out of the bedroom, which had been set up as his office. We sat at his desk and he told me a bit of IVS' history, then asked where I was staying. Frank had rented a room in a private home on north 18th Street near the zoo, and that day prevailed upon his landlord to let me move into his room even before he left for Liberia. The rental was $20 per month!

"I slowly grew into the position in the next months. My job was to receive mail and to check out applications from persons interested in positions with IVS. Dr. Noffsinger wrote up small ads for teachers' magazines and those with an agricultural audience. Some applicants had read ads or brochures, which Noffsinger's network of college professors had posted on bulletin boards. I read over the letters, sent applications to those who might have potential for the positions IVS was developing, and composed and typed 'sorry' letters for those who did not qualify."

Passports and Cover Letters

"Later I wrote descriptions of the countries, developed job descriptions and assisted approved applicants in securing passports, by taking the passports and cover letters to embassies for visas. Dr. Noffsinger believed in having a face-to-face meeting and discussion with each man and woman recruited.

"The office was actually rather quiet in those months. After Frank left, the only other person in the outer office was an elderly woman whom Dr. Noffsinger had hired out of compassion. She mistrusted people, and when he called her into his office to dictate letters, she made sure that the door was propped open. Her letters were so full of erasures that after she went home in the afternoon, I sometimes retyped them before he signed.

"Dr. Noffsinger had some health problems in the spring of 1960 and was under a doctor's orders to remain in his apartment.

I made a daily visit there and he would go over letters prepared, sign them, and advise me what he wanted done next.

"In organizing some of the office files I found and read board members' letters back and forth, discussing how IVS should operate. It was agreed that compensation should be no more than $60 per month, about the same as a private in the U.S. military, with travel, housing, and a small stipend for clothing. The word 'volunteers' merited discussion; 'IVSer' seemed more appropriate. IVS could qualify as alternative service for conscientious objectors. Several proposed logos were considered. One showed two hands gripping a short mattock against a hemisphere of the world: it was rejected as possibly representing struggle. The one finally accepted showed two hands gripping a torch of knowledge superimposed on the world, and the words International Voluntary Services encircling.

"Each month we received letters from the IVSers, telling of their experiences. With their agreement, we made correspondence easier for them by mimeographing letters and mailing copies to family and friends at IVS expense. Some never wrote; others went a bit overboard.

"Candidates were selected for specific positions after we carefully reviewed their qualifications. Dr. Noffsinger would ask me to find a person for a certain slot—say an electrician who could teach electrical skills at a national education center while wiring the buildings, or a poultry expert who could work with Vietnamese or Lao agriculturists to improve local breeds, or a public health nurse who could teach at a hospital.

"Noffsinger reviewed each letter of reference. He once tapped an open application and noted that 'A reference by one minister is fine...actually good. Two references are still good. But remember that ministers tend to see only the best in a person. If a candidate has references from five ministers, we must ask ourselves 'Why? Doesn't he know anyone else? Especially someone in his field of work?'"

An Indiana Farmer

"Early in 1960 a wizened little Indiana farmer opened our office door, and Dr. Noffsinger came out to meet him. They spent an hour in Dr. Noffsinger's office talking, and then the candidate ambled out with a few words and a quiet goodbye. Dr. Noffsinger seemed particularly pleased with him and turned and asked what I thought. 'Well,' I said politely, 'he's 48–a bit older than our usual recruits, and has no college training.' 'But he has the *experience*,' said Dr. Noffsinger enthusiastically, 'experience from farming all his life.' Mark my words; I think we'll hear quite a bit from *Edgar M. Buell*.'

"Buell flew to Hong Kong, Bangkok, and Vientiane, and was soon in central Laos, joining the IVS team on the Plaine des Jarres. He was soon nicknamed 'Pop' by younger IVSers. In a few months he was back in the capital, helping as the IVS team basically supervised the American aid program: most Americans and the USOM staff had moved to Bangkok because of a *coup-d'état*. Then Pop found the Hmong in the far north. Two years later he was the subject of a two-piece *Saturday Evening Post* article, 'An American Hero' about his aid to Hmong refugees. He was then immortalized in a book titled 'Mister Pop'."

Mister Pop

Working in Southeast Asian farmlands and rice paddies is generally a young person's game, and the majority of those who served with IVS in Laos, Cambodia and Vietnam were indeed rarely past their thirties. But as always, there are exceptions that prove the rule.

Edgar Buell, owner of a successful farm in Indiana, father and widower, was a lonely and depressed man. The death of his wife Mattie Loren had been devastating, and he needed a change of pace and of scenery. He signed up with IVS and was soon on his way to Laos.

Don A. Schance's book, *Mister Pop, The Adventures of a Peaceful Man in a Small War,* reads like an adventure novel. Buell often had run-ins with his IVS superiors and once chided an overly pious manager for playing Christian hymns before meals in their Laotian station near the Plaine des Jarres. He befriended Hmong tribesmen, 'borrowed' earth-moving machinery to create a dam for villagers, and tried (and failed) to stop the opium traffic in a nearby village. He also used money from his own retirement fund to further projects whose funding had dried up.

Buell's story involves run-ins with Pathet Lao troops, sixty-day walking journeys through Laos' rain forest, and followed in the footsteps of the famed Dr. Tom Dooley, founder of the Dooley Foundation in Vientiane.

Buell, though, had his critics. His free-wheeling ways and his association with the American intelligence community came under fire, and even within IVS, his legacy is contested.

❧

IVS IN THE NEWS

Stateside, IVS was in the news. A congressional delegation visited Southeast Asia and Vietnam just prior to President Kennedy's inauguration and reported on the success young IVSers were having in the field. IVS was recognized in early 1961 by Congressman Henry Reuss of Wisconsin who addressed the House of Representative to endorse President Kennedy's desire to establish a Peace Corps, largely based on the IVS profile. Rep. Reuss quoted at length a letter from IVSer *Don Schmidt* in Vietnam to friends in America, noting in particular the agricultural progress made in the region where he was serving as a volunteer.

Soon thereafter, and undoubtedly with IVS in mind, President Kennedy officially created the wildly successful and influential Peace Corps.

During the first decade, IVS worked in nine countries, but by the end of 1962, there were programs only in Liberia, Laos, Cambodia and Vietnam and seventy volunteers in the field.

The next ten-year period would spur a rapid geographic expansion of programs and multiply the number of volunteer assignments, particularly in Indochina.

Virtually all funding during this decade and the next came from the U.S. government, directly or by sub-contract. The Washington staff included the Executive Director, an office manager and part-time financial assistant until 1958, when staff expanded to include a program officer and a recruiter. The director traveled two to four months a year to inspect existing projects and seek new programs. This was a remarkable feat made possible by strong support and assistance from a very small, committed Board of Directors.

FINANCING PROBLEMS

The issues apparent in these first ten years set a pattern that continued throughout the life of IVS. There were almost always financing problems, and programs begun without adequate support, then often closed precipitously. There were widely scattered initiatives ranging from West Africa to Southeast Asia that should have been regional. Outreach made to countries in east and southern Africa, the Middle East and northern and southern Asia were initiated with not enough funds available for consistent development. In short, many IVS initiatives suffered from inconsistent planning and follow-through, and these limitations would have negative implications for the next forty years.

But realistically, the achievements easily outstripped the shortcomings. The first decade proudly demonstrated that volunteerism worked, and that young people, many from America's heartland, were among the best ambassadors any organization or government might want. And all in all, no one could deny that the work and responsibilities with which these volunteers had been entrusted were, beyond a shadow of a doubt, valuable and worthwhile endeavors.

Left to right, IVS volunteers Bob Yates, Richard Koegel, and Tom Luche with a local Catholic priest at the dedication of a new well near Ban Me Thuot, Vietnam , 1958

Don Schmidt and the gardener, a former French
Foreign Legionnaire, at the IVS house in Dalat, 1960

Bob Falasca, stationed at Bao Loc Tropical Research
Station, next to a laq tree being tapped as a source of
lacquer, 1960

Youngsters gathered at the IVS house, Saigon, including Lee Brockmueller at left, and Vietnamese friends. Lee was the older of two children accompanying his parents, Shirley and Gordon Brockmueller, when Gordon was Chief of Party IVS/VN. 1960

Family members in a local tribal longhouse. Vietnam, 1961

Bulbing onion trial field day, attended by numerous local officials and local farmers at Dalat Experiment Station, Vietnam, 1961. At center of photo and kneeling at left, Chuong Tsiung Yu, JCRR Vegetable specialist; standing, IVS volunteer Don Wadley; and kneeling at right, IVS volunteer Mike Chilton. Vietnam 1961

Phyllis (Colyer) Westover teaches English in Vietnam, 1961.

IVS members and staff in front of the IVS/Vietnam office/residence, Tan Son Nhut, Saigon, 1962

The first IVS Education Team boarding a plane on their way to Vietnam. From top of stairs: Bette Gau, Ann Wright (in back), Billie Lee Langley, Don Brewster, Fletcher Poling (in back), Tom Neal, Jay Parsons (in back), Forest Gerdes (in back), Roger Sweeny, Vince McGeehan, Truman Clark .

William Betts and the Malaria Vehicle, Quang Tri Province near the
North Vietnam border, 1964

Phyllis (Colyer) Westover and Nha Trang boys' high school students in Vietnam, 1964

Montagnard from the Central Highlands, 1964

Ricky Dunn teaching English to Montagnard sisters in Kontum, Vietnam, 1966

Hope Harmeling Benne at an orphanage, Vietnam, 1967

Stuart Rawlings' Christmas Card, Vietnam, 1967

Robert Hargreaves and friend, Vietnam, 1967

Boats in Hue on Perfume River, 1970

IVS volunteers demonstrating against the Vietnam War in front of the American Embassy in Manila, 1967

A young girl and her brother separated from their parents during the Tet Offensive, Vietnam, 1968

Top photo: The spoils of war, Vietnam, 1968

Bottom photo: A young Montagnard of the Bru tribe in
northwest South Vietnam going to harvest crops

Children at play with spent ammunition, Vietnam, 1968

IVS Volunteer Jimmy Bigelow and friend, Vietnam, 1968

Delores Honig with students at the IVS House in Tan An, Vietnam, 1969

THE SECOND DECADE
1963–1972

LAOS · VIETNAM · CAMBODIA · LIBERIA · JORDAN
SUDAN · ZIMBABWE · ALGERIA · MOROCCO
YEMEN · SYRIA

IVS' SECOND DECADE BEGAN amid the increasing turmoil in
Vietnam and was largely shaped by events in what was then
called French Indochina—Laos, Vietnam and Cambodia, though
projects were initiated both in Africa and in the Middle East.

TRAGEDY

The second decade was also when IVS began to internationalize by
hiring foreign nationals who were brought on to translate and
facilitate, work in the IVS offices, and become tutors. And it
saw its share of tragedy. Eleven IVSers were killed or died in
accidents. One woman was captured and released within three
weeks, while *Sandra Johnson, Marc Cayer* and *Gary Daves* were
taken prisoner in Hue by NVA soldiers during the Tet offensive
of 1968. Johnson was freed March 31, 1968; Daves and Cayer
remained captives until March 27, 1973.

Most volunteers joined IVS shortly after graduating from college. IVS offered an opportunity to live overseas and participate
in humanitarian work and this challenge was eagerly accepted.
In the early years of IVS, many volunteers also joined because of
the prospect of adventure and for the practical purpose of gaining experience in development work that would prepare them
for future careers. Later, as the American war escalated, some
volunteers regarded IVS service as a way to prove their credibility

as conscientious objectors, while others sought to understand the conflict that was so bitterly dividing America.

Certainly, for those on staff who were conscientious objectors, the decision to work in Vietnam was a difficult one. Some chose to resign, others were reassigned; others still went home to the States to campaign against the war.

The assassination of President John F. Kennedy on November 22, 1963, brought the world temporarily to a halt. IVS volunteers knew the young president as a friend of volunteerism, and his loss reverberated through the international NGO community. "The telephones lit up and we spent the next three days trying to pass on information to people in the field," remembers one volunteer. "There were areas that even radio didn't reach, much less television, and volunteers and staff were desperate for information. We were up thirty-six hours fielding calls."

The death of the young President who championed volunteerism did not deter young people from serving. The IVSers sent to Vietnam, Laos and Cambodia included engineers and administrators, but the majority of volunteers were agricultural experts and teachers.

I. VIETNAM

The initial decision to send volunteers to Vietnam had not been an easy one. Debate raged over the safety of volunteers in a war zone, and the political motivations of the government.

By 1956, Noffsinger had come to believe IVS's involvement in Vietnam would be beneficial to the country, and the first batch of volunteers arrived early the following year. It was a small group of mostly recent graduates of agricultural programs and was predominantly male except for the spouse of a volunteer. For its first years the IVS/Vietnam program remained small and continued to focus on agricultural and rural development projects.

By the early 1960s the IVS role in Vietnam expanded to include activities other than agriculture, principally education, which meant that the program grew in size, became urban as well as rural based, and included a number of women. At its peak in 1967, IVS had over 160 volunteers in Vietnam and by the time it departed in mid-1971, IVS had fielded approximately 400 volunteers in that war-torn land.

EXPERIENTIAL LEARNING
DAVE COLYER, VIETNAM 1963-65

During our first month in Vietnam, a small group of IVSers, including my wife Phyllis and I, lived in the Mekong Delta town of My Tho to learn the language. After a week or so of intensive training, our instructor declared we were ready for a field trip to town.

On our walk to the central market, we collected an entourage of local kids, calling out "Ong My! Ong My!" "Americans! Americans!" to other children running toward us from side streets and alleys. Their wide-open curiosity was funny and kind of charming at first, but then turned unsettling when it became clear they were comparing our physical appearance to theirs: lighter skin, hair and eye colors, larger bodies, big hands, big ears. It got way more personal for me when one of the kids pointed to his own nose and then jabbed his finger at my proud, prominent Scottish nose and laughed!

Finally, we arrived at the market and focused on identifying sweet lychee fruit, foul-smelling durian, plucked chickens complete with necks and heads and eyes and beaks, black-coated 'ten-year-old' duck eggs, or was that a hundred years?

Standing in front of one of the produce stands, I felt a tickling sensation on the big toe of my left foot. Looking down, I expected to see some kind of exotic bug crawling across the open-toe sandals we all wore in the Delta's smothering heat. Instead, I found two of our street escorts squatting at my feet on the gray cement floor, intently looking down at them. They glanced at each other before one reached out, spread his thumb and forefinger and measured the length of my toe. Thanks to the mind-numbing language work we had done, I roughly deciphered the boy's muttered comment to his friend: "Whaa! Lon qua!"

"Wow! It's huge!" ❦

It was in 1962 that *Charles Ross* was sitting in an industrial arts class at Los Angeles State College when the instructor read a letter from IVS, requesting people to work in Vietnam, Cambodia and Laos. "The biggest surprise that day was that none of the other twenty-two students in the class knew where these countries were located."

THE UGLY AMERICAN

Ross did, though. He had read *The Ugly American, Dr. Tom Dooley,* and *The History of Vietnam.* "I filled out the application and the reply came back asking for my wife, Louise, to also apply."

Louise taught English as a second language (ESL) and Ross worked in a technical school in Vinh Long. They left Vietnam after Louise was evacuated following the Gulf of Tonkin incident in August 1964. "We left with a beautiful Vietnamese/Chinese adopted daughter born in Saigon. This experience shaped the rest of our lives. It subsequently shaped our career choices. I ended up teaching on the Zuni and Navajo Indian reservations of New Mexico as well as the inner city of Newark, New Jersey. Louise finished her Master's Degree in Nurse Midwifery at Columbia University and started to work in the South Bronx.

"I'm sure I learned more from the Vietnamese than they from me. I never regretted going to Vietnam because it paved the way to doing many other things in life, things my wife and I might not have ever done."

John Sommer, with IVS in Vietnam from 1963 to 1967, remembers that, "I always had the travel bug, probably due to growing up in pleasant enough New York suburbs with foreign-born parents and grandparents, having numerous international visitors at home, and then being exposed to Asian cultures at college."

When President Kennedy created the Peace Corps, "there was no question that's what I would do upon graduation in 1963. But the Peace Corps took too long to respond to my application, so I accepted IVS's offer to teach English in Vietnam, thinking that the French I'd learned on a semester in Paris would help me in the then still-francophone country (it did)."

A month of language training in the Mekong Delta town of My Tho, punctuated by a few days' work camp with a lively Vietnamese youth group, was followed by another few weeks in Ban Me Thuot, in the central highlands, where Sommer exchanged Vietnamese and English language lessons with a young Buddhist monk who was later killed by the Ngo Dinh Diem regime.

STRATEGIC HAMLETS

"My assignment took me to Dalat and Bao Loc in late August of 1963, teaching English part-time. My main job was to help establish primary schools in the new 'strategic hamlets', many of them Montagnard spread throughout the rural highlands. Sixty-plus classrooms were constructed during my time there, with at least as many local teachers trained to staff them. It was a fascinating and rewarding experience that has lived with me since, and influenced my entire life and career."

In early 1965, Sommer was asked to stay on and become team leader for IVS volunteers in the northern provinces of South Vietnam, based in Hue. He also served as liaison between USAID and various Vietnamese student groups that were beginning to be involved in social service activities. "I was encouraged to do so, I eventually realized, to keep them off the streets and from protesting against their unpopular government and, increasingly, its U.S. allies."

With schisms between Buddhists and Catholics, rising overall political tensions, and the introduction of substantial U.S. troops, this was a challenging assignment. Sommer was interacting with young local leaders who were certainly different from the Montagnards he'd previously known. But in the end, he found it rewarding in terms of the alliances fostered and the service activities undertaken. He tells of his experiences in *Vietnam–The Unheard Voices*, a book he subsequently co-authored with IVS Chief of Party Don Luce.

LOOKING BACK

WILLIE MEYERS

VIETNAM 1963-65, WASHINGTON 1965-66, VIETNAM 1966-67

Looking back, life seems to be a series of doors opening and closing and opportunities taken or not. What started with IVS in Vietnam has much to do with where I am today. But volunteering with IVS was not the first influential event in my life.

I grew up in a Mennonite community in Souderton, Pennsylvania, and my international contacts were mostly through missionaries coming to our home and our church. While a student at Christopher Dock Mennonite High School, I was a member of a boys' quartet that sang in Ontario and later Cuba, Puerto Rico and Jamaica. These trips opened my eyes to other worlds, especially Cuba just six months after the Revolution. Attending Goshen College got me involved in peace movements, writing and going to Washington, D.C., to lobby policymakers in support of peace issues, particularly the nuclear test ban treaty. I applied to both the Peace Corps and IVS.

The Peace Corps offered me Sierra Leone; IVS would send me to Vietnam. In early 1963, Vietnam was not yet a political hot-spot, and I decided to go there because, though it may sound naïve or silly, my junior year roommate was from Japan, and Vietnam was in Asia too.

The door IVS opened for me led to the Education team's Hamlet School Program, designed to win hearts and minds by building self-help schools in villages to improve children's education. I grew up in a carpenter family and worked summers in the building trade; IVS felt this qualified me for the assignment. I probably knew more about building than about teaching English, but I did some of both, because English was in demand everywhere. After language training, I went off to Vinh Long to work with the Primary Education Department of the Province, then was transferred to the town of Cao Lanh, in the next province up the river. I also taught English in the local high school and my best friends were other high school teachers, some of whom joined us at summer work camps that were among that year's highlights.

After a year in Cao Lanh, IVS decided my degree in Mathematics qualified me to take over the Mobile Science Program, so in my second year I became the science teacher in Hue and the surrounding province of Thua Thien. It was an amazing change, because the work and the living environment were completely different. Two Vietnamese teachers were actually doing the teaching but I was helping to prepare the demonstrations and techniques we delivered in elementary schools around the province. The counterpart was again the Primary Education Department of the Province. I felt it was a great program, and IVS recruited proper science teachers and expanded it to three other provinces in later years.

The next door opened for me was in the U.S. when I became Recruitment Officer in Washington, D.C. This was an opportunity to share my experiences with college students around the country and invite them to join IVS. It was during this time that my friend and colleague, *Pete Hunting*, a Team Leader in the Mekong Delta region, became the first IVSer killed in Vietnam, a devastating tragedy. When I was asked to take up his position, I was honored to do so. It was June, 1966, and IVS was still growing. I led new volunteers through Los Banos, Philippines, training, then introduced some of them to their new assignments and counterparts in Vietnam. Volunteers didn't need much guidance if pointed in the right direction, so my task was to get them oriented and housed, and offer backstopping if and when needed.

During my second tour, security was deteriorating and many of us could see conditions were worsening as the U.S. presence in Vietnam increased and became a virtual parallel government. Our Vietnamese friends and colleagues felt we would help them more by speaking against the war policy than by trying to do good deeds in Vietnam. By then, I was practically a career IVSer, having worked in Washington and Vietnam, and visited several other posts in Laos and Algeria. It was not an easy decision, but ultimately I joined *Don Luce, Gene Stoltzfus* and *Don Ronk* in resigning. We, along with many other IVSers, sent a letter to President Johnson in protest of the war policies. It was a leap of faith since we couldn't know if it would make any difference. We did know it was the right thing to do.

In September, Don, Gene and I made our way to Washington. By this time the anti-war movement in the U.S. was gaining strength and we vowed to use our unique knowledge of Vietnam to inform decision-makers and the public about the folly of the U.S. war policy. Our key message, based on personal observations, was that this path was not only ineffective but actually counterproductive.

We were babes in the wilderness when it came to Washington politics. I was mostly organizing while Don and Gene were traveling around the country speaking to church and civic groups. One of my few presentations in this period was a 'point-counterpoint' discussion with (then Deputy Secretary of State) John Negroponte.

We testified before Congress and helped Congressmen plan Vietnam trips that included candid conversations with Vietnamese youth and IVSers. The Tet Offensive in February, 1968, demonstrated the truth of our statements that events were not going as well as claimed.

Gene, Don and others continued the struggle many years. Don's revelation of the Tiger Cages to Senator Harkin in 1970, and Gene's assistance to the Bella Abzug delegation to Vietnam in 1975 were among the critical actions that turned the tide of U.S. policy.

During this time of turmoil, I had some advice from John Mellor, a member of the IVS Board of Directors and a famous agricultural development professor and writer. He suggested I combine my mathematics skills and IVS-based development interests, so I went to Los Banos for an MS in agricultural economics. On the way, IVS Director Arthur Gardiner asked me to spend some time in Indonesia to check out potential IVS programs. After two weeks of Berlitz in Indonesian, I went to live in Djakarta. In time, we did set up an IVS program in partnership with the Indonesian National Voluntary Service, but only were able to fund one volunteer.

My newfound enthusiasm for agricultural economics led me to a PhD program at the University of Minnesota, but my ties to Asia were strengthened by spending more than a year as Research Fellow at the International Rice Research Institute (IRRI) in the Philippines and finally persuading Dali Cuento to marry me and move to colder climes.

In my resignation letter of 1967 (See Appendix IV), I ended by saying that I hoped to return to Vietnam 'when Vietnam has a government that is free from foreign domination and a people that is free from the ravages of war.' After moving to the University of Missouri in 2003, this dream came true at last. I have advised two Vietnamese graduate students, and helped develop collaboration with the Vietnam Academy of Agricultural Sciences that will foster annual scholarly exchanges.

It is a thrill to attend the Tet parties of our Vietnamese students every year, to visit them in Vietnam and see them realize *their* dreams. ⚬⚬

Early in 1964, after Cambodian head of state Norodom Sihanouk ended all aid programs and ousted American volunteers, *Tom Wickham* left Cambodia and headed for Vietnam. After three weeks of language training, IVS assigned him to Can Tho in the Mekong Delta as an advisor to the provincial agriculture office, and also as an assistant in the USAID-supported pacification project. "Both provided rewarding experiences. Vietnamese agricultural officials were pleased to have me, since I could sometimes provide resources or materials or safe travel on U.S. helicopters that were virtually unavailable through bureaucratic government channels." The first of a long succession of new high-yielding rice varieties was being introduced in demonstration plots showing the difference from traditional varieties. The key difference for many farmers was not the higher yield, but the shorter season to bring the crop to maturity. "The Mekong Delta was a congenial home for me since it was once part of Cambodia and still contained over one million ethnic Cambodians."

Under the USAID pacification program, undertaken to 'win hearts and minds,' were grants of up to 20,000 piasters to a village for a self-help project. But the project had to be agreed upon by a clear majority of the villagers through a series of meetings, and they had to contribute labor and local construction materials.

SKEPTICAL VILLAGERS

"During the nine months I was in Can Tho, three projects were built and two or three more likely to be approved," Wickham said. "Because government officials were often viewed with some suspicion, my role was to reassure skeptical villagers and help find a consensus view of what project to build." Generally, women wanted a medical clinic or maternity facility; men often preferred a permanent walking bridge over a canal or a concrete pad for a day market. "I reviewed the designs for some of these structures and watched over some construction details, but for the most part Vietnamese officials looked after the details themselves."

At the end of his initial two-year assignment, Wickham stayed on in Vietnam as IVS assistant team leader for agriculture. That position primarily involved finding suitable placements for new IVS volunteers throughout South Vietnam. This meant locating provincial agriculture offices that were safe enough for American volunteers to work in without military protection.

"My move from IVS Cambodia to IVS Vietnam reflected a shift in the larger picture of how IVS operated in the mid-1960s. The earlier model was a very hands-on involvement of volunteers in every phase of a development project—in my case building infrastructure at a livestock station. Many volunteers of that

period can look back on satisfying accomplishments, relationships and sometimes important improvements in village life. The
most successful volunteers then usually were practical people
with real farm experience."

Working through Others

The later phase, carried out primarily in Vietnam from 1964
on, relied on working through local agricultural or rural affairs
officials. "The role of volunteers became one level removed
from the project itself; they worked through others rather than
building projects on their own," Wickham said. "The ability to
communicate and work through others takes certain personality
traits that aren't needed and may even have been unhelpful in
the earlier model. Volunteers increasingly derived satisfaction
from the less tangible sense that someone else did the work."
The farming background of volunteers was still useful, but probably more important was the ability to know which provincial
programs and officers they could assist, and how to assist them.

"Fifty years later I can't say how successful or long-lasting
my work in Vietnam was. I'm pretty sure, though, that a number
of Vietnamese officials and villagers came to understand and appreciate what I tried to achieve, and that's enough satisfaction
for me."

Phyllis Westover was assigned as a teacher to Nha Trang in
1963 along with her former husband, Dave Colyer, a conscientious objector who worked with the malaria eradication team.

The Bed
PHYLLIS WESTOVER, VIETNAM 1963-65

The first item of commercial business in Nha Trang where
my former husband, *Dave Colyer*, and I were assigned in
1963 was to buy a bed long enough for Dave's rangy 6' 4"
frame and wide enough for two. Since we lacked sufficient
grip on Vietnamese to bargain for its making, a seasoned

IVSer temporarily in Nha Trang went with me to a carpentry shop to make the arrangements while Dave was in a meeting. We gave the owner the dimensions of the bed we wanted made and asked him if he would make it.

A truncated conversation resulted: "No, it's unnecessary to make a bed that big."

"Yes, it is. It's for a very tall man."

"No, it's unnecessary."

A day later we returned with tall Dave, which produced laughter from the owner, his wife, and an assistant. The owner agreed to build the bed and a price was agreed upon.

I returned on the date we were told to come back with a second seasoned IVSer, the first being unavailable. The owner's wife and two assistants came to talk to us. They said the bed wasn't ready yet and raised the issue of cost. We told them we'd already agreed upon a cost with the owner. They seemed disappointed and said, "But don't you want to bargain?" So we did, and the price came down. Apparently, they just wanted the novelty of bargaining with an American.

A week later Dave and I returned with a third seasoned IVSer to get and pay for the bed. This time the owner and five others came out to meet us with much laughter and conversation among themselves. We left with the bed precariously balanced on our vehicle. Our third seasoned IVSer rolled his eyes and said to us, "You know what they were laughing about?"

We didn't.

"They think you need a big bed because all the men who came in to arrange for it are going to sleep with Phyllis in it together!" ⚬

"I didn't learn for months that as the newest teacher and last on board at the Boys' High School, I got the heaviest schedule," Westover said. She taught four two-hour English pronunciation classes from eight in the morning to noon and two to six pm.

"Each class had sixty boys who ranged in age from twelve to twenty, the smaller boys sitting at the front and the older, taller boys at the back."

Since the textbooks had not arrived when she began teaching, she improvised and designed her own materials. "By the end of the day, my voice was shot. What saved my *tush* was the course on teaching English as a foreign language that I audited at San Francisco State University the semester before we left. I learned to divide large classes by sections and rows to discern those who were having trouble with particular pronunciations."

DISGRUNTLED

The younger boys, she discovered, were eager to learn but the older boys often seemed disgruntled to be in school. "Two boys in particular were sullen. One afternoon, one of these boys lit a cigarette, a flagrant act of disrespect. I strode down the aisle and snatched it out of his mouth and threw it out the window. Shortly after, when the two stopped coming to class, I learned from my Vietnamese counterpart teachers that the two were Viet Cong sympathizers and had run off to join the VC."

About this time, she was told by the commander of the MAAG Compound where she rode her bicycle each day to check for mail that her habits were well-known and that, "I was not to ride my bicycle to the MAAG Compound again. It was entirely possible for the handlebars of my bicycle to be stuffed with plastic explosives timed to go off at the MAAG.

"Sure, we knew the shifting, amorphous nature of the war. Our Vietnamese friends warned us when it was unsafe to drive into the countryside to buy charcoal for our cook's stove, and when it was safe again. But the regular demands of job and life overrode the subtle, ever-present tension of working in a war zone. It wasn't until our first vacation in Singapore, Malaysia and Thailand where we attended night events and walked freely afterwards that I became aware of the war tension by its absence—like not being aware of a refrigerator motor running until it switches off."

Most of the time, work was all-absorbing and included op-portunities to know the students and teachers better. "There was a trip into the countryside with the English Club to scatter DDT around garbage and debris sites where rats were multiplying and an outbreak of plague had been reported; a day's outing with fel-low English teachers to an offshore island where we had a picnic and snorkeled among coral reefs to view amazing fish, and visits with new Vietnamese friends at our IVS station house where we made homemade ice cream."

So many townspeople wanted to learn English for business purposes that Westover began teaching an evening course for the Vietnamese-American Association. This brought together a mixture of people who ordinarily would not associate with each other: professionals, shopkeepers, and bar girls, each with his or her own reasons for learning English.

Her teaching schedule changed radically when she contracted infectious hepatitis after eating polluted shellfish. "I became seri-ously ill just at the time President Kennedy was shot, and had to withdraw from teaching. I was touched by the teachers who came to offer their condolences for the loss of our President and to extend their best wishes for my recovery."

Following several days at the Seventh Day Adventist Hospital in Saigon and a month's convalescence, Westover returned to Nha Trang to resume teaching morning classes at the Boys' High School, and a class at the Girls' High School in the afternoon. She also taught nurses and midwives who worked with volunteer American doctors at the Provincial Hospital.

GULF OF TONKIN

With the Gulf of Tonkin bombing incident in August 1964, Westover's IVS tour of duty and that of other married IVS women volunteers was interrupted. "In an irrational and sexist decision from the U.S. government, married women were ordered to leave Vietnam, although single IVS women with identical contracts could stay. This 'women and children to the lifeboats' mentality made no sense; Dave and I had no children, nor was I pregnant. I was fully engaged in my teaching and Dave was just beginning the filming for the documentary we made, *IVS Vietnam: Commitment to Growth,** on the work of IVS in Vietnam. I was writing the script; it was a bad time to leave." Westover protested and asked for reconsideration. "Chief of Party Don Luce reported that my request was denied. I scrambled to pack amid good-bye parties from teacher and student friends and was humbled by their gifts and expression of loss." Just a few hours before her plane was to depart for Bangkok, Luce got word that the U.S. government would review Westover's request, "but he couldn't promise that the answer would not be the same. I decided to go."

For the next month, Westover and other evacuees stayed at the Christian Guest House in Bangkok where she negotiated in vain with the American Embassy to return to Vietnam. She went to Hong Kong and did volunteer work with the American Friends Service Committee and waited for her husband to complete his IVS contract. "If there was any plus to this fiasco, it was a train trip to Siem Reap to see Angkor Wat before it was shot up by the Khmer Rouge in their appalling attack on Cambodians."

...AND SO, YEARS LATER...

PHYLLIS WESTOVER

My former husband, Dave Colyer, a conscientious objector, was working with the Malaria Eradication Team in Vietnam as his alternative service. In November of 1963, Dave and his interpreter, Thanh Van Nguyen, drove from our IVS house in Nha Trang to Hue. Their vehicle might have been the buff-colored Land Rover belonging to the Malaria Office, or the powder-blue Jeep with IVS spelled out on its side in dark pink Vietnamese.

---

*The film was purchased by USAID and used as a recruitment film for IVS and USAID. It also aired on public television and was shown at universities, churches, and various organizations.

On their return trip, they were stopped on a rural dirt road
by the Viet Cong. The spokesman told them, "We know who
you are, where you've been, what you do, and where you are
going. We advise you to go back exactly the way you came;
you've already missed three land mines." Dave and Thanh
back-tracked their route exactly, following the marks of their
tires in the dust. When they reached the city, they took a
different route home.

Years pass, and in the 1980s Dave gets a call telling him
that Thanh Van Nguyen has been released from a Communist re-education camp for Vietnamese who worked with
Americans. Thanh is trying to contact Dave to see if Dave
will sponsor him and his family to resettle in the United
States. Dave agrees, and Thanh, his wife and, I think, three
children come to Oklahoma City to live in the house where
Dave and I formerly lived. The timing is perfect. Dave and
I have divorced, and I have moved to Kansas City, Missouri.
Dave is spending most of his time with his *fiancée* in a nearby
bedroom community, so our former brick ranch in a nice
neighborhood of Oklahoma City is lightly used and is available. The Thanh Van Nguyen family arrives and moves in.
I have seen photos of the family in wool caps and coats, smil-
ing in their first snow in front of our former house. Over the
years I have twice visited the family and can report that the
Nguyens have thrived. The kids all did well in school and
college and have good jobs. I continue to exchange Christmas cards with Thanh.

COOK, MAID, INTERPRETER, AND DRIVER

Mike Chilton, raised on an Iowa farm and holder of a Masters in
economic botany and seed technology, found himself on the way
to a two-year assignment in Vietnam mere days after graduating
from Iowa State College.

"I was assigned to the horticultural experiment station in
Dalat," he recalled. "I worked alone for a while, learning the
language and becoming familiar with new assignments. I was
living at the IVS house, an elegant holdover from the French

colonial period. The place came with a staff of cook, maid, interpreter and driver, which I was expected to oversee and support,
an unexpected role for a volunteer in Vietnam.

"Work at the experimental station went far beyond what I
could anticipate. The station manager seemed little schooled in
management. His purposes and direction were unclear, other
than keeping good rapport with staff and workers and the gates
open." Serendipitously, a JCRR technician (Joint Commission
on Rural Reconstruction) from Taiwan was assigned to the
station shortly after Chilton arrived. The man was an excellent
horticulturalist with many good ideas for Vietnam. Chilton soon
realized his own job was to keep his eyes and ears open, his mouth
shut, and learn. He was neither a schooled nor an experienced
horticulturalist.

"After the first year in Vietnam, I was reassigned to the IVS
office in Saigon, where I assumed team leadership for volunteers
located in the highland provinces. Still dealing with agricultural
and horticultural issues at the experimental centers, I also became responsible for an emerging project for tribal people of
the highlands who were being relocated for security reasons.
The Montagnard Development and Training program included
about eight centers in as many provinces, providing stop-gap
educational, agricultural and health assistance at the village
level." This program required a high awareness of the deteriorating security as the country's internal conflict grew.

EFFORTS EXPANDED

In 1963, Chilton signed up for a second two-year tour with IVS.
His activities reflected the growing role of IVS as American efforts
expanded in Vietnam. "A five-man malaria control component
was established within IVS, consisting of field laboratory stations, educational extension, and maintenance of work vehicles.
There was also a Rural Youth Program within the College of
Agriculture in Saigon, where agricultural students were assigned
to weekend, summer and special projects within village areas so
they could learn more about rural Vietnam."

He recalls now that, "As a volunteer, I was an insignificant entity. I had to leverage my effectiveness by making the right choices. The right solution to a known problem tended to gain its own momentum."

Mike Benge, who was in Vietnam with IVS in 1963 and 1964, recalls, "My tour with the Marines in Iwakuni, Japan, had whetted my appetite for foreign travel, but unfortunately the only organization offering overseas employment was the CIA (Central Intelligence Agency). I said what the hell to myself and submitted an application anyway. A few weeks later, I received a letter of rejection from the CIA suggesting I apply to the Agency for International Development (USAID). I did and received another rejection letter suggesting I contact the International Voluntary Services, which interviewed me and liked the fact that I already had overseas experience and proficiency for languages. IVS was subcontracted by USAID, with a $77.10 a month salary plus a food and housing allowance. I was offered a position as an 'advisor' at an agricultural school in Cambodia."

GENTLE PEOPLE

In January 1963, Benge arrived in Saigon to find diplomatic relations between the U.S. and Cambodia had soured, so he was reassigned to a Vietnamese technical school at Vinh Long in the Mekong Delta, after undergoing language training. "The Vietnamese language teacher was a bachelor just about to get married and so all aflutter—he ended up teaching us very little Vietnamese. I spent most of my time talking to fishermen and their families who tied their boats along the banks of the Thạch Hãn River separating North and South Vietnam." With only a few words learned, Benge would point to something, ask what it was in Vietnamese and then repeat in English what was said to him. "I don't know how much English they learned, but I began to pick up a pretty good command of conversational Vietnamese. After a while, these gentle people would invite me onto their boats for tea or to share a very meager meal. To this day, whenever I speak Vietnamese, I'm told I must have learned Vietnamese in Quang Tri, for I speak with an accent from there."

USAID had built and equipped several technical vocational schools in different provinces. Benge wasn't in Vinh Long long before receiving notice that he was being replaced by a highly paid USAID advisor and transferred to a technical school at Ban Me Thuot in the Central Highlands. The school had been built to train Montagnards to use high-tech machines such as lathes and arc welders. "Their agrarian lifestyle did not support the use of these skills. Also, the Vietnamese economy wasn't yet at the stage where graduates would be able to find employment, especially since the Vietnamese discriminated against the Montagnards.

"When I arrived, I found that the school had two very skilled Montagnard instructors so there was little I could do to advise them; the Vietnamese director of the school seemed only interested in my teaching him English. Nevertheless, I was able to scrounge a considerable amount of equipment and materials the school could use from USAID warehouses in Saigon and fly it to Ban Me Thuot to supplement the meager budget allocated for supplies."

Benge was also tasked with supervising USAID's ambitious program of constructing elementary schools, especially in the rural areas, training teachers and providing school supplies throughout Vietnam. USAID provided a generous amount of imported cement and aluminum roofing for each classroom, while the contractor purchased wood and sand on the local market. "The contractors received a fair wage for building the classrooms," Benge remembers, "but unfortunately too many of them increased their profit margin by skimping on the amount of cement used. Also, there was a generous amount of aluminum roofing provided for the schools, and the contractors often sold it on the local market; it commanded a premium price since it reflected sunlight and heat much better than tin roofing."

A POCKETKNIFE AND A SCREWDRIVER

Benge's job was to inspect the schools for quality of construction. "I used a pocket knife, screwdriver and small ball peen hammer. If I could strike the floor with the hammer and leave a dent or break through the floor, easily twist the screwdriver through the cement blocks; or scrape out the mortar between the blocks with a knife without difficulty, it meant that the contractor had skimped on the cement and had not used the proper ratio of cement to sand. After the first two or three schools I inspected didn't pass muster or meet specifications, I told the contractor that I would report it to the Province Chief and have his contract canceled if he didn't do it right. I forced the contractor to rebuild them; after that the quality of the work vastly improved."

The IVS agricultural advisor's departure provided Benge the opportunity to take over as advisor to a Montagnard extension team. He moved from the IVS house to the house of a team member who spoke some English. "We cut bamboo and grass and added a small lean-to onto the house where I slept on a bed of bamboo slats. We agreed I would pay for the food we ate and he would teach me the *lingua franca* of the Montagnard tribes; in turn, I would teach him English."

The agricultural extension team was a dozen men and women, the men in agricultural extension agent roles and the women in home economics, teaching village women improved techniques in hygiene, baby care, and health and nutrition. The team spent much of their time in the villages. "This was somewhat ineffective since the villagers were often not at home but out in the field. We decided the team would be much more effective by focusing activities on the school for the teacher and pupils who were there five days a week, and create school gardens and fish ponds while raising a couple of pigs. The women on the team taught hygiene and nutrition at the school and held demonstration classes for the village women."

The team's first target was the technical vocational school where meals for the boarding students were nutritionally inadequate, partially due to skimming by the contractor supplying food. A school garden project was incorporated into the curriculum, and the nutritional intake of the students vastly improved. With the exception of purchasing rice, the students consumed the product of their labors and sold vegetables at the market. The money saved from the food contract and from the excess vegetables was put into a special fund for the students, who decided how it was to be spent.

INCREASED PARTICIPATION

The schools soon became models for the villagers and centers for agricultural extension. Parents increased their participation in the school activities. If there were agricultural or health problems in the villages (e.g., disease, rat, grasshopper outbreaks), it became the teacher's responsibility to come to the province and report what was wrong or needed so that proper assistance could be dispatched immediately. Animal vaccinations were also provided. The program was very successful and similar programs were adopted in other provinces.

Later, Benge moved to Kontum province to establish an agricultural training center for the Montagnards. When his two-year tour with IVS was almost over, he went to Saigon for a little R&R, dropped by the USAID Rural Affairs Office, and was immediately offered a contract to work there. "So began my forty-one years with USAID."

MALARIA AND CHOLERA

William Betts was in Vietnam with IVS from 1963 to 1965. "IVS was seeking college graduates in science and health to work as malaria specialists in Vietnam. I applied and was accepted. What led me to volunteer for two years in the jungles of Vietnam in the middle of a war? Adventure and foreign travel!"

Betts' first year was spent at a jungle study center in the extreme northwestern corner of South Vietnam on the border of North Vietnam and Laos in western Quang Tri Province. The second year included work in four additional provinces.

"At first I was supervising and heading a team of Vietnamese malaria workers. We found the malaria vector in Vietnam and Southeast Asia. This was in a region where malaria rates were the highest in the country, where babies were not named until their first birthday because malaria alone killed fifty percent of *all* babies in a population of some 40,000 Montagnards."

Then, in 1965, following the worst flood the country was to suffer in more than a century, Betts was involved in a cholera epidemic and recovery operation.

"Hundreds of villages throughout central Vietnam were totally isolated by flood waters and few, very few, medical and public health personnel were able to reach so many in need of help. The Vietnamese government and the U.S. military agreed to support the mobilization of the malaria program teams. I was asked to use U.S. Army helicopters and what boats we could find to help scores of totally isolated villages in hopes of containing the epidemic, which had already claimed hundreds of lives."

The malaria program dispatched 220 workers to assist Betts and others in this effort. During one nineteen-day stretch, they spent eighteen to twenty hour days ferrying malaria and other health personnel with medicines and messages for communities throughout the provinces, urging all residents to boil their drinking water and protect their food supplies from flies. "The U.S. Army provided our teams with transportation to those villages cut off completely. I never counted the sorties by boats, trucks, helicopters, airplanes and on foot. During the helicopter sorties, our choppers took multiple hits from small arms fire. The bullets penetrated the chopper interior and thudded inches from our faces. We all knew why and what we were doing and while we were afraid, we never talked about it afterward." Betts and his team were credited by Vietnamese officials and attending physicians with saving thousands of lives in a month's time.

In June 1963, twelve single men, four single women and a few married couples went to Vietnam together. Among them was *Carlie (Allender) Numi*, whose original intentions had been to go to French-speaking Africa with the Peace Corps to hone her language skills. When it came time to decide where to serve, she opted for IVS, "I liked the idea of working for a small non-governmental organization that would be more personal and less bureaucratic."

TONAL LANGUAGE

Almost immediately on arriving in Vietnam, the single volunteers were taken to My Tho in the Delta region for language training. "We spent six weeks together exploring the town and trying to learn the intricacies of this tonal language After language training, four of us were assigned to stay and work in My Tho. *Anne Hensley* and I became English teachers in the local public high schools."

Hensley and Numi spent their two years there. Hensley taught in the boys' high school and Numi in the girls' high school. "I certainly had the easier assignment," Numi recalled. "That said, my classes had sixty to seventy preteen girls in each and were often two hours long. Fortunately, we'd had some coaching in the art of teaching English as a foreign language from the U.S. Information Service staff."

The principal of Numi's school was an older woman with a serious demeanor. "The students were fearful of her—you could hear a pin drop as she approached the classroom."

But in November 1963, a few months after Numi began her assignment, a major *coup d'état* resulting in the death of President Ngo Dinh Diem caused a shift of authority and positions throughout the country and the respected principal was forced out. "This was clearly a very sad occasion for her and for some around her. After all, she had nothing to do with the hated Saigon regime. A younger member of the staff took over. She was well-liked and proved to have the courage to speak out when the changes expected to follow the coup didn't occur."

That same month President John F. Kennedy was assassinated. "I was astonished at how seriously the Vietnamese reacted to this event. We received condolences and everyone had a holiday in recognition. It was commonly assumed in Vietnam that

Kennedy was responsible for the coup that ended Diem's unpopular rule."

THE TRUNG SISTERS

"Anne and I taught mainly the younger students," Numi recalls,
"those just beginning to learn English. We decided to organize
an English Club for older, more accomplished students. Both
boys and girls came to the club meetings, which were held in our
living room. We taught the kids American games, and we had
discussions. On one memorable occasion we decided to have the
students talk about a Vietnamese holiday being celebrated—Hai
Ba Trung Day. It honored the Vietnamese Trung sisters, who led
a battle against the Chinese occupiers of their land in about 40
AD. Though they lost, they were eternally celebrated for the feat.
Anne's and my naiveté were front and center on this occasion.
It had not occurred to us that some of our Vietnamese students
were from Chinese families. The discussion was friendly enough,
but we were surprised to hear these students defend the Chinese
occupation as a way to improve the lives of the Vietnamese lo
those many years before."

Numi went home after her assignment, but in early 1967
returned to Vietnam with IVS as a Team Leader. "I was shocked
at the transformation in the country during my absence of only
eighteen months. The increased crowding, traffic, garbage, etc.,
seemed completely related to the vast multiplication of American
troops in Vietnam. Any ambiguity I may have felt about the U.S.
presence when I left in 1965, was quickly replaced with a very
adamant conviction that the U.S. military had no business being
in Vietnam.

"My job then consisted of visiting and consulting with volunteers throughout the region. I was also the interface between
IVS and the U.S. government in the region, looking for new
possibilities for volunteers, and eventually helping decide which
volunteers should no longer serve in Vietnam when we had to
reduce our numbers after the 1968 Tet Offensive. Every part of

the job was a challenge for me. Fortunately, the IVS administration was supportive throughout.

"I liked visiting various places in the region. Sometimes I was talking with local officials, usually heads of schools about their desire to have a volunteer assigned to their area. Other times I was lending an ear to a volunteer who might be experiencing difficulties or giving some advice about teaching methods.

"I became aware of the ambiguity of working for an NGO that was very dependent on the U.S. government for such things as safe transport, mail service, and PX privileges, as well as the financial underpinnings of our compensation. My U.S. counterpart was John Paul Vann, and we met about once a month to discuss relations between IVS volunteers and the military in a given location. For example, the issue might be the unwillingness of a volunteer to give information to the military that he or she might have about a particular village. I'm sure Vann didn't find my responses particularly helpful, but we maintained civility and we listened to each other."

ADOPTION

"A few months after arriving back in Vietnam in 1967, my colleague, *Beryl Darrah*, who was the Education Team Leader, sought advice from a small group of us about a baby born at the maternal hospital in Saigon. Beryl's interpreter was a med student there. The mother was seeking to put the child up for adoption because the GI father had abandoned her and she was too poor to raise him. We all knew that the local orphanages were underfunded and understaffed and that the chances of adoption could decrease in that situation. I decided I would take this child, knowing we could find an American family, if not a Vietnamese one, to adopt him. In the end, I fell in love with him and adopted him myself."

This was made possible because in 1968, shortly after the Tet Offensive, Numi married *David Nesmith*, also an IVSer. They were able to cut through red tape and bring Chris (Do van Ba) back to the U.S.

In 1967, she joined the writers of the volunteer letter to President Johnson decrying the war and the damage it was doing to the Vietnamese whom IVS had come to serve. "I was involved in this effort but refrained from a public stance as I was concerned I could be forced to leave the country before the paperwork for bringing Chris out of Vietnam with me was complete. I know that at least one Vietnamese friend was struck by our willingness to speak out against our government's policies without particular fear of recrimination."

BOTH SIDES OF THE ISSUES

There were volunteers on both sides of the issue and tensions ran high. In spite of this, IVS was on track to increase the number of volunteers in Vietnam, but the Tet Offensive derailed such efforts. It became clear volunteers were all potentially in danger. "Three of our volunteers in Hue were captured by the NLF (National Liberation Front) or NVA (North Vietnamese Army) during the offensive," Numi recalled. "By then I was convinced I could be most useful in the U.S. speaking and working against the war. It was just a matter of working through the bureaucratic red tape to be able to leave with Chris. David and I left Vietnam in May 1968 with the explicit purpose of joining with others in working to end U.S. military involvement in Vietnam."

The mid-1960s became increasingly difficult for the Vietnamese and for IVSers who tended to be close to them. The war heated up after the introduction of U.S. fighting forces in early 1965, though at that time John Sommer and his IVS colleagues were relieved that these troops might turn the tide against the then-called Viet Cong. "Many of us knew of people who were being killed by the Viet Cong," said Sommer, "but when IVSer Pete Hunting was killed in a delta ambush that year in November, we were stunned and anguished as the horror really hit home." Sommer ended up temporarily taking Hunting's place as IVS team leader for the southernmost part of the country, as well as holding that position for the Hue area. He also inherited Hunting's bullet-ridden vehicle.

By 1966, however, "Many volunteers began to have doubts about the efficacy of the U.S. role in Vietnam, though I remember that in a speaking tour of the Middle East and Europe, arranged for me that spring by the U.S. Information Agency, I was still supporting the overall effort while expressing concern about the methods being used to 'pacify' the country."

During the 1966-67 academic year Sommer began graduate school in Washington, D.C., and in the summer was invited to return to Vietnam to lead a group of some twenty U.S. university students funded by USAID to persuade them of the rightness of U.S. policies. Student protests had begun a couple of years earlier. By then, though, "I was turning against the policies myself and agonized over becoming another American who could be seen as part of the problem." Sommer went to Vietnam with his group of students after consulting with a few Vietnamese friends who said that 'good Americans' like IVSers were needed. "My assumption that the U.S. students would oppose the American intervention proved true; I think all of them returned to their universities radicalized."

DESTRUCTION OF THE CULTURE

In the summer of 1967, momentum built among many IVSers to protest U.S. policies. They were seeing the damage being done; countless lives lost, tens of thousands of refugees, and the destruction of the culture itself led a large number of volunteers to gather at the IVS house in Saigon for a couple of days to consider what they should do. "I'd been asked to moderate the discussions and found the depth of commitment to the Vietnamese people and the sincerity of all who spoke profoundly moving," Sommer said. At one session, "we had invited some especially close friends on a Vietnamese advisory group to hear their views and advice as to what we should do—stay and quietly do our assigned jobs in agriculture, community development, and education, or publicly protest U.S. policies.

"As I recall, they were as conflicted as we were, but one theme that clearly emerged was that if we really wanted to help

Vietnam, we should speak out to our fellow Americans on what we were seeing and experiencing. That September, a group of IVSers composed a letter—really a *cri du coeur*—to President Lyndon Johnson, delivered it to Ambassador Ellsworth Bunker, and gave it to *The New York Times,* where it made the front page. At the same time, the top four leaders of IVS in Vietnam publicly resigned in order to be free to speak out."

This was a traumatic event. "I was returning to graduate school at the time and was in close contact with Executive Director Arthur Gardiner and others at IVS's Washington headquarters, including board members. One of the recommendations of the Saigon group had been that IVS internationalize its funding and its volunteers, who were almost all Americans, so as not to be seen so much as part of the U.S. government establishment."

Both Gardiner and board members had been reading volunteer reports, and understood the complexities of the situation, even as they managed to keep the remaining IVSers operating with AID support.

A LITTLE WAR

While in San Diego, California, in 1962 *Forest Gerdes* got an offer from IVS to become part of the first Education Team in Vietnam. "I still have a copy of the letter I wrote to ask if there was some kind of little war going on there! I was fresh out of the Stanford teacher training program, excited about starting my career, and worried about being drafted." Gerdes had applied for and received conscientious objector status, with the help of the Palo Alto Unitarian Church, and would have been in the medical corps. "When I went to my draft board, the retired colonel in charge accused me of not wanting to go into the army, but when I told him I wanted to teach English in Vietnam with IVS, he changed his tune and gave me permission."

Gerdes had wanted to go to Hue, but was sent instead to the Teachers' College in Vinh Long. "It worked out for the best. The first thing I did was split my classes of fifty students in half. The other teachers thought I was looney, as I doubled my class hours, but I was far more effective teaching twenty-five than fifty. Most of the students had a couple of years of English, but they could not process spoken language. By the time I left, all could speak, read and understand English at a new level. I used an aural-oral pattern practice approach with lots of repetition and student participation. I made a pattern practice chart with the help of a local artist, which had ten pages of pictures. It was quite effective. One of the beginning patterns was, 'This is a...' The first time I used it and pointed to the mango, the class broke up. They had been saying, 'This is a mango' for weeks without knowing what they were saying! After that, when anything funny happened, it was 'this is a mango!'"

Gerdes spent the first month living in MAAG headquarters, which occupied the upper story of a former French seminary. He learned more than he wanted to know about military life, eating with the officers. "I'm sure they thought I was either young and crazy or working for the CIA. I was thinking, 'What great arrangements IVS makes for volunteers!' when a house opened up. It seems the USOM advisor and his wife, for whom a new duplex across from the school was reserved, were reassigned to Saigon. My cook was really the ex-gardener for the local missionary, who decided he wanted to be a cook. I didn't learn until much later that he went every day to his brother, who was the missionary's cook, to get directions for the day. In a short time, he became quite talented."

The next USOM advisor was willing to live in Vinh Long, so Gerdes had to move to a former Chinese shop house nearer town. "I could lay on a canvas bed on the roof to get cool and sometimes watch planes noiselessly drop napalm in the distance."

TEMP JOB

When his school shut down for the summer, IVS found Gerdes a temp job. "I took the place of the IVSer who was taking the place of the USOM man who was the coordinator for small U.S.-sponsored village projects in the Quang Tri area, near the border with North Vietnam. A four-dollar-a-day, 23-year-old volunteer English teacher, doing a job formerly done by a highly paid USOM man! I had a really good time, traveling around by Jeep with a driver, a translator and a public works counterpart, authorizing small projects like a community water project, about which I knew almost nothing.

"The second summer, I found my own job. Upon the end of my second year teaching at Truong Su Pham, I said a fond good-bye to my friends in Vinh Long. I took a letter of introduction from my local Buddhist leader to the main Buddhist temple in Nha Trang. I stayed at an IVS house and rode a bike up to the lovely Tu Duc temple, met with the lead monk and some bonzes, and introduced myself as their volunteer teacher! The price was right, so we settled on a book and a schedule. This turned out to be my most enjoyable teaching time in Vietnam. Nha Trang in 1964 was close to unspoiled. It was not so long since the French had left. The beach, the bread and the lobster were good. Before leaving Vinh Long, I had sent in applications to grad school at Cal Berkeley and the University of Oregon. It was while I was in Nha Trang that I got my replies. Cal sent a form letter which began, 'Dear Foreign Student...' The University of Oregon sent a telegram offering a full tuition paid Teaching Assistantship. Guess where I went?

"A few years ago I returned to Vietnam," Gerdes continued. "I was able to travel by hydrofoil through the delta to Vinh Long. So much had changed, and so much was the same. I took with me copies of student photos from 1963, and a current teacher at the greatly expanded Su Pham recognized one. He took me on his Vespa to meet my student from so long ago. We were both surprised by the emotions that surfaced. I couldn't recognize my second house, but I found the duplex built by USOM. In Nha Trang, I found a chain-smoking monk who'd been my student. He told me of another who had translated a book of Vietnamese Buddhist teachings, and gave me a copy. I learned that my best teacher friend in Vinh Long had been blown up."

S ELF-RELIANCE

"How much did my time in Vietnam change my life? I continued to be a teacher all my life. I have always shared my learning with others. Surely the many hardships, adventures, successes, and friendships with the Vietnamese taught me self-reliance. I was part of an important history lesson, still ongoing as the Vietnam of today springs up from its past. I was able to become fully familiar with one Asian culture, which led me to explore the similarities and differences in others."

Philip and *Cathy Walker* were both raised in families that were members of the Church of the Brethren; Cathy in Wenatchee, Washington State, and Philip in Long Beach, California. In 1957, at eighteen, Philip registered with the local draft board as a conscientious objector, and after completing college with elementary teaching credentials in 1961, he and Cathy were married and became teachers in Southern California. At twenty-three, he received his draft notice for military service.

"Because of my previous registration as a CO," he says, "we made arrangements with the Church of the Brethren to join Brethren Volunteer Service. BVS sponsored community service programs that were recognized and approved by the draft boards, allowing young men to serve out draft requirements in a manner consistent with their beliefs.

"In October, 1962, we traveled from the West Coast to Baltimore and New Windsor, Maryland, where the Church of the Brethren volunteer training headquarters was located. It became apparent following three months of training that BVS had no openings for professional teaching positions, and they told us about International Voluntary Services."

Both Walkers, after being accepted by IVS and while waiting to receive government clearance to go to Vietnam, helped with typing and general office work. "This experience provided us with a unique opportunity to become closely acquainted with the IVS staff." They went to Vietnam in March, 1963.

"Our first placement was in the small and quaint sea-coast

village of Rach-Gia. We stayed in the home of *Les Small*, (IVS Agriculture) for six weeks of intensive language study with Les' interpreter. We also had the opportunity to join Les on a few of his IVS projects." Most people in this little town had seen very few Caucasian women before and were intrigued by the young American couple. "When we were walking along the waterfront, children would follow us, excitedly yelling 'Om/Ba Mi!' (Mr. and Ms. America).

"After the completion of our language study in Rach-Gia, IVS placed us in the provincial capital of Can-Tho, about eighty miles south of Saigon. Prior to our teaching position, we were assigned to the only hospital in Can-Tho. We assisted American physician friends in providing services to patients who were mostly local militia."

The following are excerpts from the Walkers' newsletters to IVS headquarters.

CAN-THO, VIETNAM, OCTOBER 18, 1963

School has been underway now for close to two months. Phan-Thanh Gian High School was originally a French boarding school. About 3,000 students attend at this campus. We became aware that many of the students live in Viet Cong controlled areas and therefore often need to identify with whatever political system they are exposed to in their community. Our classroom furnishings consist of narrow wooden benches attached to tables that extend to the wall. The students have to crawl over each other to get to their seats. Furnishings are simple, a teacher's desk and a blackboard—the old slate variety that makes the chalk squeak. Books are kept in the Principal's office, requiring students to retrieve and return them daily. All our students have studied English grammar and can read and write fairly well.

One of our tasks is to teach pronunciation and conversation with only a minimum of grammar. In Vietnam, the status of a teacher is one of the highest in the social order, so students stand when the teacher enters the room and are seated at the teacher's command. School uniforms are universally required.

Our daily schedule at school goes from 8 a.m. to noon, followed by a lunch break. Then we resume teaching from 2 to 5 p.m. Our evenings are involved in teaching informal English classes in our home to our teacher colleagues as well as to local business owners. We became aware that for the Vietnamese, mastering the English language opened doors for higher paying positions in various American enterprises in the country.

BI-NATIONAL SEMINARS

A valuable activity sponsored by IVS was the monthly bi-national seminars held at the IVS house in Saigon. These meetings provided for informal sharing of experiences between IVS volunteers and their Vietnamese peers, as well as for in-service training for ESL (English as a Second Language) teaching skills. "On a return trip one afternoon from Saigon to Can-Tho," the Walkers remember, "Our flight landed about twenty miles from our home. After being dropped off at a small American air base, we approached some mechanics working on a Huey combat helicopter who, after hearing our predicament, agreed to fly us home. An American Colonel joined us apparently for security. As we engaged in discussion and advised him of our mission with IVS in Vietnam, he responded, '…well you know, if there were more people like you in this place and less of us, perhaps this country would be better off.' A rather remarkable observation from a military officer!"

DEPENDENTS

"In March 1965, our government contrived the Gulf of Tonkin Crisis to promote more popular American support for the war. Consequently, American wives were re-identified as 'dependents,' allowing the government to require their evacuation from Vietnam within twenty-four hours!"

Upon their return to the USA, the Walkers shared their experiences with Vietnamese life and culture to show the contrast to the war-torn Vietnam portrayed in the media. "We helped with the resettlement efforts of Vietnamese refugees in the Fresno, California, area after the fall of Saigon. Cathy's teaching profession was centered on ESL once again, to Vietnamese, then Hmong and Lao immigrants.

"Cathy and I entered Vietnam as an idealistic young couple unsure of what type of impact we might have on our host culture. We became immediately aware of the appreciation felt by our Vietnamese friends toward our eager attempts to learn their language. We also learned the value of embracing another culture and observing how the sometimes shallow priorities in our U.S. life style sharply contrast with the priorities of a culture that is different in socio-economic and religious orientation."

Charlie Henderson was attending Ohio Wesleyan University in 1968 when he heard Vietnamese Ambassador Tran Van Dinh speak about IVS. Henderson opposed the war but wanted to serve. "My older brother was in the Navy and he and his friends advocated for the war. Our political discussions were hot and heavy and always ended with, 'You don't know what the f--- you're talking about. You weren't there.' I felt I had to be there to shut them up."

During high school Henderson's elective classes included woodshop and he earned money for college "by slamming nails and pouring cement." IVS/Vietnam wanted to add a vocational education unit to its English instruction and Henderson was picked for the job. After three weeks' language training at Hickam AFB in Hawaii, followed by one month at Nha Trang, he was assigned to the orphanage school outside Tan Son Nhut. "I also checked out schools at the Buddhist Center and at the Vietnam amputee center. The orphanage was ARVN run with a major for the principal and a captain as vice-principal."

After a few weeks at the orphanage Henderson found a Vietnamese assistant, an ARVN soldier who had studied at the Vietnam vocational school for six years. During the next several months, the assistant taught while Henderson planned the projects. Together, they wrote an ongoing vocational training manual.

FORWARD PROJECTS

"Since I lived in Saigon and could be spared from the school, I sometimes escorted supplies to forward projects. Once, I rode alone in the belly of a C-130 with a generator bound for the Highlands. Other times it might be schoolbooks or motorcycles or cement. These trips gave me the opportunity to see what other volunteers were doing and to carry their reports and requests back to the IVS/Vietnam Headquarters in Saigon."

Henderson had been fighting illness for several months. "My weight had dropped from 170 pounds to 135 pounds and I was visiting the 3rd Field Army Hospital every other week. The army doctors recommended I return to the USA, so in August, 1969, I was discharged from IVS and began my trip home.

"The IVS experience left a powerful impression. For the past fifteen years I've served with the Federal Emergency Management Agency (FEMA) as an external affairs officer. I cannot tell what impact my meager IVS contributions may have had, but the benefit to me was incalculable. It opened the world to a provincial twenty-two-year-old. I've worked all my life and made many friends, but it's my IVS and FEMA associations I deem family."

In 1966, twenty-nine-year old *Janice Guenther Kavadas* saw an article in an Arizona newspaper about teaching English with IVS in Vietnam. She wrote for details and as soon as her second school year of teaching high school in Arizona ended, IVS sent her to the Institute of Modern Languages in Washington, D.C., for training in ESL, then to Vinh Long for Vietnamese language training. She remembers that, "None of my family or friends approved of my choice because of the danger in a war zone, as well as the unimpressive volunteer salary, but I considered it an opportunity to enrich my life. Forty-six years later, I still believe it was one of the best decisions of my life."

She was assigned to Dalat where IVSer *Kay Haberlach* was already settled, so moving into the same house was easy. "My teaching assignment was at Bui-thi-Xuan Girls' High School where most of my colleagues were women, but there were also

some men on the faculty. The principal and assistant principal
were both women. They were all very competent and conscientious in their school responsibilities and helpful to me in many
ways. They included me in school activities, including Tet parties
and parent open house meetings. I was amazed that our audito-
rium was always full on parents' nights."

INQUISITIVE

"I enjoyed teaching all the different class levels. In the beginning levels, I taught pronunciation with sentence practice, and a
Vietnamese teacher taught the grammar and vocabulary translation on alternating days. The older students were inquisitive and
knew enough English to lead to interesting discussions.

"In one class of the youngest girls, a little girl was a constant
talker and giggler," Kavadas remembers. "My usual attempts to
correct this behavior did not work, so I asked one of the Vietnamese teachers what she did in this situation. She told me to
send the girl outside to stand in the sun. I tried my colleague's
suggestion. I could not imagine how this would solve the problem, but soon found out. From the time the girl reached the sun
until the bell rang to end the class, she cried her heart out. I knew
the Vietnamese girls tried to shield themselves from the sun, but
did not know how serious they were to avoid darkening their
skin."

The Political Warfare College class of twenty-two students
studied English for their officer training program. They were
going to work with American advisers, and so had a specific
book that dealt mostly with learning terminology. "We never
had political discussions."

At the Catholic orphanage, Kavadas taught English to two
nuns who managed the facility with more than 200 children.
These women, though very busy, made time once a week to
practice their English and used their new language skills to get
help from the American soldiers at the small U.S. military base
in Dalat. "The nuns persuaded the men to make repairs to the
orphanage buildings and always gave each one of them a beer

after their work. The men also helped the children celebrate Christmas by decorating a Jeep to look like Santa's sleigh and one of them dressed in a Santa suit to greet the children. It was hard to tell who enjoyed this contact more, the American men or the Vietnamese children.

"Teachers never really know their impact on students or understand the students' impact on them. There are no tangible forms of measurement that can be used for the long-term learning and understanding that improves the lives of both teachers and students. However, I have enjoyed regular communication with one of my Bui-thi-Xuan students. Thai thi Mo finished Dalat University and teaches English in an American school in Ho Chi Minh City. She calls me her 'lifeline to the rest of the world'. In one email, she referred to learning as food for the soul. Such communication with a former student has certainly fed my soul."

GOATS ON THE RUNWAY

Vietnam was a crucible for IVS, a country at war with itself and needing an ever-widening set of skills from its volunteers. *Robert Hargreaves* spent two years there as an expert in animal husbandry.

"In September 1965 I arrived in Phan Rang, a small provincial capital of 18,000 on the central coast. There was only one telephone in town and it was usually out of order. The trains had stopped running several years earlier because of Viet Cong activity. The small airport opened in the morning four times a week for the arrival of the ten-passenger Air America shuttle flight that flew from Saigon to Danang and back. As soon as the plane left, the resident herd of goats would wander back across the runway.

"When I first arrived, the only other American in town was Larry Laverentz, the USAID representative and a former IVSer. This gradually expanded to a small American population that included three more IVS volunteers. A Military Advisory Command Vietnam (MACV) compound of one hundred American soldiers was just outside of Phan Rang, and they showed American movies once a week. I could also eat there whenever I got tired of rice and nuoc mam.

"Most of my work was with the Vietnamese Animal Husbandry and Crop Science Services. I also conducted some experiments at Nha Ho Experiment Station. The Animal Husbandry Service had seventy people asking for American chickens. I began monthly trips on the shuttle flight to get chicks and other supplies, bringing back four or five hundred chicks on each trip."

GRAPES

"My most successful project was with grapes. When I first arrived in Phan Rang my neighbor across the street had a huge old grapevine that had never borne fruit. I found the blossoms were being killed by mold. I tried spraying with Bordeaux mix, an old French remedy of lime, sulfur, and copper sulfate, a concoction originally created to keep Paris picnickers from helping themselves to the grapes, and it turned out it also prevented mold. It worked!

"The grapevine was badly in need of pruning. I gave a lesson in pruning techniques to the Vietnamese specialists I was working with. I then took the cuttings to Nha Ho and planted a small vineyard. Grapes take at least two years to reach bearing age, and I left before I got any fruit. When I returned twenty years later Phan Rang had thousands of acres of vineyards!"

Hope Harmeling Benne was one of 7,500 American women who lived in Vietnam during the war. "I went there to teach English. But the more complicated reason as to why I ended up there lies in my upbringing as the daughter of an army officer. My six brothers and sisters and I moved from place to place living in several different states and also traveling abroad to Okinawa and Europe. We rapidly gained a cosmopolitan outlook."

After graduating from college in 1966, she went to Vietnam as a member of IVS. "My application letter to IVS stated simply that I majored in Asian history and wanted to go to Vietnam to teach English and learn Vietnamese. I didn't realize at the time how serious the war was and that in 1965 the U.S. had made decisions to greatly escalate the number of American troops."

A PAINFUL CONTRAST

Her group of about twenty volunteers arrived in September, 1966 at Tan Son Nhut airport in Saigon. "From the moment we alighted and stepped out on Vietnamese soil, my senses connected with balmy tropical air, brilliantly-colored orchids, lilies, hibiscus and gardenias, and the marinated grilled meat sold by street vendors. It was a tropical paradise with white sandy beaches ringed with palm trees, and majestic mountains in the central highlands. But the luminous, radiant beauty of the scenery was terribly marred by pervasive and intrusive American tanks, planes, helicopters, and barbed wire. Oh what a painful contrast! It would haunt me for years and make me realize right from the first week I was there that the American presence and the war were all wrong."

After a short orientation at the IVS central office in Saigon, her group traveled to the Central Highlands resort city of Dalat for Vietnamese language training The teachers were northern Vietnamese so the IVSers first learned the northern dialect.

"The more Vietnamese I learned, the more I came to view the world from a different point of view reverential of family, respectful of nature, and proud of historical traditions.

"Upon returning to Saigon, I was assigned to teach English at the Saigon Normal School. There was a pressing need for well-trained teachers to teach the nation's youth, and I was very pleased to think if I did a good job it would have a ripple effect."

With a monthly salary of eighty dollars and a clothing allowance of $150 a year, Harmeling had to find living arrangements. IVS Director Don Luce found an ideal place with a group of South Vietnamese nuns, Lovers of the Cross, in a convent adjacent to a Catholic school and church. In exchange for room and board, she taught English four evenings a week.

"I loved teaching at the Saigon Normal School. Every day

was challenging, and my students' love for learning made it a pleasure. My classes, called Practical English, were geared toward conversation and pronunciation. I conducted repetition drills for pronunciation and the students made rapid progress. We practiced sayings, quotes, and idioms and conducted role-play and oral reports.

"My students delighted in American pop music. Their favorite song was *Love Potion Number 9*. They also loved Salem menthol cigarettes."

But there were problems. The school was overcrowded, noisy, and lacking books. Many of the students' lives were unsettled, with young men being drafted and too frequent funerals of relatives and family killed. At times teaching English became a sideline to more pressing work Harmeling undertook at a refugee center and orphanage. "I drove sick children to the hospital and took them for appointments and surgeries when needed. I brought amputees to a center for artificial limbs. I picked up donated goods and clothing from the airport and wrote thank you notes to the donors."

TIME MAGAZINE

Occasionally journalists in Saigon would contact IVS and ask if they could meet with some volunteers and learn about their work. One day a *Time* magazine reporter asked a group of IVSers what they thought of the war. "My fellow volunteers were saying the war was all wrong, that the U.S. should never have become involved in the internal affairs of Vietnam," Harmeling remembered. "I said a lot of Vietnamese didn't know why we were fighting there. The reporter asked me, "Do you mean you think American efforts are a matter of unrequited love?" I replied, "Well, yes, you could say so." The next week in *Time* magazine there was a headline, *US Effort Unrequited Love*. Fortunately the Vietnamese government did not expel me from the country, a credit to their tolerance."

TRAPPED

In 1968, for Tet, the Vietnamese New Year, Harmeling traveled to Dalat to visit two IVS friends. They found themselves trapped in their house when the North Vietnamese and Viet Cong attacked the city. Harmeling and her friends moved to the villa of the province's senior USAID advisor, who was in radio contact with U.S. military authorities. They spent two weeks there, often in fear the North Vietnamese and Viet Cong would destroy the house as they had done to other westerners' homes in Dalat. "We could sometimes see them in their tanks on the street in front of the villa. We rationed all of the food at the house, and did not go out for two weeks."

They were finally evacuated to Nha Trang by helicopter. There Harmeling was asked to be an interpreter at the U.S. military hospital in Nha Trang. "My role was to speak with wounded North Vietnamese soldiers and tell them they would be operated on before being taken to prison. Even those who were taking their last breath smiled and told me I spoke beautiful Vietnamese and thanked me for learning it. I will never, as long as I live, forget their absence of anger and their willingness to be so cordial to me."

In 1967, *Carlyle Thayer* had been assigned by IVS to the English Language Program. "I studied Vietnamese in Saigon and did some teacher training at the Catholic School of the Holy Spirit. I then opened the first IVS station in An Loc town, Binh Long province near the Cambodian border. I taught English as a second language to oversized classrooms of secondary students. At night I taught English to ethnic Khmer children, the sons and daughters of the security force protecting the compound where I lived."

The 1968 Tet Offensive disrupted South Vietnam's school system. "I was at IVS headquarters in Saigon when the first attacks took place. We were evacuated to a billet in central Saigon. When the second wave of attacks subsided I returned to An Loc only to find that the school was closed. Many teachers had gone home for Tet and not enough returned to resume teaching. I returned to Saigon with an intestinal disorder and had to return to the United States for treatment."

A LETTER TO THE PRESIDENT

After some time in Vietnam, many of the volunteers concluded the U.S. involvement there was ill-fated. In the summer of 1967, they drafted a letter to President Johnson, which began,

> "As volunteers with International Voluntary Services working in agriculture, education and community development, we live with Vietnamese and have learned Vietnamese. We have watched and shared their suffering since 1958. What we have seen and heard of the effects of war compels us to make this statement. The problems the people face are too little understood and their voices too long muffled. We are finding it increasingly difficult to pursue our main objective: helping the people of Vietnam. Our small successes are being negated by the violence and destruction around us. To stay in Vietnam and remain silent is to fail to respond to the first need of the Vietnamese people—peace."

The letter was signed by forty-nine IVS volunteers and on September 19, 1967, sent to the NY Times, U.S. ambassador in Saigon Ellsworth Bunker, and President Lyndon Johnson. The country director and three senior volunteers resigned and returned home when the Board of Directors did not make a political response to this letter. The Board pointed out that IVS did not engage in political activity according to its charter.

Harmeling now says, "As I look back I have a plethora of mixed feelings on my years in Vietnam. I wouldn't trade anything for having known Vietnamese people on their own terms in their own country. My stay in Vietnam has left me with lasting twinges of nostalgia for that enchanted countryside, and the sweet people with their languorous lifestyle."

"Good English"

Sally Benson was another IVS woman on hand to witness the developing conflict. Assigned to teach English at the National Institute of Administration in Saigon, she remembers that, "A special assembly was called and I was instructed to sit with the newly 'elected' President Thieu. Stunned to see no one sitting near us, I wondered if that had to do with security, or whether no one wanted to be seen close to him and the American. He told me I spoke good English, which I took as his effort at conversation and a touch of humor."

Later, fighting broke out in the alleys and Benson's landlady's son came to tell her his nearby home had been bombed. Along with *Steve Nichols*, another IVS teacher, Benson took refuge in a building adjacent to the school where she taught.

With access to an IVS vehicle, "I helped student refugees transport lumber and bread, driving across the river to areas where Americans were not supposed to venture. Some of my students must have come to trust me—and I them—because I was once hidden on the floor of a small truck and taken to the far outskirts of Saigon to enjoy 'the very best crab place'."

A refugee camp had sprouted on the IVS grounds; there was street fighting around her and threats from planes overhead. "I scribbled a 'will' on an envelope re: my car and a few pieces of family jewelry at home."

The document, fortunately, wasn't necessary. Benson decided it was time to go home. "Things I was experiencing and suggestions from Vietnamese acquaintances made me increasingly uncomfortable with my role in Vietnam."

"A Very Nice American"

Amal Chatterjee remembers being in his last year studying to earn a Bachelor of Science in Agriculture from the University of Sri Ram Pur in India when, "I noticed a small advertisement on the bulletin board of our agronomy department. It said that a non-profit international philanthropic organization in the USA was looking for young agronomists to work in developing countries as volunteers. I found the fellow who had the necessary information and application forms. I had seen him around but never talked to him. He turned out to be a very nice American named Lawrence who explained that he had been a volunteer in Laos."

The man gave Chatterjee an application to fill out and said it would be a good opportunity to get some real life practical experience working in another country. But he could not say where Chatterjee would be sent if selected.

Chatterjee waited for a response from Washington to his application. "One day a letter came saying I was selected to go to South Vietnam as an agronomist for two years and asked me to get my travel documents as soon as possible.

"But in those days in 1965, there was a terrible war raging in Vietnam, and the Americans were fighting the North Vietnamese. Everyone knew that Vietnam was not a place to go to at that time. I told Lawrence this but he assured me that many young people were working in Vietnam as volunteers in areas that were not dangerous. I was convinced, but no one else was; they said I was a fool to jump into such a mess and should instead work in India."

STRANGE AND FOREIGN

Cultural issues were also at stake. No one in his family had ever gone abroad and jet travel, passport and visas were strange and foreign. "My father told me I was too young so it would be better if I took a graduate degree before starting to work. He said I should forget about Vietnam."

Six months passed and still Chatterjee could not get a passport. "So one day, in October 1966, I went to Lucknow and asked the passport officer what was really the problem with my application. He told me that my case had been sent to Delhi. The Indian Government did not encourage anyone to go to Vietnam due to their disagreement with the Americans on the war there."

Chatterjee took the name and address of the person to see in Delhi and boarded a train the same night. "This was my first solo trip to Delhi and I did not know a soul. When I arrived at the Ministry of External Affairs, I demanded to see a certain Mr. Chakrabandhu. After what seemed like a long time he came over; I told him the whole story and asked if he would look into my case. He listened to me very attentively and asked his secretary to bring my file. He asked why I was going to Vietnam of all places and what in the world was this IVS organization? So I told him. He was not convinced."

The official then asked how much Chatterjee was going to be paid to which he replied that it was only $80 a month. "I was going more for the experience than money but he kept shaking his head and asked why I was going to risk my life for $80 a month."

Chatterjee replied that, "If the Japanese, Americans, Canadians and many other young people from so many countries could go to Vietnam for only $80 a month, then why couldn't an Indian?" He returned to Sri Ram Pur and received his passport within a week.

When he finally arrived in Saigon, "I was met by a big bald American fellow called Robert. He had no trouble recognizing me because I was the only Indian off the plane. At that time there were over 200 volunteers spread out all over South Vietnam but quite a few lived in Saigon in the IVS house dormitory. I had arrived at a time when the entire team in Vietnam was undergoing some serious discussions about the whole philosophy of working there, as the war was all around us. A general meeting was called that was attended by all the volunteers and the executive director from Washington.

"The outcome of this meeting was that Don Luce, the country director of the IVS team in Vietnam, resigned along with a few others who then returned to the U.S. to protest against the war and its negative effect on the people. Some saw IVS as tacitly supporting the war by simply being in Vietnam. But most did not agree and said we were doing humanitarian work that needed to be done. I sat through the meetings absorbing everything. Only later would I start developing a strong sense of what was right and wrong and what we, as individuals, could do about it. But in June, 1967, I kept mum and listened."

RICE, PIGPENS AND COMPOST PILES

Chatterjee's first few days in Tay Ninh were hectic, even as his job proved not too arduous. "I was an agronomist so I involved myself with rice research and extension from the start, but I also built pig pens, compost pits and chicken coops for farmers in many parts of the province. The rule was that we had to be back in town by five p.m. and could not drive before seven or eight a.m. for security reasons. I was told that the mine sweepers cleared the roads early in the morning but the Viet Cong were known to be very industrious."

At night he could hear the sounds of bombs dropping from the B-52s west of Tay Ninh in Cambodia, through which the Ho Chi Minh trail passed. "But sometimes the sound was much nearer, meaning parts of our province were being bombed." The incessant traffic of helicopters and army planes told them the war was all around, but volunteers took everything in stride. "We learned to ignore the sounds."

Chatterjee busied himself with the rice extension program benefitting local farmers who were getting good yields from the new IRRI (International Rice Research Institute) rice varieties. "Many farmers asked me for seeds so I started a seed multiplication program where a farmer would give me back part of his harvest so that I could give it to someone else. The Ministry of Agriculture in Saigon appreciated my efforts and gave me rice kits to spread new varieties in the province."

Then, suddenly, he found himself in a war zone. "In February 1968, I was in Saigon but returning to Tay Ninh the very next morning. When I got there, the guards at the gate started shouting and pointing their machine guns at us. We had just gotten inside the gate with our heavy luggage when all hell broke loose and bullets started flying in all directions. We dropped to the ground and stayed on our bellies, I don't know for how long. This was the start of the infamous Tet Offensive and we were right in the middle of it."

The IVS field director asked a few volunteers to work in Saigon to help with the refugee relief operation. "I went every morning to the ministry of social welfare and loaded whatever relief goods they gave me to distribute to various centers. Food, soap, nuoc mam (a smelly fish sauce), mats, medicines, fuel, rice, etc. I got to know the University of Saigon students who started calling me Anh Phuc, Happy Brother. They were my guides. I tied a Red Cross flag on the Jeep lest someone shoot at us and I drove like a madman all day long. This went on for a month. I got to be very street savvy and good at the cat-and-mouse games of avoiding trouble."

Back in Saigon and finally in Tay Ninh, it was the same routine of working and listening to the sound of B-52s bombing at night. The whole of 1968 would pass like this.

DISTINGUISHED SERVICE AWARD

One day a cable arrived from Washington saying Chatterjee had been awarded the International Distinguished Service Award by Macalester College in St. Paul, Minnesota.

After receiving the award in the U.S., Chatterjee returned to Tay Ninh, then settled in a small village called Go Dau Ha near the Cambodian border. "Here I was free to carry on my rice research. But finally the time came for me to say goodbye. In July of 1969 I visited the volunteers who worked in the agricultural team and wrote about their work so that it could be included in the annual report. I welcomed this job and went to Ba Xuyen to set up the language training program for the new arrivals there."

The Vietnam chapter was closing but Chatterjee's IVS service was far from over. He went on to serve with IVS in Algeria from 1971 to 1973, then worked for various development agencies on agricultural projects in the Philippines, India, Mali, Haiti, Burundi, and Sudan.

In the autumn of 1966, *Rich Fuller* drove to Johns Hopkins University in Baltimore to hear the monk Thich Nhat Hanh speak out against the war. That same year, in a social-psych class, his professor played a 45 rpm record of Peter Paul and Mary's *The Great Mandala*, "which changed my life forever."

Three years later, "my late-dad's family in Canada told me I could stay with them until the war ended. Earlier, my mom had offered to get our family doctor to say I was unfit for the military due to a heart murmur discovered when I was 17." But three Mennonite volunteers back from Vietnam spoke at his college that same year, which led him to IVS.

Fuller joined IVS in 1969, "to find out what the Vietnam War was all about. I was 1-A draft status and about to graduate from Western Maryland. I took the rice training at Los Banos, Philippines, in July of that year. We saw the Apollo moon landing on TV while there. When I reached Vietnam shortly afterwards, Don Luce, the former head of IVS, told me to go back home."

Fuller said that if he did that, he would not learn anything first-hand about Vietnam. Luce then suggested Fuller learn Vietnamese thoroughly, "to understand what the people were saying."

IVS sent Fuller to central Vietnam in July to study Vietnamese for two months. He taught conversational English at the local high school in Dien Khanh District, about ten kilometers from the coastal city of Nha Trang. "I then started my agricultural work there with one of my students from the countryside."

MINI-OFFENSIVE

"A mini-offensive took place while I was away on leave in May, 1970. This led IVS to re-assign me to the delta. *Ron Moreau, John Ameroso* and *Vic Svanoe* had built a rice-growing cooperative based on the high-yielding rice seeds Amal Chatterjee had reproduced in Tay Ninh. I joined them in 1970, but their contracts were up and I was alone after about two months."

Fuller took sick with hepatitis A in 1970 in Saigon, and

was treated at the Third Field Hospital of the U.S. Military. "While recuperating from hepatitis in the special ward, I met U.S. soldiers. We all wore the same color hospital clothing. One man jovially told how he and his U.S. military convoy of trucks played a game on the mountain pass road to Dalat, pushing a Vietnamese passenger bus closer and closer to the abyss until it fell off the cliff."

During a mail run to Saigon, Fuller met and sang with Vietnamese students, Mennonites and Quakers, all supporting peace. "I met the Bob Dylan of Vietnam, the late composer Trinh Cong Son, through some students in Dalat. They had me sing one of his songs for him in Vietnamese.

"From there, I was encouraged to learn more of his songs about the war and translated eight of them to be sung in English, some in 1972-73 and others, later, in 2004-2008. I met him again in 1993 and sang the earlier translations for him at his studio, and together at an outdoor concert." Fuller would go on to perform the songs at charity concerts in Vietnam, Europe and the USA, to bring attention to Agent Orange victims in Vietnam.

"I returned to the Mekong Delta in early 1971 after recovering from hepatitis. Rice extension was the most rewarding job in my life, being a sort of Johnny Appleseed stepping into the shoes of John Glass who developed the low-lift pump, and John Ameroso, the agronomist who was my model for doing agricultural extension."

One day, Fuller met *Alex Shimkin*, a volunteer in nearby Chau Doc. "Alex liked to go out on patrols, and in 1970 he heard of an incident related by a bearded, split-thumbed monk named Thay Chanh, who said that in his village, the villagers were forced by the Americans and the Saigon army to walk through paddy fields to blow up mines. Alex arranged for *Ron Moreau*, then a stringer with *Newsweek*, and Gloria Emerson, to go there in a helicopter. Emerson wrote the story in the *New York Times*. Six months later, Alex and I were in the living room of the IVS house in Saigon. He had been fired for going to Ba Chuc, he said, and I told him I admired what he had done, sacrificing his job to save lives in Ba Chuc.

"He then said that if I really believed that, I would follow this up, as I was the last volunteer in Chau Doc, then working in Hoa Hao."

After refusing several times, Fuller agreed to go. "Alex went to his bunk bed which was covered with files, notebooks and papers, and drew a map and told me what to do. First, I would go to the IVS house in Chau Doc and stay overnight, saying nothing to anyone. The next day, I was to go to the bus station, dressed in black pajamas and a hat. I got on the bus for Tinh Bien unobserved, and got to Lac Quoi on the Vinh Te Canal that runs along the border with Cambodia."

MOTORCYCLE

At Tan Quoi, Fuller took a motorcycle taxi up to Ba Chuc, then went to the Filial Piety Temple. "I did what the people there did, bowing when they did, and sitting when they sat."

He found the bearded monk with the split thumbs sitting in the village. "I told him I was a friend of Alex and was asked to check if everything was OK. He was very thankful, and said nothing had happened in the six months since Alex was there with the reporters.

"It was getting late, so I excused myself and started the trek back to Chau Doc. The problem was, the bus wasn't running, so I hitched a ride with a truck. When the police stopped it, I said hello and the cop was so surprised that he didn't collect his usual bribe."

An American military Jeep arrived and the driver told Fuller to get in, chiding him for being in a war zone close to sunset. "They took me to their camp, saying I could not get to Chau Doc safely. They asked me why I was there and I told them I lived near Long Xuyen, was an IVS volunteer, and worked in rice agriculture, all of which was true. I feared they would inform

IVS and I would suffer the same fate as Alex. I left the camp the next morning. IVS never found out about this."

In August 1971, Fuller says, "IVS was asked to leave Vietnam. I returned home to the U.S. for two years before going back to Vietnam in mid-1973, believing the Paris Peace Agreement had brought peace and I could continue my agricultural work.

"I joined Vietnam Christian Service (VNCS) in early 1974 and worked with them until we all had to leave the country toward the end of the war in April 1975."

Fuller then worked resettling refugees with the International Rescue Committee (IRC) in the U.S. from 1975 to 1976. He went to grad school at the University of California at Davis and in 1978 earned a Master's degree in tropical agricultural development. In 1978, he traveled to Malaysia to interview Vietnamese refugees with Church World Service (CWS), the Malaysian program headed by ex-IVSer Galen Beery. In early 1979, he went to Bangladesh to do development work.

PRISONER OF WAR

Marc Cayer, a French-speaking Canadian national, was sent to Vietnam in October, 1967, on a two-year IVS contract as an agronomist. "I arrived in Saigon on November 13, 1967, exactly at noon". Before going to Dalat to study the language, "I went with Russ Bradford to Tay Ninh to meet some IVS members. During that first night, the Viet Cong made a foray just a short distance from the IVS house. I was concerned but the IVS members told me there was no danger—the Viet Cong did this from time to time and would leave a few hours later.

"Russ Bradford brought me to Hue at the beginning of January, 1968. We met a person from USAID, and I began to plan projects for that winter. I can still remember the first time I went to the market to buy some fruits and vegetables, and I had to use the Vietnamese language I had learned to be understood.

"On January 31, the VC attacked Hue, and Gary Daves and

I were surrounded. What to do? We just had to wait. There was no food, no light, just a lot of noise outside. On February 3 at about three o'clock in the afternoon, the VC knocked on the door and we had to surrender. It was the beginning of my five years and ten days as a prisoner of war."

After a short time in Hue, Cayer and Daves were brought to a small house just outside the city. "I did not have pants—just underwear—and Gary gave me a pair of his pants. We stayed there a few nights. Then, we were taken to the mountains, a long day of walking with our elbows tied tight behind our backs. About a week later, we were joined by *Sandra Johnson* who, just before our capture, had invited me to go with her to a party!"

Soon after that, Daves, Cayer and Johnson began walking toward Laos. For 13 days they slept on the ground with just a plastic tarp to shield them from the morning rain.

BOMBS

Cayer and his captors stayed at Valley Camp near Laos for four days. During the last meal one afternoon, American planes flew over them and dropped bombs. Cayer was badly wounded on his left foot.

"A few days later, we were taken by truck for a nine-day journey on the Ho Chi Minh trail. It was a terrible experience; rough roads, bombings, no sleep and very little food.

"We called the first prison Bao Cao and it was very bad. I spent my days in a very small room, three feet by six feet, with no windows. We had to ask for everything in Vietnamese. This was not a real problem for me but for the American prisoners who did not know Vietnamese, it was very hard.

"I was lucky. Because of my wound, I had the first room and often the guard left the door open so I could look outside and see the people and the animals around the camp."

After three months, the captives were sent to a prison about ten miles from Hanoi. "We called that prison Camp 77 and my new room was six feet by nine feet with a small window. I spent the first nine months in solitary confinement. I was allowed to go outside to take my meals and to shower. There was nothing to do, nothing to read. I slept and I dreamed. Then, I began to play with the spiders and mice and the insects in my room. I can remember one mouse that came in my cell every afternoon and then retreated to her hole.

"Eventually I went to another section of the prison where there were three Americans. I had the chance to learn English and play cards with them. It was much better but we were still in solitary confinement. We did not get news from home; there was no radio, no newspapers."

Time passed slowly. Cayer began to exercise every morning. The camp regulations did not allow the three to communicate with other prisoners in the next cell, and Cayer became best friend with Jim Thompson, one of the American POWs, who had been captured in March, 1964, and released nine years later in March, 1973.

FRENCH LESSONS

"In July, 1971, we were moved to Camp Rockville, a prison between Hanoi and Haiphong. There, we were allowed to go outside every morning and afternoon. It was so nice to see the sun and to plant a small garden! Then, three of my American friends escaped and were soon recaptured. Our group couldn't go outside for the next 12 months. It was terrible; there were fights between prisoners and a lot of words exchanged." To pass the time, Cayer gave French lessons every morning to five Americans and after one year, his students could read, speak and understand French quite well.

In October, 1972, camp conditions changed. Cayer and the other POWs were allowed to go outside. The food got better but bombings around the camp increased. The captives could hear the B-52s every night. One day, a plane came in low on a bombing run. "The guards ordered us to go back very quietly to the camp.

"On January 27, 1973, they told us that a peace agreement would be signed the following day, and that our entire group would go to Hanoi. I was in the Hanoi Hilton by the end of the afternoon. I stayed with two Germans prisoners, a boy and a girl, for 10 days. They were originally in a group of five that was captured not far from Danang. They walked sixty days towards the north and three of them died on the trail. I was with a group of about forty-five prisoners when it was time for me to get released. What a nice day it was!"

FREEDOM

"I had breakfast and was getting a haircut when I was told the camp director wanted to see me. He gave me a package from my parents, the first since my capture five years earlier. Soon after that, they told me to go to my room and put on fresh clothes. That's when I knew it was the day of my liberation. I was handed over to Canadians working for the ICC (Commission Internationale de Contrôle) in Hanoi. I was free!!"

There were no planes to or out of Hanoi, so Cayer waited three days. "But I had good food, and I sent news to my parents for the first time. The next day, I received a message signed by my Maman and Papa. They were alive!

"The chief of ICC told me at the time that I was more important than the Prime Minister of Canada! My story was in all the newspapers, and on radio and television!"

Cayer slept one night at the IVS Office in Vientiane and two days later was on a plane bound for home. "I slept in San Francisco and the next day, I flew to Quebec City. All my family was there and I saw my father crying. I will remember that day forever. In Quebec, I was told everyone was talking about me because I was the only Canadian prisoner of war in Vietnam."

Cayer spent a week at the hospital being checked over, and during the next four months was the subject of multiple interviews. He gave speeches and eventually wrote a book.

FLOODS

Dyle G. Henning was an IVS volunteer from 1967 to 1969, and then again from 1970 to 1971. He was studying law at Columbia when, "Going into a corporate law course final in December 1966, I almost walked out! I promised myself I would finish the second year and leave. Vietnam was the place I felt I should go; it was where other people my age were going by choice or by chance. I wanted to do something constructive to build that country."

USAID suggested he contact IVS and, "IVS accepted me in March 1967. Orientation at Harpers Ferry started in August with further training at Los Banos in The Philippines." After three months of in-country language training in Tan An with twelve other new IVS volunteers, he was sent to Dien Khanh District as a member of the IVS Community Development Team. "I arrived in November just in time to see a flood cover part of the town and the remnants of a battle in a nearby village. I had hardly begun when Tet changed things.

"Although there was no attack in Dien Khanh and not much success for the NVA and Viet Cong in Nha Trang, the male teachers, both locally and nationally, were called up for military training. I found myself teaching many Basic English classes for a while. Facing sixty students in some classes was quite a shock; I had no formal teaching instruction or experience. When the male teachers returned to serve in place, I still did some English pronunciation and conversation with classes at teacher requests." Most of Henning's work centered on working with local government staff, teachers and high school students.

By the summer of 1968 a variety of project activities had emerged which carried into Henning's second year and were picked up again more than a year later during his second tour. "After returning for the third year at Columbia Law and working several summer months for the American Friends Service Committee (AFSC) to influence U.S. government policy on the development of a United Nations Volunteer Program, I returned happily to Dien Khanh in late 1970."

Among the most significant local program efforts were: Support for youth sports; organization of after-school and summer English clubs in the local public, private, and Buddhist high schools; and working with teachers and students to create a student lending library at the public high school. "The lending library was started with some donated books, most in English from the Saigon Vietnamese-American Cultural Center." Student members helped suggest books to buy and by 1971, the library had over 1,000 titles in Vietnamese. "I remember riding my bike one day out to several distant hamlets to retrieve books that had not been brought back by students; in the next few days nearly all the delinquent books were returned by these and other students!"

Henning recalls that, "A lot of specific activities were accomplished over three years. However for me it was the obvious personal growth of the student volunteers that really was the important impact. I kept in touch with some of these students and active teachers during the year I returned to finish law school, and from 1971 until being evacuated out of Saigon in April 1975.

"IVS service had a huge influence on my life. Although I went back to Columbia Law to finish the Juris Doctorate in 1970, I knew by the end of the first tour that practicing law and going into politics were no longer goals. My career interests had shifted to youth work."

After IVS/Vietnam was terminated in 1971, Henning stayed on with three Fulbright teaching grants. "The first two years I worked at the National School of Social Work in Saigon; the last year was at the new Coastal Community College in Nha Trang. In 1974 I hired one of these college graduates to help me operate a CARE International daycare training class. Oanh Thu became my wife in April 1975; now in our thirty-eighth year we have three kids and five grandchildren."

Serving in Vietnam toward the end of 1967 was *Stuart*

Rawlings, born in 1943 to "a high society family" in San Francisco. He was sent to school for a year in Switzerland at the age of 12, and then on to four years at the Phillips Exeter Academy in New Hampshire. After spending a summer helping build schools in a remote village in Togo, Rawlings went to Stanford and majored in Latin American Studies. During that time, he took leaves of absence to study Indians in Peru, do civil rights work in Mississippi, and reflect on life in Rio de Janeiro, Brazil.

"The main reason I applied to IVS to do volunteer work in Vietnam was a sense of curiosity. The war there was featured in daily news broadcasts, and I wanted to find out for myself what was happening. Adventure and a sense of injustice were also part it."

CONSCIENTIOUS OBJECTOR STATUS

Rawlings applied for conscientious objector status, and hoped his IVS work would count for this service, "but my draft board in San Francisco rejected my application because I was found to be 'insincere'."

Rawlings' service in Vietnam was from September 1967 to May 1968, and cut short due to security concerns after the Tet Offensive. "After one month of language training in Tan An, I was sent to Phan Rang, where I lived with a Vietnamese family and worked in agriculture." His job was to help Vietnamese farmers acquire seeds, fertilizers, water pumps and other materials not available due to the closure of most of the country's roads.

He worked closely with a Taiwanese agriculturalist and a few USAID agriculturalists. "I have fond memories of the Vietnamese family I lived with, and of other Vietnamese and Americans with whom I worked. There are also less pleasant memories of the crassness of American soldiers, who were looking for sex and drugs while trying to avoid the fighting.

"My main accomplishment was probably introducing the Vietnamese people I met to a different type of American from the

500,000-plus American soldiers there. I was sincerely interested in the Vietnamese as people, and had no desire to kill them or force American politics onto them. My Vietnamese friends called me 'Ton Tuat Hoa Binh' (the Prince of Peace), and many of them supported my view that this war and America's involvement in it were crazy.

"I am still close to *Stu Bloch*, one of the IVS volunteers in my group. While in Vietnam, we performed rock and roll songs together, and were known by Vietnamese as 'The Two Shi-Toos'. After we left Vietnam, we worked on The Vietnam Education Project to try to get our government out of this war. After seven more long years, we were glad to see the American government finally withdrawing all its forces from South Vietnam."

SHAMEFUL POLICIES

Rawlings now believes that, "IVS itself was fine in coping with USAID politics and allowing protestors like me to work there. But the American government policies there were shameful. We were killing thousands of innocent people every day and making enemies around the world, for no good reason.

"Looking back, I think that this IVS experience confirmed my belief that militant nationalism and militant religion are destructive forces in this world, and that somehow we need to view the human race not in terms as nations, or races, or cultures, but as one large family."

Ron Beahm had been accepted to the Peace Corps, scheduled to teach biology in Nigeria, but learned this would not qualify as alternative service.

He taught school in York, PA, and got to Vietnam with IVS in the summer of 1967. "I spent six weeks in intensive language training in Saigon and then went to Long Xuyen with the Mobile Science project to teach elementary education teachers science methods. Our system of hands-on experiments and interactive methods teaching students to think was far better than the old French system involving pure rote memory."

Things were not easy at that time, but Long Xuyen was less affected by the war. "The indigenous people hated the Viet Cong who years before had killed their leader (the Hoa Hao people). I was able to interact with teachers, students and my IVS colleagues. I was also active with students in the English club.

"Like many IVSers, I was looking for answers to some of life's questions and trying to grow up. I was very idealistic, hoping to do some good before settling down. Teaching was a possibility, though the salary was not enough, even then, to live on."

BOY'S HOME

The Tet Offensive put a stop to the Mobile Science project and Beahm and his team were asked to leave. He chose to continue his service with Brethren Volunteer Service in Germany where he spent seven months in a boys' home before returning to Bethany Brethren Hospital in Chicago to finish his alternative service.

"During my time of wandering in Vietnam with IVS and Germany with BVS," Beahm said, "I somehow developed the confidence to go to med school. Perhaps I always wanted to, but I wasn't sure I could do it. My time with IVS, I believe, showed me I could. I'm not sure how much good I did for my Vietnamese contacts; I'd like to think I helped some. We just don't know how much good we do for the people we touch. My time in Vietnam was short, and the circumstances difficult."

By 1968, the Tet Offensive had, in the words of IVSer *Ron Gould*, "disrupted everything. The IVS team in Vietnam was in chaos, and more than half of the volunteers there decided to leave. But I was still interested in going there, and by July things had settled down enough that the new group of volunteers could leave for Vietnam."

Gould served three tours with IVS. His first assignment was in Pleiku, Vietnam, to teach English in a high school; the second was in Savannakhet, Laos, again as a high school English teacher; and the third was in Vientiane as a teacher and teacher trainer.

"In the summer of 1968, the IVS/Vietnam team had been

seriously reduced in size, and many of the new volunteers were assigned to posts where they were the only IVSers in town. That was my situation in Pleiku.

"My formal assignment was to teach English; the understanding was that the high school headmaster could use me in any way he saw fit. He thought it would be great for all the students at his school, and this meant hundreds of them, to hear and practice speaking with an American. Of course, this meant that each student would at best have only a few minutes a week of personal interaction with me, but the headmaster thought this was the most equitable way to use me. In effect, I was a human tape recorder. It took a year to convince him that I could be much more valuable if I focused on the students in the higher grades who would actually be using English in the near future, but finally he came around to my way of thinking."

THE AMERICAN TEACHER

While his first year in Pleiku was a trial, "the second year was just delightful," Gould said. "I taught the middle and upper grades at the Boy's High School (which had girls in the highest grades), and I added several classes at the Girl's High School. I still had a lot of students, but we could actually communicate quite well. Of course, it also helped immeasurably that I was much more fluent in Vietnamese the second year. The Girl's High School published a yearbook and it included an interview with their American teacher in both English and Vietnamese. Several evenings a week, I had groups of the oldest students come to my house for extra lessons, which might be about American music, family life, meals, sports—whatever they were interested in. We would also go out on picnics and visit some of the tribal villages."

Pleiku is located in the center of the southern Vietnamese highlands, which are inhabited primarily by tribal Montagnards. Many of these people were desperately poor, and most Vietnamese considered them to be very primitive. A few of the school-age Montagnards were students at the Boy's High School, and Gould felt one of the small things he could do was show he valued them just as much as he valued the ethnic Vietnamese.

"If a Montagnard student was in danger of dropping out of school because he was too homesick for his family, I would drive him to his village for a visit every month or so."

While it wasn't part of his formal assignment, Gould also spent quite a bit of time with members of Vietnam Christian Service, who operated a clinic in Pleiku. There were five Americans on the VNCS team—a doctor, two nurses, a general handyman, and a team leader. "They were often overwhelmed by the number of patients who needed medical help, and I helped them whenever I could."

William Seraile, originally from Seattle, was living in New York when he joined IVS, after earning a BA from Central Washington State College and a stint with the Peace Corps as a social science teacher in Mekelle, Ethiopia. "That experience from 1963 to 1965 whetted my appetite for overseas adventures which is the reason I went to Vietnam.

"My service in Can Tho was from October 1967 to late April 1968. I was 26 when I arrived. I taught English at Phan Than Gian high school with a schedule that resembled a college professor's light teaching load. Additionally, I was engaged in language tutoring. The school with 3,000 students was formerly a French fort and a World War II Japanese barracks. As the only American on the faculty, my classes were very large."

Before Tet, Seraile became disillusioned teaching English and thought he could better serve the country by working in a refugee camp. "These feelings were so strong that I informed IVS in Saigon that it wasn't right for me to teach students who were using their acquired language skill to quit school and work for the U.S. military or for USAID. My threats to resign at the end of the school year unless I was given a transfer went unanswered."

REFUGEE CENTER

The Tet Offensive curtailed his teaching as the school became a refugee center until mid-April. Seraile, along with *Jerry Kliewer, Roger Hintze,* and *John Balaban* volunteered to assist overwhelmed American Air Force doctors and nurses in the local hospital. He was quickly trained as a scrubber in the operating ward where he cleaned wounds prior to surgery. "I witnessed surgeries of all types including amputations. This was my volunteer assignment for about six weeks, with a short leave to Saigon, until the number of wounded patients returned to normal.

"After all these years, I harbor some regrets for leaving Vietnam before completing my assignment. But there were mitigating factors. *David Gitelson,* whom I met once in Can Tho, was murdered on January 26, 1968. He was well known in the Mekong Delta for his saintly demeanor and the Viet Cong had no reason to kill him. I believe he was killed because he had information for Senator Ted Kennedy relating to civilian deaths committed by the Vietnamese military. A meeting with Senator Kennedy, scheduled for January 12, 1968, with Gitelson, Hintze, Balaban, Kliewer, Roger Montgomery and I, was abruptly cancelled when our Jeep was blown up. We all rushed out and Hintze jumped into our Land Rover to take injured Vietnamese to the hospital but quickly jumped out when a Vietnamese shouted, "NO!" A dog walked too close to the right front tire and the vehicle was blown up by a mine. I had sat on the Land Rover's passenger seat 30 minutes earlier. To this day, I don't know how mines or explosives were placed by the vehicle. A few days later, an explosive was discovered outside my school. Was it meant for me? Overly cautious, I checked my scooter for stray wires before kick starting it."

IVS offered all volunteers the opportunity to leave by April 25, 1968, at the organization's expense. "If we remained, we would have to finish our assignment or pay our way home if we left early."

BASKETBALL

"My final reflections about Vietnam: The war was surreal," Seraille said. "Seeking safety in Saigon, I flew on Air America—

a CIA aircraft—February 6, and approaching Tan Son Nhut airport, I saw in Cholon, the Chinese section, explosions and gun fire of an intense battle, while at a base about a mile from Cholon, I saw American soldiers playing a fierce basketball game.

"After Vietnam, I earned a PhD in American History and taught African American history at Lehman College, City University of New York from 1971 to 2007. Sometimes, when I think of Vietnam, I visit New York's Chinatown to capture again the smells and sounds of Asia."

Roger Hintze's family was imbued with a sense of giving, sharing and volunteering. In the small rural communities of Minnesota where he was born, neighbors and relatives would always be there to help out in case of need. And, in the Kennedy years of the early 1960s, he remembers, "There was a wave of fervor among young people to serve outside of our realm of comfort, and to do this abroad. I felt I had been given a good life so far, and that I should give back to someone in return."

One of his college roommates had moved to Canada in protest against the U.S. policy in Vietnam. Although Hintze didn't care for the country's involvement there, he felt he could do better by perhaps helping the people in that country.

Raised on a small farm, Hintze studied horticulture at the University of Minnesota, where he received BS and MS degrees in 1963 and 1966. He had applied to the Peace Corps and been offered a chicken project in India, and then a community development project in Panama. "My university advisor had pointed out the presence of IVS recruitment efforts on our campus. I decided to apply to IVS because of what appeared to be its smaller, more personal and focused programs."

Hintze served in Vietnam in the Mekong Delta (Can Tho) as an agriculture advisor, where he worked with counterparts in Ty Nong Vu and with teachers at the local agriculture high school. "On the way to Vietnam I had studied rice and tropical agriculture briefly at the University of Philippines and the International Rice Research Institute (IRRI) Our Vietnamese language study was held in the delta city of My Tho, where we studied for six weeks, six hours a day, six days a week. In the evenings we'd spend time in the local restaurants, where we could practice the Vietnamese we'd learned so far."

SOMETHING UNIQUE

In 1966 the concept of a foreigner attempting to learn the language was something unique, so he and his colleagues were persons of much curiosity. It was there Hintze discovered that the concept of volunteerism was particularly foreign to the ordinary Vietnamese.

"IVS, I found, was not keen on holding your hand and telling you what to do. I was introduced to the local agriculture people in the province and was left to find my own way. Early on, I tagged along with Filipino agriculturists who were working on irrigation and mushroom growing projects. As time went by I spent much of my time reporting to the Vietnamese Ag Service that dealt with plants. There was also a service in Can Tho that dealt with animals (Ty Muc Suc), which I decided was not my specialty. The Ag Service personnel often traveled into the province to the rural hamlets, teaching new methods of farming. I was able to travel with the service people when it was safe to do so."

In the fall of 1966 there was a flood on the rivers that fed into the Mekong Delta. Much of the farm land, being only a few feet above sea level, was under water. This destroyed the rice crop. The teachers at the ag high school organized a student trip to distribute *mung* bean seeds, which could be planted as a quick growing crop as soon as the water receded. Hintze traveled with the students to do this and, later on, helped the teachers organize a tomato trial of new varieties he had obtained from the Philippines, as well as a trial of the new high yield IR8 rice being promoted by IRRI.

"Working with the ag service, I became involved with the introduction of the Sugar Baby watermelon to a group of farmers on an island in the Bassac River. This particular melon with its almost black skin and deep red sweet flesh was in high demand and sold for a high price for the Tet New Year celebrations."

During the second year of his IVS contract, Hintze became IVS Ag Advisor for volunteers in the Mekong Delta area. "As part of staff, I spent time introducing new volunteers to their stations and arranging for additional ag training for IVSers. This took time from my own projects, as I also had occasional meetings in Saigon with other staff members."

Then, in the spring of 1967, Hintze became infected with Japanese B Encephalitis. He was confined to an army field hospital north of Saigon and fortunate to recover without after-effects.

"The Tet Offensive that occurred in late January and early February of 1968 pretty much put an end to traveling into the province. My vehicle, as well as another at our headquarters, was mined, and portions of the city were burned. The IVSers who were in the city then spent time working at the local hospital, helping American surgeons in the operating room and caring for wounded patients. We were quickly trained by medical personnel and were able to do procedures that no one in the U.S. medical world would ever have allowed unschooled persons to do."

At this point the decision was made to close down some of the volunteer sites in the delta, so Hintze spent time doing this. "The tomato trials I had set up at the ag school were eaten by hungry refugees housed there. The canals were not safe for me to travel. We later found that some IVSers had been put on a hit list by the VC. Also, after signing a letter to President Johnson complaining about the treatment of ordinary Vietnamese during the war, the teachers at the ag school confessed that they thought we were with the CIA. I decided to leave Vietnam in April of 1968."

Hintze now questions IVS's decision to place volunteers in the politically unsettled countries of Southeast Asia, particularly when a war was escalating in Vietnam. "By the time I left Vietnam there were over 500,000 American military troops participating in the war. Because of this, anti-Americanism among the Vietnamese was at an all-time high." Still, he feels fortunate to have arrived in-country in 1966. "I could still make what I thought were trusted co-workers and friends. I felt sorry for newly arrived volunteers who had this animosity to deal with."

LISTEN TO OTHERS

"At times I was torn between being there and maybe 'doing good' and being 'used' by the Vietnamese to further their own personal wants and goals," Hintze said. "I suppose I helped some of the farmers raise their living standards by increasing their crop yields. I learned to listen to others, and to adjust to a different concept of time. I became known to some of my co-workers as 'the mild American'.

"I feel sorry for the Vietnamese with whom I had contact and who suffered repercussions for having worked with Americans.

"There is one incident I particularly remember. Several days before I left to come home, the farmers and the ag service people had a going-away party for me. One of the farmers was blind, and I had arranged to have a large goiter removed from his neck. As he held my finger over the surgery scar, he said to me, 'Whenever I feel this on my neck, I will think of you.'

"I'll never forget the Vietnamese and their beautiful culture."

Jacqui Chagnon grew up comfortably in Meriden, Connecticut, an industrial town largely populated by, "Parochial Catholic European immigrants, whose main connection to international issues was through missionaries. My formal studies in International Relations at George Washington University in the mid-1960s and later at Johns Hopkins School of Advanced International Studies widened my perspectives and intensified my desires to work overseas, preferably for humanitarian organizations."

THE EFFECTS OF WAR

Her interest in overseas work in war zones started when she was six years old. "My introduction was a photo album hidden behind our family couch. The pictures showed dead bodies and skinny adults and children. Years later, as I was heading off to Vietnam my father told me that those photos came from the Ordruf Concentration Camp near Buchenwald, Germany. During its liberation in 1945, my father's military unit had spent days interviewing French-speakers, in order to help them head back home. 'I hope you never see the horrors of war in Vietnam,' he told me. Being undecided at that time about the necessity of war, I simply told him about my desire to study the effects of war on ordinary people and its legacies."

Chagnon's first job overseas was at Catholic Relief Services (CRS) in Saigon in October, 1968, six months after the Tet Offensive. She resigned from CRS after, "I found its private humanitarian work disturbingly embedded with U.S. military and intelligence operations."

From May 1969, until December 1970, she served with IVS in Saigon as the Associate Chief of Party for Administration. "This was a rather puzzling title to me at the time, which I later learned came from USAID jargon. For a barely experienced 22-year-old American woman, my appointment startled everyone, including myself, as I had never been an IVS volunteer and was hired in-country. I attribute my appointment not to experience but rather to luck. IVS-VN needed urgently to fill the administrative position and I was available and in Saigon."

As expected, the administrative part of her work was rather mundane. She arranged visas, orientations, and finances for some eighty volunteers and staff and acted as a liaison with USAID. "The best part was witnessing the volunteers at work in the field and hearing their perceptions about the struggles of common Vietnamese. Gratefully, the work bonded me with life-long friends with extraordinary accomplishments and personal values."

GRENADE

Chagnon's most vivid and memorable incident as the team

administrator occurred when the social backlash of warfare impacted directly on the IVS Saigon office. In 1969 and 1970, families of war-injured disabled veterans of the Saigon government began squatting on vacant land. About a dozen families had done so in front of the grassy IVS compound. "The Vietnamese veterans were angry about their insufficient welfare support, and the vet families wanted to extend their cramped quarters into the IVS yard. IVS staff organized a discussion team to explain to our vet neighbors that the land belonged to the Ministry of Agriculture. During the meeting, one severely disabled vet who had buried his pain in alcohol, started yelling slurs about Americans, and then suddenly pulled out a grenade, threatening to pull the pin.

"In seconds, the IVS men ran back towards our building, leaving me standing alone before the small group of vets. I continued to talk calmly to the vets and their wives, sensing that they might feel less threatened by a lone American woman wearing a Vietnamese traditional dress. I suggested that IVS staff could go with them to the Ministry to help them make their request. After about five minutes the vets agreed and got the drunk vet to put down the grenade."

Chagnon also remembers that, "A well-known Vietnamese Catholic priest who worked with several IVSers once said to me, 'You will not do much for us here except to learn about us. Take the lessons and go home to tell them to your people.' I agreed with him, but did not have a clue how this could be done.

"Nonetheless, I began to raise questions which have nagged me to this day. What were the long-term psychological ramifications of conflict for ordinary citizens? How long does post-war reconstruction and reconciliation take? Why does history fail to teach us about the deep ramifications of war for civilian populations? After forty-five years of searching for answers to these questions on international relations, be they focused on Vietnam, Laos, Cambodia, Afghanistan, Iraq, or El Salvador, I am still struggling to find answers."

MOBILE SCIENCE

In early 1967, *Hugh Manke* was closing in on a Master's degree in International Studies at American University, and living with a former Peace Corps volunteer who had friends visiting on a regular basis. An overseas Peace Corps-type of experience was high on Manke's postgraduate options, and Vietnam was at the top of everyone's list of political concerns.

"Ken Landon was one of my professors at American University. He met with Ho Chi Minh in 1945 and in 1953. Couldn't get the State Department to focus on his nationalist credentials rather than on his communist connections. Dr. Landon helped with IVS orientations and encouraged me to head in that direction, which I did. Mobile Science seemed an appropriate fit for a person with a Bachelor's degree in biology and chemistry."

MEMORABLE THRILL

In October, Manke boarded an airplane for Vietnam. "The thrill of flying into Vietnam was memorable. As we approached Tan Son Nhut, an airport outside of Saigon, the jungle canopy hid what I had read so much about: the strategic hamlets, the search and destroy missions, the people of Vietnam."

The IVS house in Saigon, a former government Agriculture Experiment station, was a momentary stop before heading to Vinh Long for language training with Gary Daves, another Mobile Science volunteer. "*Mike Fairley*, a seasoned IVS agricultural expert, was our host. *Jim Westgate*, an IVS English teacher and his Thai friend were our neighbors. I can't help but recall two rites of passage. The first was addressing the gastrointestinal issues. Gary, a former Peace Corps volunteer, Mike and Jim thought it was funny. Everything eventually worked itself out, as they say. The second was the first time I successfully used my newly acquired language skill to negotiate a meal and a price for the meal in the market."

CAPTURED VOLUNTEERS

The two-month language instruction was over too quickly. "Gary and I drew straws to see who was going where in the Mobile Science program," Manke wrote. "There were two openings: Hue, the Imperial Capitol and home of a famous university, and Quang Ngai, a backwater Central Coastal provincial capital controlled by the Viet Minh during the war with the French. Gary drew the long straw and chose Hue. In what turned out to be the ultimate irony, he was captured during the Tet Offensive two months later, not to be seen again until 1975 when the North Vietnamese released him and *Marc Cayer*, an agricultural volunteer from Canada. In 1970, as chief of party, I went to Paris with A.Z. Gardiner, our Executive Director, to try to learn the status of Gary and Marc in a meeting with a representative of the National Liberation Front. They professed ignorance and said they knew about IVS and would let us know if they learned anything about our two volunteers."

The two months of intense language instruction were just enough for Manke to socialize with Vietnamese co-workers who patiently listened to him speak their language and gently corrected him. "In three months I began to bond with two young teachers and one older one, each of whom was assigned to work with me by the former Provincial head of the Department of Education, who came south after the division of the country in 1954. His accent separated him from others in the local school system and, as I soon learned, his politics separated him even more. The evening of the Tet Offensive I was invited to a party attended by one of my co-workers in a village on the outskirts of Quang Ngai City. After about an hour of drinking beer and eating dried squid, my friend's face went from relaxed to tense as he excused himself. I was left alone to glance through the window and see several people crowded around the visitor."

POSTPONED CELEBRATION

The friend returned to explain that the celebration would need to be postponed because there might be some trouble. He then told Manke to go to his residence and not anywhere else. Sometime after midnight, the VC made an all-out assault on the city and by daylight was in full control of the streets. There was a Viet Cong cadre in the water tower that rose high above the buildings in the center of the city.

"It took several days before gunships and soldiers drove the VC out. As I walked through the streets looking at bullet holes in all of the buildings along the main street, the bombed out schools which served as the base camps for the VC, and the piles of dead VC bodies covered with lime on every other street corner, two light bulbs went off in my head.

"The first was that my government did not know what it was talking about when it reported that they had turned a corner in the war. The corner that had been turned led to a blind alley. The second was that my Vietnamese co-workers were not loyal Government employees—they were either people struggling to survive in that dangerous area between the anvil and the hammer, or active supporters of the VC. They probably were in the first category with strong sympathy for the old Viet Minh, now VC. I also realized these co-workers who only knew me for three months cared enough to keep me out of the line of fire. Somehow they knew I had no political agenda and worked for an organization that had a good reputation and no political agenda. IVS was not the CIA."

After several weeks, Manke and his team returned to work preparing a teacher plan for elementary school teachers in science instruction, "A program that ran smack dab into a century of Vietnamese instruction by memorization. Who came up with this program of aggressive challenges to a strong tradition and an outreach to rural school districts that were presumptively controlled by the VC at night? The village of My Lai was on our list of places to visit."

IMPRESSED BY THE IVS LEGACY

"The war took a respite in my province for most of the following year," Manke continued. "I did what was needed for my Mobile Science Project and spent a lot of time learning the language and trying to understand the culture around me. Every new word properly used and idiom understood was a step closer to the threshold of basic acculturation. When I arrived in Vietnam, I was impressed by the legacy of IVSers Don Luce, Gene Stoltzfus, Willie Meyers and John Sommer, all of whom knew so much about the differences between the various regions of the country, the diversity of religious and ethnic groups, and the nuances of the language. In my mind they had crossed that threshold that is so important in the implementation of successful volunteer development projects. I wanted to be like them. I never got there, but my time in the field led me to formulate some basic requirements for IVS program development in Vietnam."

Number one of these requirements was to find local agents for change and determine what they considered priorities, "Not only for themselves but also for their communities, and take the time required to thoroughly develop a project.

Number two was the need for safety in the communities targeted for projects. "Change is difficult in times of peace and nearly impossible in times of war.

"Halfway through my second year, my vision for IVS/Vietnam, which I shared with senior staff in Saigon, included continuing or developing programs in areas where there was some level of security. We should not expect to effect change in a community fighting for survival. The second goal was to put some distance between our programs and the war effort in order to maintain credibility with our local co-workers and our personal safety. Top-down central government programs backed by a foreign government with funding are not generally acceptable to village level leaders in the developing world."

NON-AMERICAN VOLUNTEERS

In order to meet these goals, IVS recruited more non-American volunteers in 1969-70, pursued private funding sources, and enhanced its programs among ethnic and religious minority groups that were low priorities for both sides in the war. Manke recalls that, "The U.S. and South Vietnamese governments soon realized that IVS was no longer an integral part of 'the team'. In 1971 the security situation in the Highlands closest to the Ho Chi Minh trail deteriorated and the South Vietnamese government forcefully relocated tens of thousands of Montagnards to coastal areas. This undermined the IVS programs there. IVS had worked hard over the years to steer away from refugee programs and could do nothing but protest the relocations and the destruction of the Montagnard cultural fabric in hearings before the U.S. Senate Subcommittee on Refugees. The U.S. government response was to not renew the IVS contracts. I was asked to leave two weeks after the notice was given and all of the programs were shut down several months thereafter."

II. CAMBODIA

IVS efforts in Cambodia begun in 1960 were cut short when Prince Sihanouk ordered all Americans out of the country in 1963.

Tom Wickham, graduate of a Quaker boarding school, left college in 1962 armed with a degree in agricultural engineering. "I felt an affinity for the hands-on rural development volunteers who made up most IVS teams at the time." The recruitment letter offered him a position rehabilitating parts of the irrigation structures underpinning the ancient Cambodian kingdom of Angkor Wat. "It was everything I could hope for: a position in which I felt I had some expertise, in a remote and historically exciting place." He was also drawn to the fact that, "This was a newly-independent country that had staked out a cold-war position of wariness to both super powers, especially the U.S." In September 1962, he bought an airline ticket to San Francisco and joined *Harlan Grosz*, another volunteer departing for Cambodia.

A PIPE DREAM

Upon arrival in Phnom Penh, it became clear to him that, "The position I had been recruited for was a pipe dream, wishful thinking, perhaps, on the part of the IVS team leader in Cambodia," who had not taken into consideration the wishes of local authorities. "I was dispatched to the opposite end of the country, to a new livestock station USAID and the Ministry of Agriculture were trying to carve out of a jungle not far from the sea and the border with Vietnam. I had no clear direction on what I would do there."

He arrived at this station in Kampot Province, a three-hour drive from Phnom Penh, just in time to hear the crash of a big livestock barn collapsing while under construction. "Fortunately, no one was hurt. The local contractor blamed the U.S. plans for the building; USAID blamed the contractor for shoddy work. I was asked to be a resident building inspector to ensure the work followed the plans for the barn and several other reinforced concrete buildings. This suited USAID, which was trying to enforce a U.S. regulation against the use of building materials from communist countries. Cambodia was building its first and only cement plant at the time and bartered rice for cement from North Vietnam." It was the first of many instances where he saw ideology impede practical development.

Wickham and Grosz gradually came to supervise most of the work done by the fifty-some Cambodian laborers. Grosz tended to pasture plantings and animal husbandry. Wickham maintained three heavy bulldozers and several tractors, and trained three or four young men in their operation.

COBRAS AND WILD ELEPHANTS

"Our houses, like almost all houses in rural parts of the country, were built six feet or more off the ground for protection against cobras, tigers and boars. We all saved rainwater in large clay pots during the rainy season, but during the six dry months we had to share water with the livestock from a mud hole in the bed of the river running through the station." The riverbed never dried out completely, so they dug a horizontal trench under the mud hole and installed a pump to move water uphill into a reinforced concrete tank. The system provided water for all the workers, livestock and families at the station when it was completed.

But, Wickham discovered, "Life on a government livestock station was not what I signed up for, so late in 1963 when I was offered a transfer to Lomphat, a town in Ratanakiri Province, to advise on agricultural extension, I accepted." Getting there meant a thirteen-hour overnight boat trip up the Mekong River from Phnom Penh to Kratie, and then a bus ride along a heavily forested route toward Vietnam. The last fifteen miles were off-road and impassable during the rainy season, except for travel by elephant. Wickham found it impossible to carry out any meaningful work there, in part because there were no government officials to work with, and because of sensitivities resulting from active use of the Ho Chi Minh trail nearby.

While Wickham was there, Ngo Dinh Diem was deposed and killed in Vietnam, and Cambodia's head of state, Norodom Sihanouk, "claimed the U.S. was behind the killing, denounced all Americans and terminated all aid programs including IVS. I waited a week and then left for Phnom Penh to see what we should do." He was one of the few Americans still in the country, "So I arranged my transfer to IVS Vietnam in six weeks, and bought a ticket to Bangkok, Singapore, Jakarta, Bali, Darwin, Hong Kong and Saigon. I never returned to Lomphat, leaving behind almost all my clothes, books and an old Jawa motorcycle.

"I visited Cambodia for Oxfam America shortly after the Pol Pot years but was unable to visit Kampot or Ratanakiri Provinces. It's likely that little remains of the livestock station because it was such an outsize Western target for the Khmer Rouge. I suspect a number of the men working with us on the station would not have survived the upheavals of that period."

Tracy Atwood arrived in Cambodia shortly before Sihanouk's edict and remembers: "My time in Cambodia was probably the shortest of any of the volunteers as I arrived a week after the others in my group."

He was sent to the Stung Keo livestock station, which had a sizable contingent of IVSers. The team leader suggested Atwood study Khmer in the mornings with an interpreter and work on the farm in the afternoons.

"There were eleven Murrah water buffalo on the station that Sihanouk had bought from India. He wanted to start a dairy industry in Cambodia. The buffalo were initially kept at a livestock facility just outside of Phnom Penh. No one knew what to do with them so they sent them to Stung Keo. I decided to milk them. That was a niche no one else was filling.

"The Cambodians would not drink this very rich milk unless it was laced with gobs of sugar, making it similar to the sweetened condensed milk they drank in their tea. We made some great ice cream with it using a hand crank freezer."

ASSASSINATION

Atwood was at Stung Keo for a little more than two months when everything fell apart. Ngo Dinh Diem, the President of South Vietnam, was assassinated on November 1. Then Sarit Thanarat, the Prime Minister of Thailand died, and his death was shortly followed by the assassination of President Kennedy. At the same time Sihanouk, the Prince of Cambodia, decided he did not want any more American aid. "He declared this very loud and clear in one of his nationally broadcast marathon speeches. USAID's work ended the next day. A USAID official drove to Stung Keo and told *Charlie Simmons* and me—the two remaining volunteers—that he was to bring us back to Phnom Penh and we had an hour to pack.

"Charlie and I were sent to the Mondial Hotel. The next

morning the desk clerk told me in Khmer that President Kennedy had died. I was sure I had misunderstood him. Then, later that afternoon someone arrived from the IVS house with mail that had accumulated. There was a letter from my father telling me that my favorite cow, Dolly, had died. It was an eventful twenty-four hours that I will not forget: my favorite cow died, I was pulled out of my first overseas assignment, and my President was assassinated.

"We sat in Phnom Penh for more than a month. Eleven volunteers signed a letter to Prince Sihanouk telling him that we would like to continue to work in Cambodia. Eventually there was a reply that we could stay as long as we had no funding from the U.S. government. IVS secured sufficient private funding for one volunteer who stayed on for a year-and-a-half at his station in Cheri Dong."

III. Laos

Robert Zigler arrived in Laos in April 1961. "This was the time of the Kennedy election. I was in the IVS/Washington office in the spring of '61 and went to Laos with IVS about April of that year. By this time, the Peace Corps bill had been passed and IVS began to receive delegations from the new Peace Corps organizational teams. An insurance group would come and see Dr. Noffsinger and ask, 'What do you do about insurance?' Then another group would ask about recruitment and another still about travel. For the Peace Corps, it was important useful information based on experience."

In Laos, Zigler headed a group of about twenty-six Americans who were scattered around the country working on agricultural construction, health, and educational projects.

A Neutralist Laos

"The American objective was to create a neutralist Laos. It was supposed to be a tripartite kind of government, left and right and neutral. We tried to get the village people to make group democratic decisions because of the stimulus that came from offering outside resources. That's what AID provided, opportunity for something different and practicing democratic action in their community. That was the rural development side of things."

Fighting raged in the country's interior regions. "That was a bad situation that affected project performance in several ways. One was when it came to people, particularly the Montagnards. They would get their upland, dryland rice started and ready for harvest. Then they were frequently attacked by the enemy. They had no rice crop for the coming year for survival. That was one impact. Another had to do with the limitations on travel because of security, and there were a number of people that got killed in different ways. Then, occupation of territory by the so-called enemy could prevent you from access to the people. Those were limitations caused by the internal war in Laos."

At the time and in spite of its difficulties, Laos was, "Essentially self-sufficient in agriculture with the exception of some people who lived in the city. In the Mekong River valley area, that was paddy rice. You had one crop a year and that was about it. They would also fish and hunt for survival. As I remember the income was about $100 a year. Once again that doesn't mean you had a poor life, but you just had a limit on life. Some people called Laos a 12th century civilization. We were trying to get the country to the 15th."

BILL RUFENER*: FISH TALES

BERNIE WILDER, COP/IVS/LAOS EDUCATION 1963-68

In the summer of 1963 I arrived in Laos as the newly minted Chief of Party of the IVS Education team. Bill had just finished a two-year tour and was beginning his second two-year tour. He was a steady and unflappable presence who was a big help to me as I was trying to figure out my role at Don Dok.

———

*Bill Rufener died in June, 2013.

The USAID officer who was responsible for assistance to Don Dok was a particularly pushy individual. Over the objections of the Lao, he had a road built through the student garden plots. When we sought permission to build some fish ponds behind the school so Bill could teach fish-raising, the officer refused to provide any USAID resources and adamantly told us that under no circumstances should we build the ponds. There were only twelve houses completed in the compound. The only residents were IVS/Education volunteers and Bureau of Public Roads (BPR) personnel, one of whom had become friends with Bill. Bill learned that his friend was going to conduct a training program for bulldozer operators. He thought he had the perfect place to conduct that training. We got permission from the head of the school for BPR to conduct their training program behind the school, and did not see the need to seek permission from USAID. By some strange miracle, when the training program was finished, Bill had his fish ponds. The USAID officer was furious. We had figured from the beginning that it would be easier to obtain forgiveness than permission. As it turned out we didn't get either.

ANOTHER TRUE RUFENER FISH TALE

HOWIE LEWIN, LAOS, 1963-65

When I first arrived in Laos, Bill Rufener was at Dong Doke, an American-inspired, comprehensive high school that taught both academics and manual skills. At the fish hatchery, which consisted of six fishponds, Bill was teaching the techniques of raising and breeding fish. When I went to visit him, I noticed three-foot-high fences covered with fishnets all around the ponds.

I jokingly said, "What are you trying to do, keep the fish in?"

"No, we're trying to keep fish out," he replied. I wasn't quite sure what he was telling me. But then he described a fish called pa douk (Clarias batrachus) that walked out of water. It actually could come out of a pond and crawl into another pond, he told me.

"Sure," I said, "I know I'm new in the country, but you can't expect me to believe this."

"Well, stick around," he said, "because it's going to rain in a little while and you'll see what I mean."

I stuck around and it started raining pretty hard. There was a pond just on the outside of the school campus, a little lower in elevation than the six ponds in the fish hatchery, and, sure enough, fish began crawling out of the lower pond and up the road looking for another pond. It was the damnedest thing I have ever seen. They used the fins on their sides like little feet and pulled themselves along with their tails wiggling like mad. They were walking fish. ⚮

Though almost all of the IVSers in the area were influenced one way or the other by the spreading conflict, *Val Petersen's* tours in Laos were largely trouble-free. "I departed the U.S. on April 17, 1962, arriving in Laos on April 21, to fill an undefined position as the first generalist for IVS/Laos. During that first tour I did everything from loading rice on airplanes for refugees to serving, for four months, as acting USAID Area Coordinator in Luang Prabang."

TEAM LEADER

"My second tour, technically as a Team Leader, started in June, 1964, in the village of Muong Cao (also referred to by Americans as Borikhane) up the Nam Sane River from Paksane, three-and-a-half hours by long-tail boat in the rainy season, forty-five minutes by road in the dry season. I chose this second tour with IVS because I wanted the grass-roots village-level experience the IVS position offered. This I got, and while at it, I taxed and developed my skills at community development, agriculture, Jeep-winch operation, snake evasion, and plumbing, to name a few, for eight months.

"About the time I felt the 'cluster village' community development effort had some chance of getting organized enough to have long-lasting value, I was moved to Thakhet to be temporary

USAID Community Development Area Advisor (a misnomer for pushers of U.S. and Lao government papers), and to take over a rather infant refugee resettlement program from IVSer *Al Bashor*." Petersen was soon able to concentrate primarily, and then solely, on refugees, but it was always a mixture of relief and resettlement work. "In this work I was soon, for all practical purposes, working for USAID, with minimum contact with IVS."

At the end of this tour, USAID offered Petersen the same position as he had had with IVS, "plus money. However, believe-it-or-not, I took them up on it not for the money, but because I had a feeling of accomplishment and thought another two years there should see most of the people with whom I was working well on their way to self-sufficiency. (This was in a relative way, since they had marginal soil, no place to grow paddy, few water buffalos, etc.) In fact, by the time I left Thakhet in 1968, I felt this had essentially happened." In January, 1969, Petersen rejoined the IVS staff, and spent "one mostly enjoyable year in Luang Prabang as Associate Director for Northern Laos. In 1970 I moved to Vientiane, and remained there until my termination Jan. 31, 1974. I suppose my most important contributions during my time on the IVS staff were, one, contributing to the general effort to work closely with the Lao people in planning the IVS program in Laos; two, attempting to use this relationship to help Lao planners look more incisively at the needs of the Lao people; and three, helping develop systems for more effective communication within IVS Laos."

LAOS: **1965-1966.** THE FORWARD AREA TEAM AT XIENG LOM

GALEN BEERY*

The Forward Area Teams were small teams of IVS men assigned to rural villages in areas a bit further away from the

---

*Galen Beery served at IVS Headquarters in Washington, D.C. from 1959 to 1962, then in Laos from 1962 to 1967.

usual provincial capitals. One of these was in Xieng Lom, northern Sayaboury province, where I was assigned in the mid-1960s. Four or five of us occupied a cabin about four meters square, with a view south towards the landing strip.

Here we lived, ate and slept, using an outdoor squat privy. We had five or six cots, each with a mosquito net. We had folding chairs and sat around a crude table for meals, which were bachelor cooking on a battered tabletop kerosene stove. Rice was a staple, plus eggs and vegetables such as pole beans that we bought at the rudimentary market every day or so, and canned food from the commissary in Vientiane. A normal meal was scrambled eggs, 'beanie-weenies' and rice.

We also used the table for typing or writing, and when we brought up canned seeds from USAID Agriculture and spooned small amounts into little plastic envelopes for distribution to villagers. New varieties of corn and beans were very happily accepted when we talked to farmers in the villages. Lettuce seeds didn't do well and no one could ever get any celery seeds to germinate.

Life being rather relaxed, villagers would come by and visit. I once woke up from an afternoon nap and discovered five women squatting around my cot, not disturbing me. It was a bit of a problem to get dressed in the sleeping bag but I accomplished it while they giggled.

After about six weeks, we began to realize that little cuts and sores in our hands were not healing; rice and beanie-weenies weren't providing enough vitamins. So we bought and cooked more vegetables and the sores cleared up.

We ignored the building next door, which seemed deserted. I once went over to find out when an aircraft was coming in. A man in jungle-style uniform at a desk looked up and said something to an associate who went to a large map of the area and drew a curtain over it. Colored map pins showed the location of special guerrilla units of two or three Lao military.

We had several bicycles but enjoyed walking to the villages

on all-day trips. In my spare times I wrote up the history of the valley, and produced a rough map showing where the villages were. Our emphasis was on improving the wells, and we had a good program going, digging wells and helping the villagers create concrete rings that were lowered into them.

Before I went to Xieng Lom, I interviewed candidates for interpreting positions with IVS. Most were young men who had graduated from the equivalent of high school and had studied English on their own. One who I felt was rather good was Boutsy Bouahom. When I was asked to go to Xieng Lom, I arranged it so Boutsy would go with me.

We landed on the Xieng Lom airstrip, loaded our bags and boxes into the Jeep, and were driven to a long building.

The next day we walked to the office of the Chao Muong, a Vientiane-appointed local governor, and told him about our assignment to help rural development in Xieng Lom. A house was being built; the frame was already up, and a group of men were involved in a good old house-raising.

We helped by carrying panels of grass to workers on the roof and spent most of the afternoon with me learning how to tie the grass panels. That evening we were invited to join the building crew in a nearby home for food and obligatory rounds of lao-lao whiskey. The workers were discussing the Chao Muong and how bad he was! Boutsy and I agreed not to get too cozy with the Chao Muong, given his reputation.

Several more IVSers were assigned to Xieng Lom, and we welcomed them into our little cabin. Since the wells were old and new ones were needed, this became our primary program. It was a halcyon period. Boutsy and I sat at a village campfire one evening with a dozen men and enjoyed the camaraderie and the starry night. They asked about my family. I said that I had two younger brothers, both married. One had two children, the other had three but he and his wife had decided not to have any more. Now this was of interest! How did one decide not to have any more children? I explained 'the pill,' and Boutsy taught me the term 'birth control' in Lao. Everyone absorbed this bit of information, and then a quieter man in his twenties spoke up: "Uh, where can one get this pill?" The older men chuckled and made a mild joke or two, but he was serious. He told us, "Well, we have three kids already and this valley is running out of arable land."

As we began to contact villages further away, we were given a CJ-6 long-bodied Jeep to carry cement and tools. The roads were merely trails, and sometimes we had to widen them. One creek, no more than ten feet wide, posed a problem. The Jeep became stuck in mud while we were trying to ford the creek. A villager suggested an elephant, and in an hour one came in, was chained to the front bumper, leaned forward and pulled the Jeep up the bank with a giant sucking sound. I was steering the Jeep and knew I shouldn't touch either brakes or horn. Finally the elephant came to a stop and the owner unhitched him. Later, we took two gasoline drums from the airport and made a culvert. A week later we drove back, only to find it had been smashed flat by an elephant!

A new man hired by the Rural Development Division came to live with us. Sam Adams had been Peace Corps, but didn't speak Lao, and was earning about five times what we were paid! But he took to the program. He was intrigued that there was almost nothing except first aid kits and so in Vientiane checked with USAID Public Health. He returned and soon a carpenter hired by USAID came and hired some of the villagers to do construction. Sam insisted on nailing a metal plaque with the USAID logo on one of the roof supports, which rankled the rest of us a bit: we had been trying to help villagers with their own programs and give them the credit!

The Chao Muong was really disliked in the villages. One afternoon Boutsy came in with a big smile and told us that the Chao Muong, irritated by his lazy wife who was sleeping, had kicked her in the head! She grabbed her bags and went to the airport and caught a ride out to Vientiane. The Chao Muong was around a few more months and finally he too departed for Vientiane, leaving the villagers a lot happier.

A U.S. Army Colonel nicknamed Haff worked with the

Embassy, USAID and IVS to make the Forward Area Teams (FAT) successful. He was thoughtful, observant, and intelligent. At the time some IVSers were put off by the idea of working in villages where it could be dangerous, though others entered wholeheartedly and quietly joked about being 'FAT men' under 'Col. Halftrack'.

One evening at Xieng Lom, Haff mused about giving each man on the FAT some training in firing an M-1 rifle. I thought about it for a minute, then gently suggested that to villagers, IVSers with guns would undoubtedly be considered soldiers. There was also the danger that they might shoot themselves or someone else by accident. Also, if captured, it would be their advantage to be unarmed. Several days later, dining in the American restaurant in Vientiane, I heard Haffner explain to someone that "we don't want our men to carry guns."

He restated my comments, point by point. ◦◦

Lucy Hollinger (Basler) remembers, "My exposure to IVS started in the early months of 1963. I began to receive postcards from the Adventist Hospital in Bangkok, Thailand; then the cards began to come from a dusty screened-in porch which housed IVS volunteers who lived and worked in Vientiane, Laos, or were visiting from out of town." Hollinger knew IVSers Galen Beery and *Val Petersen* from the Brethren Voluntary Services, which she had joined in 1959. "They bombarded me with postcards full of propaganda about how wonderful IVS was and that I just had to join up."

Hollinger was scheduled to graduate from college at the end of the summer session. "My closest friends were studying at Elizabethtown College, and I would stop in occasionally. What I enjoyed most was talking with my friend, *Dee Dick (Quill)*, who was a nurse/student at the college. She asked me what I was going to do when I graduated, and I told her about IVS. Dee was taken with my sales pitch and on Labor Day 1963 we were flying from our homes in Pennsylvania to D.C. in a rickety two engine airplane for the IVS orientation."

"SURE, WHY NOT?"

Hollinger received a letter from IVS asking if she would go to Jordan to teach. "Sure, why not, I said to myself. A month or so later, I received another letter asking if I would go to Cambodia. I ran to our family's outdated World Book Encyclopedia, looked up Cambodia, read the three descriptive paragraphs, studied the photo of the Cambodian dancer with pointed hat and long fake fingernails and again replied, 'Sure, why not?'

"Dee was asked to go to Laos and so together we traveled to the other side of the world. In Hong Kong, Dee flew off to Laos and I, with twelve other IVSers, flew to Phnom Penh. In Phnom Penh, four days a week were spent in learning how to teach English as a Second Language in the mornings and Khmer language classes were in the afternoons. To get to our classes, most of us bought bicycles or Vespas. Our long weekends were spent visiting the fantastic major attractions in Cambodia."

Hollinger became ill, was admitted into the Calumet Hospital in Phnom Penh for surgery, and "soon after my hospital discharge, Prince Sihanouk ordered all Americans out of Cambodia. Because of the surgery and possible repercussions, I was given a ticket to return home to Hershey, PA, to my extreme disappointment. My ticket was about three-fourths of an inch thick, with tickets to Laos, Calcutta, New Delhi and many, many more stops. I did not want to waste this opportunity."

On December 14, 1963, she landed in Vientiane, Laos, and there met Pat Basler, "a stranger with whom I was to fall in love and marry ten months later."

IVS told Hollinger there was no work for her in Laos, so she was hired to teach at the American School. "Since the school hours were from 7:30 a.m. to 12:30 p.m., I became a volunteer ESL teacher at the Lao American Center in downtown Vientiane. I also enjoyed trips to Luang Prabang and Pakse, where I drank lao-lao (village rice whiskey) for the first time. It truly tasted like white lightning! Although I no longer was an IVS volunteer, I experienced IVS through those who shared their quarters with me."

Dianna Quill, a student at Elizabethtown College working on a B.S. in Nursing, was employed by the college as one of three nurses in charge of student health when she met Lucy Hollinger, whose cousin was also a nurse. Hollinger was in the process of applying to IVS and told Quill about the organization. "I called IVS in Washington, D.C., for an application. I was accepted to go to Laos. Lucy went to Cambodia.

"After a week of orientation at George Washington University we left with our group on September 9th. IVS had told me I would be teaching obstetrics to midwives and nurses."

The infirmary at the school had a Lao male supervisor, Thom Phan, who would transport the students who needed to see a doctor, and two female nurses working in the dispensary.

FIRST AID BOOK

"Life with the IVS team was great. We were invited to many USAID and Lao government functions; vacation time was generous, and we could travel to many places in Southeast Asia, but I wasn't happy in my assignment. I did write a first aid book that was translated into Lao and published by USAID, and I spent a summer in Thakhet teaching first-aid to local teachers, but I felt I wasn't using my nursing skills and not contributing anything to Laos."

In February 1965, the Director of Public Health USAID, Dr. Charles Weldon, was looking for an American nurse to go to Sam Thong, a refugee village in North Laos with a thirty-bed hospital employing seven Hmong nurses. Better facilities were needed because the Vietnam War was spilling over into Laos. Weldon wanted to start a nursing school at the hospital to train Hmong girls in basic procedures and assist doctors as needed. "The hospital was being enlarged to a 130-bed unit. IVS gave permission for me to finish out my tour.

"USAID built me a house to live in across from the hospital as I was the first woman to live on site. In March 1965, I began an incredible experience working twelve to fifteen hours per day, seven days a week. The hospital grew. The girls became excellent nurses and we treated many different diseases and military personnel. Now I was doing something!"

After her tour ended, Quill extended for six months, then signed on for another two years. In January 1967, she met her future husband, Terence (Teny) Quill, and they were married in the States in 1968.

"During my time in Sam Thong, the original seven nurses, myself, and *Carol Mills*, received the King's personal Medal for Service to his country.

"Then, on July 4, 2013, in St. Paul, Minnesota, there was a Hmong nurses, medics and USAID reunion. About 200 people attended. It had been forty years since I last saw many of the nurses. I was really proud when I heard that almost all of them had nursing careers after relocating to the USA. That day brought back many memories of Laos that I have cherished."

A COMPELLING CANVAS

Howie Lewin's experiences in Laos began in 1963 and would culminate in a book, *Sunsets, Bulldozers, and Elephants: Twelve Years in Laos, the Stories I Never Told.* He was with IVS from 1963 to 1965.

One of his school acquaintances invited him over for a slide show. A college friend had just come back from overseas and was going to tell them about his adventures in Vietnam, a country at that time not yet totally engulfed in war. He painted a compelling canvas in Lewin's imagination.

IVS had contracted with USAID to provide volunteers with expertise in education, agriculture, construction, engineering, animal husbandry, agronomy—basic skills that could be taught to the peoples of the host country. It was an unexpected opportunity but one that fit Lewin's needs and aspirations. Tours were two years, with $80 per month and a $125 cost of living allowance.

"That sounded pretty good to me, since I had been living on

student's wages for six years. Besides, I could take just about anything for two years; university life had tested me to that extent."

Lewin flew to Tokyo and then on to Saigon where he spent a couple of days as guest of IVS/Vietnam. Next he boarded a Royal Air Lao DC4 and flew first to Pakse, and then to Vientiane. "It was a strange flight—a taste of a life that was a bit too real for me. Some of the passengers were chickens and pigs, and with no air-conditioning the aroma on board was a bit... well, let's just say unpleasant. When we landed in Vientiane and the stewardess opened the plane's door, I felt a blast of hot air the likes of which I had never experienced in my life. It literally sucked the wind out of me. Coupled with this was the blinding brightness of the sun. I did not have sunglasses, and the light reflected off anything and everything that was light colored. We had arrived in the middle of the hot season."

The first night in the IVS hostel was hellishly memorable. Not only was the heat far beyond anything he'd ever experienced, but during the night he was assaulted by the Lao mosquitoes. "I became their pincushion and by morning was covered from head to toe with bites as big as quarters. To this day, I have never suffered as much from mosquitoes as I did that first night. I tried to get rid of them with mosquito repellant, and bug spray, for which I was criticized by one of the IVSers sharing the same room, who was more worried about the effect of breathing the spray than the potential for contracting malaria from the mosquitoes. I prevailed, however, and had a much better second night."

WINNING HEARTS AND MINDS

The next few weeks were spent at in-country orientation, which consisted of Lao language classes for about six hours a day, visits to the morning market, to various religious shrines, Lao ministries and government agencies, and finally a field trip upcountry. The Deputy Director of USAID gave all new IVS arrivals an orientation lecture to explain the role IVS was going to play. "We were to demonstrate that what the Lao Government could do for its people with USAID assistance was definitely more than what the Pathet Lao and Vietminh could do for them. 'Winning the hearts and minds of the people,' so they would stand with their government, was the basic concept."

Still, Lewin had questions. "If we are successful," he asked, "Won't the PL and Vietminh see us as a threat and seek to shut us down?" The answer was yes, but the volunteers were assured the Lao military would provide protection.

"We reached our destination, Muong Khao in Borikhane Province, by air and by water. We flew from Vientiane on an Air America chartered C-46, which serviced all of the major cities of Laos twice a week. Its first stop was Paksane, a small provincial capital on the Mekong River where our support base was established. After landing there, we arranged transportation to go up river to Borikhane Province, our new home."

It took eight hours on the river. The road to Muong Khao was only thirty-five kilometers long, but the river meandered for at least three times that. "We arrived in early October, 1963. Our village rested on the banks of the Nam Sane River, which was a clear green river when it wasn't raining hard. After a heavy rain, it turned chocolate brown.

"The purpose of many of our projects was to help the local people become healthier. One such project was to get potable water supplies by digging water wells and lining them with concrete well rings. Another was to develop a water-seal privy program." Other projects were to improve nutrition and agricultural techniques, supervise the construction of self-help schools, and build a training center and medical dispensaries.

Every evening the IVS team would wander to the river to bathe. It was an idyllic scene. "What stood before us was the pink glow of a sunset, monkeys playing in the bamboo thickets across the river, a perfect water temperature, clear green water, and a sandy beach. At this time of the evening, gongs and drums from the Wat would begin calling the villagers to prayer. That sound is indescribable, so pleasant and so peaceful that it seemed to fit into the picture seamlessly. It was hard to believe that a war was going on."

Every village in the cluster area eventually dug at least one well and lined it with concrete well rings. Round steel bar was scarce so they used bamboo as reinforcing rods. "I also experimented with making a bamboo bucket pump out of rope and wood. It worked pretty well. I fabricated a pump out of a bamboo pipe, a bolt, and an old inner tube. It worked pretty well, too. The idea was to get villagers to pump rather than draw water out of the wells in buckets, so that the wells could be covered. Open wells allowed many undesirable things to fall in. For instance, the villagers just dropped their buckets that had been set on the ground into the well. One time a big water buffalo defecated in the well near our house, which defeated the whole purpose of having a concrete-lined well. It took about a week to get the water back to safe drinking levels."

PATHET LAO

At that time, the Royal Lao Army (RLA) stronghold at Tha Thom had fallen because of mass defections. The defectors had joined the Pathet Lao. The fall of Tha Thom left the road wide open to Paksane, and to the volunteers in Borikhane Province. Muong Khao became a target of the Pathet Lao, who started attacking south from the Plain of Jars. They seemed invincible.

Lewin remembers that, "The women IVS team members were evacuated, and for a while it looked as if the men would have to as well. But the Royal Lao Army (known as FAR, Forces Armées du Royaume, in French) counter-attacked and drove the PL back. I vaguely recall a battery of 105 howitzers being set up in an open field at the north end of the village." In a letter to home Lewin wrote: "Here in Muong Khao, things have settled down again, and there is hardly a trace of the 3,000 troops that were in our village. The PL have withdrawn almost back to their attacking positions. The IVS team remained on post the whole time and was given letters of commendation by the USAID director."

Borikhane was the center of defense for the entire area, set up as the main supply base and last defense line. There were trench works, large guns, small guns, just about everything needed to carry on a war, except the enemy. The enemy came down from Tha Thom until they were about thirty kilometers north. Then they retreated, after causing considerable panic in the FAR. "At first they just ran. Then one week later, the FAR counter-attacked and retook a village that the PL had left one week before. The FAR are scared to death of the Vietminh; they are like the *Pi* (spirits), very powerful. So powerful are they that all the troops have to find out is that there are Vietminh in the area, and they are gone—poof—as if by some feat of prestidigitation."

The village experience in Muong Khao gave Lewin insights that helped throughout the next eleven years he was in Laos.

Lewin's next assignment was supposed to be in Thakhet, but he was there only a few weeks. "Our project just did not seem to get off the ground. I'm not sure what happened. Perhaps my stunning personality and machismo attitude caused some anxiety on the part of my new colleagues? Actually, I think an administrative problem as well as serious security issues delayed the start of what was to be another cluster program. When I was in Thakhet for that short time, the Pathet Lao made another one of their periodic forays. I was beginning to think that I walked around with a cloud over my head—either it rains or the PL make a sortie somewhere nearby." Soon Lewin was sent off to Vientiane. There he worked under the Area Coordinator, Jim Clark, to complete thirty-two self-help schools. "This project had been on the books a long time, and little if any progress had been made. I was put in charge of completing them or bringing them to a stage where they could be taken off of the books."

Another project was a little farther north in an area of questionable security, about eighty kilometers from downtown Vientiane. Lewin was driving by himself. "Barreling along on a main road at a pretty good clip, I encountered an army deuce-and-a-half (a two-and-a-half-ton truck with eight wheels in the back and two in the front). I kept my distance trying to avoid its dust cloud. Finally, the driver pulled off the road to drop off some passengers. I passed, waved to him in thanks, and sped by. Pretty soon I could just see the truck in my side view mirror. He must have pulled back onto the road shortly after I passed."

LAND MINE

"When I heard the explosion, the shock wave rattled me so I almost drove off the road. I wasn't exactly sure where the explosion came from, other than somewhere behind me. I looked in my rearview mirror, and through the dusty haze, I saw the army truck turn a somersault and land upside down with a sickening crunch. There was no hope for the driver. I realized I had just driven over a land mine and it had not gone off! Either my Jeep was not heavy enough to detonate it, or it must have been triggered by someone lying in ambush. Either way, it meant enemy troops were nearby—not a comfortable feeling—so I put the pedal to the metal. The realization that I had passed over a mine, perhaps twice, once coming and then returning, without it going off really made me wonder what kind of luck I had."

Louis Wolf received his draft notice in the fall of 1964 when he was twenty-four, a year out of college and involved in the civil rights movement. "I already knew I was opposed to war. I had to plan my next step quickly because my draft board gave me only two weeks before I was to be drafted into the military. I wasn't thinking about avoiding the draft but was clear in the realization that I didn't want to put on a uniform or kill people. So I applied for conscientious objector status with an application to IVS."

Wolf was living in Indianapolis, so IVS personnel director *John Hughes* flew in and interviewed him at the airport. He told Wolf there were job openings for volunteer assignments in two countries, Vietnam and Laos, and the pay was $150 a month. Wolf responded that he didn't want to "go to a war zone or be involved in a war, so I chose Laos and was accepted on the spot. Hughes told me IVS was contracted by the U.S. Agency for

International Development to do rural development work with the Lao people. He never mentioned (nor did he really know at the time) that Laos was a major war zone but the war was Top Secret, at least to the American people and the Congress."

WAT LUANG TEMPLE

"In October I arrived in the sleepy capital, Vientiane, site of a bustling public marketplace, and the grand Buddhist Wat Luang temple that purportedly contains Buddha's bosom bone and boasts a spectacular Golden Stupa, the symbol of the Lao nation. At that time, there was just one traffic light. On my fifth day, I was sent north to a remote mountain place called Sam Thong where I was to teach English to poor, uneducated Hmong nurses who were working at a very small Filipino hospital."

Each day, he saw two-engine Air America aircrafts land and unload stretcher after stretcher of battle—wounded. "I abruptly learned I was in the middle of a war zone. Within forty-eight hours, I realized Air America was run by an obscure U.S. government body called the Central Intelligence Agency, and that the bloodied and maimed people being carried into the four-room clinic were part of a secret army of local Hmong tribespeople enlisted by this agency to do battle with 'the Communists,' the Pathet Lao and their North Vietnamese allies."

QUESTIONS

Wolf began asking questions about the pallets of rice and military ordnance piled on the landing strip. These were being ferried across the mountains to small landing sites. "In no uncertain terms, I was told, 'That's not your business.' Then I learned that the rice was being flown across the mountains and dropped just ahead of the Hmong fighters in a way calculated to make them march toward the rice rations and inevitably into battle." The dead and wounded men were flown back each day for medical treatment.

"The larger picture of this 'secret war' became obvious to me.

"At the end of my second week, I was falsely accused of sexually harassing the nurses and ordered to leave Sam Thong and return to the capital." This turn of events may have saved Wolf's life as he came down with a near-fatal bout of malaria, dengue fever and gallstones. Wolf lived for a time in Vientiane working on the first-ever census of the capital.

His next assignments were more in keeping with the idealistic 'helping people to help themselves' IVS motto that first attracted him to the job. "I learned to love Lao food and became fluent in the Lao language, though due to a measure of laziness, I never learned to write or read the Lao script."

B-52s

"Then I lived and worked with another IVSer at Muong Cao, a small village about 150 miles south and east of Vientiane on the Sane River, a Mekong River tributary. This work took us to sixteen villages in the area, helping to build water-seal latrines, deep-water wells, and a school. We also distributed seed and fertilizer."

Nearly every day, they heard and saw B-52 aircraft flying overhead from U.S. Air Force bases in Thailand, Okinawa and the Philippines, headed north on bombing missions in North Vietnam.

One day, Wolf heard there had been a bombing in one of the villages where he'd worked. He rushed by Jeep about twenty miles on rutted dirt paths and across rice paddies to reach the devastated village some ninety minutes later. "There were dozens of bodies and body parts all over. The villagers' thatch hut dwellings were laid to waste among the carcasses of water buffalo, pigs and chickens. Knowing the American pilots would routinely circle around for a second run on their target, the surviving villagers had fled for cover into the jungle nearby.

"I ran east into the dense jungle until I heard the haunting wails and cries of survivors. I saw a friend, Phanh, with whom I'd worked just the week before digging the hole where we and other villagers were building a thirty-foot deep well. Phanh was badly wounded by shrapnel, gasping, bleeding through his ears, and fast losing consciousness."

LAST WORDS

"As I took him in my arms, his last words were, in Lao, 'Please understand that I am not dying for your country; I am dying for my country.' I never knew if he could hear me, but I swore aloud that I would find out why this village of eighty-five people had been destroyed. I learned in subsequent months that the bombing had been called in by the CIA.

"My life was forever changed; I decided I would devote myself to investigating this secret instrument of American foreign policy."

In time, occasionally drinking beers with the pilots at local watering holes, Wolf discovered that bombers sent out on missions would return in the mid- or late afternoon, "But, because they often still had unused bombs aboard, the pilots would dump them in Laos so the planes could safely land back at their home bases.

"This and other military bombing meant that on a per capita basis, more tonnage of ordnance was dropped on Laos than in the entire history of warfare, including during World War II and the Vietnam War itself. Even now, from the air, much of northern and eastern Laos resembles a moonscape. Today fully thirty-nine years after this secret war, ended, unexploded ordnance—known in Laos as UXOs—still maim and kill innocent Lao who accidentally encounter the remnants of these weapons in their soil.

"While efforts continue to clear the land of the UXOs, reliable estimates are that it will take seventy years to make much of Laos safe for its people again. Former CIA Director William E. Colby once proudly asserted, 'Laos was one of our success stories.' Precisely what Colby meant with this judgment is a really tough call."

Wolf now says, "Many years later, it's my opinion that at

the time, IVS, and we as individual volunteers, were used by the American government as window dressing for a much wider strategic war agenda in Laos and Vietnam. Whether it was volunteers writing monthly reports disseminated without our knowledge beyond the offices of IVS, or in a few cases in Laos, being deployed to the 'Forward Area Program,' resulting directly in several deaths of volunteers, these were unquestionably consequences which none of us signed up for."

Larry L. Lehman first heard of IVS in 1965 when Willie Meyers and John Witmer came to his college to recruit volunteers. They told him IVS was a nonprofit organization designed to promote people-to-people cooperation in foreign development projects. "I was happy to hear that my experience farming, my high school major in agriculture, and my college degree from Goshen in biology were enough to qualify me for rural development work in Laos." He was recently married to *Kristin Troyer* and joined IVS out of a sense of adventure. It was also a chance for him to do alternative service to the Vietnam War, "Although I wasn't required to do any service since I'd failed my physical."

In the Lowlands

IVS was not sending married couples to work in Vietnam at the time and the Lehmans were assigned to Laos with the IVS Rural Development Team working with lowland Laotians. They attended Lao language training in September and October 1966, in Washington, D.C., and another two weeks of training in tropical agriculture, rice cultivation and community development in the Philippines, then were sent to Laos. "Kris and I landed in Vientiane November 19, 1966. *Ken Lewis* was our supervisor. A few days later, Kris and I flew south to Savannakhet, the provincial capital where we met Jack Huxtable, our USAID Community Development Advisor (CDA). I remember how surprised I was at the cold, dusty conditions of the dry season as we drove east on Route 9 for thirty-six miles to Ban Dong Hene, where I thought we would live and work for the next two years."

USAID in Laos was following a strategy called the Cluster Concept. It was up to the CDA to visit villages in the cluster, to survey felt needs, to develop plans with local leaders, and then start small projects. It was hoped enthusiastic villagers would support the Lao Government and overall efforts to contain Communism. Dong Hene was one of the on-going Cluster Areas.

Two other IVSers were already there. "*Lew Sitzer* was working in Muong Phalane eighteen miles east of Dong Hene. This village was as far east as we could go, eighteen or twenty miles from the Ho Chi Minh trail. *Fred Cheydleur* was in Ban Phakkanya located thirteen miles north of Dong Hene. We all had Lao assistants to help us translate as needed. Kris got two Royal Lao Government (RLG) home economics agents but due to poor security they basically worked in Dong Hene and did not venture out into surrounding villages. The Pathet Lao were stealing rice in our area.

"It was really satisfying to assist villagers to improve their wells by installing cement well rings. We supplied the well ring form, the cement, and the Jeep to haul sand and gravel. The villagers supplied the labor. I think they were surprised to see me help shovel sand and gravel and get down into the well to pump out excess water. I helped finish the dispensary in Dong Hene, pour a new concrete floor in the market, and hauled sand for a concrete floor for a school in Ban Chelamong. I also started an experimental vegetable garden in Jack's yard."

On March 25, 1967, they learned that Fred Cheydleur and his Lao assistant Chantai Onphom had been assassinated by the Pathet Lao. The Lehmans left with their assistants and RLG agents later that day.

PIGS AND DUCKS

"In early May 1967, Kris and I were assigned to work in the Vang Vieng cluster, located in a beautiful valley approximately 120 miles north of Vientiane. My job was to work with the veterinary and agriculture agents assigned to this cluster by the RLG." Lehman and the veterinary agents vaccinated water buffalo against shipping fever and distributed pigs and ducks to selected villagers, who were expected to share some of the offspring with other villagers to perpetuate the program.

Lehman and the Lao agriculture agents gave vegetable seeds, set up rice paddies to demonstrate improved rice varieties and improved rice growing methods. They held a week-long training program for farmers in preparation for a dry season rice program.

"I also had some contact while at Vang Vieng with IVSer *Jack Donnan* who was working country-wide with fish production. He was teaching people to raise fish in their paddies along with the rice. This double cropping provided villagers with some extra protein."

In June 1968, Lehman accepted a position with IVS/RD as the Training Officer. It was his job to arrange and coordinate the orientation and Lao language study of new volunteers. "I extended my contract with IVS for four months before heading for home, with a great sense of relief at being alive, in March 1969."

POLITE AND PATIENT

In retrospect, Lehman writes, "I found the Lao people polite and patient as I stumbled through their language. They were friendly and hospitable as we introduced development projects or asked them to provide overnight accommodations for new IVS recruits." His counterparts, particularly the RLG agricultural agents, were not always as accommodating. "They seemed more interested in bossing villagers around and collecting their pay rather than getting into the paddy with the farmers and me."

He feels that his most notable contribution was that, "I represented a nonmilitary American. I think very few Laotians could grasp the concept that a rich American would volunteer for two years to live out the motto of IVS: 'Development through people-to-people contact.'

"I consider the twenty-eight months I spent with Lao villagers to be one of the highlights of my life. I still appreciate their politeness and the courtesies shown to me. I enjoyed learning their language and practice it when I can. The Lao have an expression *'Bau phen nyoung'* which could mean 'never mind,' or 'it is not important.' They often say this when things do not go as planned. I soon learned that patience was a required virtue to work in Laos."

Lehman also recalls the ingenious excuse voiced by a Lao farmer who did not want to participate in a program to plant rice in the winter time, when the farmers had time off. "It always made me smile. 'Sir,' the farmer said, 'I cannot plant rice in the dry season; my buffalo is tired.'"

Paul E. White, who served from 1965 to 1967, went to Laos with the words of President Kennedy ringing in his ears. "I believed that with U.S. dollars, U.S. technology, and U.S. goodwill, the youth of America could change the world. As I reflect back now, I may have touched a few lives, but more than changing the world, the world certainly changed me."

He joined IVS, studied Lao for a week and soon was on his way. "Floods shut down international travel into Vientiane so our IVS group was sent to Saigon until the water subsided. We finally found our own way to Pakse, to Savannakhet, and finally to Vientiane. There I was told there was no IVS refugee program in northern Laos." Eventually, he found his way to Sam Thong, Xieng Khouang Province, on a trial basis to teach at the Sam Thong Teacher Training School.

THE SECRET WAR

Across the valley, the aircrafts of the "secret war" filled the sky. Sam Thong was a hub for the refugee assistance program in northern Laos. Refugee officers flew in and out, providing rice, cooking oil, salt, tools and shelter to the hill tribes—Hmong, Lao Theung and others.

"Education quality in northern Laos was limited by the primitive condition of school buildings and school furniture, and a complete absence of educational material in the hill tribe schools. My first non-English project was to teach basic mechanical drawing to the village youth who had been recruited to become primary school teachers. They learned to measure, draw simple school furniture designs, and then I provided them with the saws, hammers, nails and plywood to help them learn to make school desks, benches and blackboards.

"The next phase of the project was to teach basic construction skills and produce teachers who, with village self-help, would have the tools, wood and roofing sheets to build more substantial classrooms. These projects were all highly demanded and were very successful."

White helped move the education system from the French-style rote memorization of things to a series of activities that would give teachers a status beyond that of just being educators. Also, recognizing that physical education was not in the curriculum, he introduced the idea of recess via a simple playground rope climb and ball games. "Eventually I taught teachers how to build swings, teeter-totters, and other games. The Hmong children loved this addition to their curriculum.

"A final project was a library stocked with all of the Lao books I could buy, and also with Thai books (written Thai and Lao are similar), and of course with English language picture books. While most could not read the English books, they were popular."

Then White was given the opportunity to move from the school to the airstrip where he could begin to work as a refugee relief and rehabilitation officer.

"That had always been my goal. This came at a time when IVSers in forward areas were being withdrawn for security reasons. I was asked to return to Vientiane. I opted to stay. I was placed on a USAID contract which eventually led to a direct hire position in the Agency."

Stephanie Merritt Stevens was born in San Francisco and spent her early years mostly in California. In September 1964 she married "my best friend, *Lauren Merritt*, an electrical engineering graduate from Caltech. I was in my senior year at Cal Western University near San Diego, majoring in sociology. Lauren and I decided that prior to starting a family, we wanted to do a volunteer project somewhere in the world."

They first applied through their church and were turned down as not suitable for missionary work. "We weren't interested in aggressive proselytizing!" They considered the Peace Corps but decided against that as being too closely associated with the government. "We weren't too happy with the government at that time, during the Vietnam War. Then we learned about IVS and thought, 'This is for us!'"

Their plans met with some disillusionment. In a newsletter printed by IVS to friends and family, they wrote about what they felt were too close ties between IVS and USAID. *"When we signed up with IVS, we had the impression that we would be working for IVS on IVS projects and that there would be several levels of IVS command between us and USAID. It turns out that we will be working very closely with the USAID man in the area and will have to turn to him, rather than to an IVS leader, for material support such as Jeeps, cement, seeds, etc. Exactly how free this will leave us to be ourselves, rather than just U.S. government officials in the eyes of the Lao, we do not know. As we go into Laos we want to be private citizens, or representatives of a group that is basically interested in persons, rather than official representatives of our government. This is one reason why we did not join a government agency, per se."*

They applied to IVS, were accepted and arrived in Vientiane in April 1966. "I was scheduled to begin immediately teaching English as a second language at the National Education Center (NEC) at Dong Dok, nine kilometers outside of Vientiane. Lauren was to continue with his Lao language studies while supervising electrical construction at the NEC and was slated to start teaching at the French Technical High School in Vientiane in the fall."

The assignment did not materialize as planned and he was then assigned as an advisor to the electrical shop at the NEC.

LAO, HMONG AND CHINESE

"My most vivid memories are of teaching Lao students who were very eager to learn English. They were enthusiastic, joyful, and such fun to be around! They taught me so much about the various cultures represented in my classroom. Among them Lao, Hmong, and Chinese!

"I loved teaching! Lauren and I started an English Club for the students. We shared books, magazines, games, music, and even introduced them to field trips to Vientiane. And, prior to our leaving to return home, we helped get a badminton court built near our housing apartments."

At times, Merritt Stevens wondered if her time in Laos was well-spent. "I have to admit I am truly not sure what I accomplished. Since Laos was taken over by the Communists in the mid-70s, and hearing that Lao people were being sent to 'education' camps, tortured, or killed, I feared the worst. What had I done? By teaching English, I may have put my students in harm's way. It was a burden I felt for nearly forty-eight years."

But then, she adds, "Recently, I had the opportunity to go to Portland, Oregon, and by virtue of persistence and luck, I was able to locate one of my students.

"I learned that most of them not only survived the Communist takeover, but are leading very successful lives all over the world. Engineers, restaurant owners who provide Lao refugees a place to work, teachers, and farmers in France, Australia, the United States, and Luang Prabang. I was amazed and overjoyed!"

Her husband, after some discussion, became Electrical Advisor at the Teacher's College where Merrit Stevens was teaching English. She recalls, "This was fine for a while but did not particularly challenge his scientific talents."

They returned home to southern California in October, 1967. "We were amazed that folks really weren't interested in our stories. These were stories of a world that was too foreign to them and too far away."

What could or should have been done better during her IVS years? Merritt Stevens still believes IVS was too close to USAID. Her End-of-Assignment Terminal Report recounted her wish for clearer expectations: *"One of my basic reasons for joining IVS was that it was a 'private, non–profit organization' interested in people-to-people contacts rather than government-to-government contacts. I soon realized that IVS/Laos worked more closely with USAID than I had expected. In fact, if we had realized that our contacts might be so deeply USAID-oriented, we might never have joined IVS."*

"One of the things Lauren and I wrote about in our various required reports was that we felt the top-down approach to managing the volunteers was in many ways counterproductive. If there could have been more collaboration between everyone, we would not have felt so isolated and we quite likely would have helped each other in our various tasks. As an example, during our orientation and language training in Washington, D.C., we met a couple that was assigned to the Rural Development Team in Laos. We became good friends, even to this day, and when some gadget was needed to make something work, Lauren would help. With Lauren's problem-solving skills, they were able to come up with something that worked splendidly."

Russell Marcus grew up in Greenberg, a suburb of New York City and an unincorporated town with no post office, "So we used the address of the town on the other side of the tracks, Scarsdale." He attended Earlham College in Richmond, Indiana, and majored in Sociology, then grad school in Library Science at USC in Los Angeles.

"I was twenty-four when I joined IVS in 1966 as a way of performing my alternative military service, and I served in Laos. Actually I volunteered and was accepted to serve in Vietnam, but when I got to Washington, D.C., for language training I found I was assigned to the Lao class. I was told it was a mistake and to go to the Vietnamese class anyway." That same night he was given the option: Go to Laos where his background in libraries was needed, or go home. He switched to the Lao language class the next day.

LAO DICTIONARY

"I was trained in teaching English as a Second Language and assigned to the Lycée Dong Dok, a high school in Vientiane under Dr. Sampou. I taught English there and helped organize the school's library. I was all fired up about learning Lao and so went to find a dictionary. I was told that USIS Vientiane (United States Information Service) published a Lao dictionary. When I got there, the Cultural Affairs Officer informed me the dictionaries were out-of-print, and that he wanted to update it. I checked back two weeks later to find out how the update was coming and he told me the project was on hold because there was nobody to run it, and besides, qualified Lao people weren't available since they were immediately hired by the U.S. Embassy." Marcus volunteered to take on the project in his spare time, using the students at Dong Dok as language informants.

"And that's how the dictionary project started. As I got to know people in Vientiane, I talked some of them into assisting the project. The most helpful person turned out to be a Japanese linguist named Tatsuo Hoshino who was working with the Japanese equivalent of IVS."

At the end of the first year, Marcus was released from IVS and went to work for the Asia Foundation in Vientiane. "I moved into a small house on a rural street in Vientiane. A Vietnamese man saved the dictionary project one day by locating a hundred pages of typed manuscript that had accidentally blown into a rice paddy." When Marcus finished the dictionary, he thought his work was done, only to find it had entered a new phase—publishing. "That, I had to do in Bangkok. I traveled there by train from Nong Khai every weekend to supervise the work. Eventually I got pretty good at switching between the Lao and

Thai language dialects. The printed books became available in 1968 and I was able to sell the entire printing to USAID."

THIRTY-FIVE EDITIONS

"The *English-Lao:Lao-English Dictionary* was my major achievement in Laos. It was soon picked up by the publisher Charles Tuttle. Over the years, it has gone through more than 35 editions and it is still available as a useful dictionary of the Lao language."

Several years after publication, an incident occurred which brought home the significance of what Marcus had achieved. After the Pathet Lao took over the government in 1975, many Lao became refugees. Marcus was on a plane from Bangkok to Tokyo and happened to sit next to a Lao who had been given asylum in the US. Marcus and he chatted in Lao. "At one point he asked my name and I asked if he had a dictionary. He wouldn't believe that I was the editor of his book, but was amazed when I showed him my passport. I was happy to learn my project in IVS would be contributing to his life in the USA as well as the lives of many others."

Marcus' own life has been totally impacted by the time he spent in Laos. Over the years he has continued to write books as spare time projects, including *Lao Proverbs*. In Japan where he married and now lives, he wrote *The Guide to Japanese Food and Restaurants*.

James Archer went to Laos with IVS in 1966 and was first stationed in Ban Houie Mun in southern Savannakhet Province. After a few months, he was pulled out of the area when the Pathet Lao attacked the village where he was stationed. He spent the rest of his first IVS stint in Hongsa in north Sayaboury Province with *Tom Tufts, Ken Steiner, Chandler Edwards, Mike Flanagan*, and *Jerry Lewis*.

"Our house there was old and on stilts and it had a lean to it from the wind. The floor planks had huge spaces between them. No ceiling; just rafters and an old tin roof. We had the usual water filter and kerosene stove and canvas army cots with wolf fur-trimmed full-body sleeping bags. The sleeping bags were great. It was winter and the wind was terrible and blew up through the floorboards. It was very cold at night and the days weren't much better."

Squat Toilets

The first thing they did was to put in a water seal toilet "We took the bottom out of a forty-five gallon drum, and wired it to another drum with no top, but which still had the bottom. Both barrels were then perforated with a hammer and cold chisel. The barrels were lowered into a hole we had dug and a cement pad with an Asian squat toilet was placed over that. A small shelter was built over the whole thing."

Water was a problem in the dry season so every year the villagers built two rock-and-earth dams. One reservoir was for drinking water and the other was for bathing, livestock, and washing clothes. Archer remembers that, "Before I found this out I went bathing in the wrong reservoir in the evening. I was corrected the next day. Kind of embarrassing.

"We were there to oversee a well drilling program. The first place to get a well was Ban Houie Mun. That made life a lot easier as we could now get our water from a pump."

Choosing the villages that should get the wells was a difficult and stressful exercise. "We had promised ourselves we would be objective. Every village we went to had a similar tale to tell. The women walked kilometers for water in the dry season and the children were sick because they could not bathe enough. It was obvious that they all needed the wells and I would lie awake at night trying to decide where we should build.

"We did make the choices and five wells went in. It was like a gift of life to those poor villagers. They were ecstatic."

Enemy Activity

After Archer and the others had been there a few months, they began to hear rumors of enemy activity in their area. One evening, Chandler Edwards, Archer and Jerry Lewis hosted visitors, so that five foreigners were staying in the IVS house, with two interpreter/assistants in the room below. The Pathet Lao attacked the village and shot up their house.

"About 6 a.m., all hell broke loose. There was firing and explosions everywhere and it seemed you could hear the rounds whistling by. At first, I dropped into the drainage ditch we had beside the house, and then decided I wasn't going to lay there while someone came up and shot me in the back. I got up and ran back and hid behind a pile of firewood under the maid's house. Chandler came out dressed in jeans and nothing else and Jerry was in undershorts and a T-shirt. The two interpreters came out much later. They were fully dressed and had taken time to comb their hair. Talk about cool under fire. While I was hiding under the maid's house, she came out fully dressed and with her little suitcase all packed. Without a word she headed away from all the noise, leaving me cowering behind her woodpile. She later returned as if she had been out on a simple shopping trip.

"Finally it all died down; we got dressed and learned that a band of PL had sneaked into the nearby army camp, killed a soldier, and then taken off in the face of a wild counterattack. The army fired off every shell they had in the camp and were still firing long after the PL had departed. We had to leave until the Area Coordinator gave the all clear to return."

DOGS, PUPPIES, AND A LEOPARD CAT

"Since I had lost all my livestock and some personal possessions the first time I was evacuated from Ban Houie Mun, this time I decided to take my animals with me to Luang Phabang (LP). That included my dogs, Haff and Lady, some puppies, and a leopard cat. The helicopter was not too happy with me, but they let me take them. Jerry Lewis and Chandler went on to Vientiane. After a week or two I was informed that we could return to Hongsa so I loaded up all the animals and returned, alone.

It was one of the most nerve-wracking times of my life. The dogs were totally paranoid and spent all night barking at the slightest noise or movement. This went on for a couple of weeks and then I was told Jerry was coming back in and I could go to Vientiane for some R&R. Jerry called in and asked to be removed from Hongsa for good. When I returned there I was alone for some time before more IVSers were sent."

One day Archer went out as usual to supervise the loading of people into a helicopter that had landed on the airstrip near the IVS house. "I had worked out a system of priority so that sick people could go first and the helicopter crew depended on the IVSers to tell them who should get on." When the helicopter was fully loaded and the pilot had enough passengers, he signalled no more could get on.

"There was an MP (military policeman) trying to put his son on the flight so he could go back to school in LP, but there was no room for the boy who, at his father's urging, was standing right beside the helicopter. I took the boy by the arm and led him to the side so the helicopter could take off safely. The MP went ballistic. He was carrying a gun and threatened to kill me! He finally left with his son, but not after more screaming and threats. I was left with a severe nervous tic on my left eyelid and a desire to do something about this idiot. IVSers willing to work in such difficult places had power. I called Vientiane to complain about him and soon he was removed from Hongsa. My eyelid tic remained with me for several years."

HMONG REFUGEES

Archer also worked with Hmong refugees whose move from the mountains to the relatively lowland area of Hongsa had serious repercussions. "They soon were riddled with malaria and dysentery. I became their medic and every day dispensed pills, gave animated lectures on sanitation to uncomprehending Hmong families, and did triage, deciding who should go to hospitals in Houie Sai, Luang Prabang, Sayaboury, or Vientiane."

He found he had to hand each person their pills for the day

and watch them take at least their morning dose. The Hmong had a tendency to share and to hoard. "If you gave them three days' worth of pills, they might take just one and then share the rest with the family." When doing the triage, Archer remembers, "If I sent someone out to a hospital and they then died there, none of the other Hmong would go to that hospital. Rather than run out of hospitals I had to decide what a person's chances of survival were. Not a fun job..."

The Hmong were animists who would kill a pig or pigs every time someone got sick. Since they were refugees, they had brought only a few pigs with them from the mountain. "Running out of pigs made a big impression on these Hmong. They decided that since they had no more pigs and could not buy any more, they could not practice their religion. One day they asked me for my recommendation. Should they become Catholics or Evangelicals? They had been contacted by people from both religions. I told them I thought they would be better off as Catholics as the Catholic fathers I had met were in it for the long run. They lived with their flocks and formed cooperatives, introduced improved agricultural practices and crops, and even had tractors. The Evangelicals as far as I could see, all they were offering was salvation."

Archer was told by the Hmong that they were soon going to be moved to Sayaboury onto an irrigation project. "I asked them what they would be doing there and they told me they would plant paddy rice. They had never planted paddy rice, so the adjustment was going to be difficult. I proposed that they learn how to plant paddy while they were marking time in Hongsa. They agreed, so I set up a training program for them."

There was land close to a creek that could be used for irrigation. The owner agreed to let the Hmong use it. Archer found a farmer who would show them how to plow the land and supply the plow and other implements. "I paid him both for the use of the land and for the instruction. I bought two white bull buffaloes trained to the plow—white buffalos were not very desirable as the people said they couldn't work as long hours as the blacks. I think the buffalo cost me 40,000 kip each, which would have been about $80. I was using my own money so I asked IVS if they could help. They gave me the amount that a volunteer could get for his or her own project, but USAID and other NGOs all turned me down.

"That was interesting, because we soon got a number of visitors from IVS and USAID to see what we were doing, and we received many compliments on the efforts, but no additional money. Everyone seemed to think it was a great idea, but nobody could help me out."

LEARNING THE ROPES

The Hmong were eager to work on the rice paddies. "They thought it was a great idea and they had a good time learning the ropes of lowland rice culture. There was lots of laughter and joking and all I had to do was talk to the headman and the needed people would show up for work. They set up a labor rotation system so people had time to provide for their families but still took their turns sleeping in the paddy hut at night and weeding the rice when needed."

Soon it was time to weed, watch over the rice, check the fences erected against buffalo and other herbivores, and wait for the harvest. The rice grew well until the elephants decided it looked good enough to eat.

"Down went the fences and in came the elephants," Archer said. "The Hmong could not cope. Neither could I. The elephants were unafraid so the Hmong refused to sleep in the paddy house." About this time the Hmong were sent to their new home in Sayaboury and they hiked off to the south with their buffalo and few possessions. Archer, along with his assistant and some others, harvested the remaining rice and ended up with a forty-five-gallon barrel full of paddy for the livestock.

He remembers that, "Our own health was a problem in the

beginning. I found that I had a case of the runs about every three days. I suffered from roundworm, tapeworm and hookworm at different times. I was in Houie Mun for only a couple of months before I came down with a serious case of dysentery. I was evacuated to Vientiane and spent about two weeks in the hospital on a diet of saltine crackers and tea. I was finally released, but was not allowed to leave Vientiane until I had a negative test. At that point I was down to about 140 pounds, the same as when I was fifteen years old."

Archer returned to Canada in December of 1968, but then went back to Laos in June 1969 and started to work as an Extension Agent at the National Veterinary Service in Vientiane. "The lifestyle was great, but the work situation was very unsatisfactory and I was granted an early termination in 1970."

In 1973, Archer returned to work with IVS in Bangladesh. "That's where I did my most rewarding work. The lifestyle 'sucked,' as they say, but the work was great. I left Bangladesh in 1975, but the start I had given to duck raising in Bangladesh was carried on by IVS." (See Appendix III.)

Loren Finnell and his Ecuadorian wife, Pilar, were with IVS in Laos from 1966 to 1968. In his book *Still a Country Boy, After Embracing the World,* he wrote, "A Brethren friend from North Manchester let me know about a job opportunity with International Voluntary Services. There was a staff opening for an Administrative person in Vientiane, Laos, where they had 120 volunteers on the ground from various countries, albeit the majority was Americans. After looking at the map to see where Laos was, we decided to do it, in spite of the fact that there was a war raging in nearby Vietnam. Until we got there, we did not know that there was a secret war also taking place in Laos.

"IVS had two contracts with USAID, one for a rural development team, which was the larger of the two, and the other for education. Each had their own Chief of Party and separate staffs, and I was hired as part of what was to be an effort to begin unifying the two. The education team had no administration person, but I was replacing a person on the rural development team who had been there for seven or eight years. As Associate Chief of Party, I handled all of the administrative duties for both contracts, and I was the communication link between them.

"After settling in, Pilar began spending a good deal of time as a non-paid volunteer at the orphanage where two IVSers were working.

"Neither of us knew any Lao, and we had only a very limited understanding of French, the second official language. However, over the period of two years, Pilar not only perfected her English by speaking with the IVS staff and volunteers, she also picked up a decent amount of Lao and French. My own work situation only allowed me to say enough in Lao to greet people and say 'Thank you.' This was probably better, as Lao is a tonal language, with wide-ranging meanings for the same word, depending on how it was pronounced, and I have had a hearing problem all of my life. For example, Pilar once asked the cleaning lady to help serve one evening, telling her that we were going to have some pigs over for dinner, instead of friends."

A GLORIFIED HIGH SCHOOL

"Most of the volunteers with the Education Team were working at Dong Dok, a glorified high school referred to as a university. Many of the students were taught in Lao and some in French. The IVS volunteers obviously handled the English. It was a fairly new facility, thanks to USAID, situated some distance outside of Vientiane. A complex of two-story apartment buildings had been built for the faculty, and it was there that we found lodging. USAID also provided a small van that made regular trips back and forth to the USAID compound in Vientiane, but one could get from place to place in the city via *samlos*, a three-wheeled bicycle with space for two passengers behind the bike rider. We also bought a 125cc motorbike, and I had a Jeep at my disposal for work-related activity.

"We soon got to know all the volunteers very well, especially since we were living so close to the Education Team. Since we were staff, they also saw us as persons who could do something about their concerns and problems. Our apartment was a favorite gathering spot.

"My days were split between the two offices in the beginning, but then in the spirit of trying to unify the two teams, I began to encourage the education volunteers to come to the larger office in Vientiane. I had a staff of six to eight Lao employees to assist me. My basic job was to make sure that the volunteers had everything they needed for their work and for their living quarters.

"Given the fact that a 'secret' war was going on in Laos, and that a good number of volunteers were living in rural areas, it was extremely important to know where everyone was at all times," Finnell said. "The ones in Vientiane were fairly easy to track, but those living throughout the country were obligated to call me by radio and let me know the exact hour when they were leaving their post. I had a radio on all the time in the office, and another one in our apartment. Upon arriving in Vientiane, they were required to report to me before doing anything else. If they were overdue by more than sixty to ninety minutes, I was to notify the office responsible for sending out a helicopter search, something I had to do more than once."

T-28 PLANES

The Lao Air Force had a fleet of WWII T-28 planes that bombed the Ho Chi Minh Trail twice a day, and their engines could be heard for a long distance as they took off and returned from their duty. On occasion Finnell could hear the thud of the bombs exploding in the distance as well.

"During my tenure, two of my colleagues on the staff were killed, as were four volunteers and two Lao assistants. All of these losses were hard to take, but the one I remember most of all was related to a volunteer whom I visited near Pakse in the southern part of the country. He was a new volunteer, so I was there to check out his living and work conditions. He took me out to one of the communities, where he was involved, which we reached by driving across the dry rice paddies. He made his visit, and we then sat around drinking lao-lao, a potent local liquor, before we left. On the way out, he told me that it was a Pathet Lao village, in other words, one that was sympathetic to the communist forces. I highly recommended that he not return there, but I guess I didn't get through to him. A short time later, he was shot and killed in that same village.

"In spite of the conflict that surrounded us during our tenure in Laos, we had a tremendous experience," Finnell said. "The Lao people were beautiful and very peaceful. They had a simple life and enjoyed it. While we would consider their general condition to be one of poverty, in reality they had few needs. For the most part they had adequate shelter and sufficient food. Education and health services were however, in short supply.

"The landscape was breathtaking, displaying an abundance of flora and fauna. We had a hanging orchid garden in front of our apartment with more than a hundred varieties, some of which we helped gather in the forest. The small lizards that lived in our home helped us deal with insects and, as long as we kept all the food in the refrigerator, the ants did not invade us. Even the large green geckos were harmless, but one did manage to give Pilar a large scare when it showed up less than a foot away from her face while she was putting on her makeup in the bathroom."

SNAKES

Finnell recounts, "The snakes, both large and small, were to be taken seriously. While tending the orchids one morning, I failed to see a small snake referred to as the 'two step,' for if bitten, you would likely die within that time period. Someone else did see it and yelled out to me in time. I also remember coming back to K9 on my motorbike one night, when I very abruptly came upon a large snake that was crossing the road. I could see neither the head nor the tail, and there was nothing I could do but continue to ride right over it. No one ever believed my story.

"On our own, we visited Chiang Mai in the northern part of Thailand. On another occasion, we took some vacation time in Penang, a lovely island off the coast of Malaysia. I too had a side trip during the second year of our stay, when I was asked to spend a month in the Philippines to accompany four new volunteers receiving training at the International Rice Research Institute.

"For recreation, there was usually a Sunday softball game at the K9 compound, where the majority of the USAID workers lived, and sometimes we challenged the Japanese at their own version of softball. There was also a basketball and a volleyball league. I participated on the IVS teams for both. We regularly beat everyone in basketball, especially the Lao team that was so short in stature, but when it came to volleyball, we were totally outclassed by them."

Erwin (E.J.) Johnson was born and raised on a farm near Charles City, Iowa. As he was completing his studies at Iowa State University in late 1965, he met, "a couple of IVS/Vietnam volunteers in an Agricultural Economics graduate course. They had recently returned to the U.S. from serving with IVS in Vietnam and I had just come back from Venezuela where I participated in a 4-H International Farm Youth Exchange experience."

Johnson's Selective Service Board had scheduled him for the draft. "I was in a limbo as to which branch of military I would join after college graduation. The two former volunteers told me of their work in Vietnam and suggested that I could be of greater service to people in Southeast Asia by using my agricultural education and farm background than by joining the military. It was an easy sale! Within two months I was scheduled to participate in an IVS orientation in Washington, D.C."

In early 1966 at Harpers Ferry, West Virginia, Johnson's group of twenty-plus volunteers completed IVS orientation. "We were to leave the next day from Washington, D.C., to go to Vietnam. That evening, *John Hughes*, IVS Deputy Director, came to my room. He said IVS needed an agriculture teacher to join the IVS/ Laos team and asked if I would consider serving in Laos instead of Vietnam. I had no special agenda or vision other than to work in Southeast Asia, so I said yes."

After teaching agriculture for a few months at a Lao Teachers Training School just outside of Pakse, Johnson transferred to IVS/Laos Rural Development and went to the Bolovens Plateau in southern Laos, a unique area about 3,000 to 5,000 feet in altitude which receives around 160 inches of rain per year. The volcanic lava soils there are rich and fertile and can grow multiple kinds of crops, shrubs, and trees.

Working with Nha Hueng and Loven tribal villagers, he and his team built bridges, roads, schools, and an irrigation dam and canal system. They trained a cadre of local tribal young men as medics to provide basic medical care to the villagers and developed an agricultural training program for fourteen- and fifteen-year-old boys to come live and train at their demonstration farm. They introduced corn and cattle production and American style pigs (boars) to the area. "We even purchased a Massey-Ferguson 165 tractor plus implements to till the rich soils of the flat area."

CREATIVITY

"I reveled, excelled, and grew in this remote assignment. We used resources and ideas from USAID, IVS, NGOs, and the CIA to conduct our projects and work. We had large amounts of creativity and ambition to accomplish the rural development work, but the war held much of our efforts back. The villagers understood hard work due to their slash and burn crop production practices and daily foraging or hunting for food."

The Ho Chi Minh Trail was located off the eastern edge of the plateau and heavily bombed nightly by U.S. forces. Security was a major concern and made the area there even more isolated. "I rarely left the plateau during my tour. No Lao government officials lived in the Houei Kong area, though there were soldiers stationed in Lao army bases along the eastern edge of the plateau. We kept our distance from them. Our safety depended on the local Nha Heung part-time soldiers," Johnson said.

"IVS volunteer *George Viles* arrived to join us my second year and took over the projects and programs when I left in 1968 to work with USAID/Laos up north in the Sayaboury area.

"Three things stand out from my time spent with IVS in Houei Kong. First, I developed a positive sense of self. Second, I learned to like who I was and gained confidence in my talents and abilities even as we were isolated and removed from the language, culture, and environment from the world that I grew up in. It was a tremendous growing experience for me as an individual.

"Third, credit needs to go to the people in Houei Kong who worked and cooperated with us in our projects and activities."

Johnson returned to Laos on two separate trips. "We traveled to the Houei Kong area in 1998 and 2002. On both ventures in the area, we located villagers and co-workers that remembered us from the late 1960s. Those individuals spent months and years in the Communist re-education camps partly because they worked with the Americans. Amazingly, they remembered me and greeted me back into their lives as we shared meals, lao hai wine, laughter, and conversation together. Their acceptance and remembering is a great gift to me!"

Johnson believes the years spent living and working in Laos changed his life. "I survived. I matured. I grew stronger and more able. Does this have significance? Did I make a difference? The Loven and Nha Heung people I met during our trips back to Houei Kong gifted me with a positive response to these questions."

THE RICE EXPERTS

E.J. JOHNSON

Mark Bordsen and I lived in Pakse, Laos, at the IVS House. We both had experienced rice production training at Los Baños in the Philippines in early 1966, and thus became rice production "experts" upon our arrival in Laos.

Realizing that the expert label didn't fit too well, we decided to produce rice ourselves as a hands-on experience. We rented a few rice paddies in an old, unused irrigation system that was within walking distance from the IVS House. We repaired the canals, diverted the water, and flooded our paddies during the dry season to get a second crop. It was meant to be a learning experience for us and a demonstration plot for the local rice farmers to show them that rice could be grown when the rains did not fall. If this all sounds a bit naive and idealistic, it was!

We grew our rice seedlings, tilled the soil with a buffalo-powered plow, spread some fertilizer, transplanted the seedlings, and sat back to let it all grow. This relaxed phase ended abruptly with the invasion of four-legged critters into our lush green oasis. Water buffalo, cattle, goats, all arrived to munch on our beautiful green rice, so we built a fence which slowed them down. Then a winged invasion began. It seemed every bird in southern Laos knew of our bountiful waves of grain and had breakfast, lunch and dinner in our paddies of maturing rice, so we built scarecrows, waved flags on ropes, and stayed near our rice plots to scare the birds away.

Amazingly, we ended up with a crop of rice. Mark and I became rice production experts! When I returned to Laos in the late 1990s, vast fields of rice were being produced in the dry season using irrigation.

Can Mark and I lay any claim to this now common practice of growing dry season rice in the Pakse area? Probably not. But we were among the first to try it. ❧

Mark Bordsen, who served from 1966 to 1968, worked with the Royal Lao Agricultural regional office a few kilometers from the IVS house in Pakse. The office had jurisdiction for six southern Lao provinces. "I had been told I would work in entomology, but it turned out the office had no idea of how an entomologist could help. They didn't even know how to give me work.

"It also became strikingly clear that my inability to communicate in Lao was a huge obstacle. IVS did pay an assistant, Boun Suey, to be my translator, and that helped. But I could never be certain that he was getting the Lao message correctly into English, and vice versa. Due to my previous experience as an IFYE (International Farm Youth Exchange) delegate to Poland in 1964 for six months, where I had learned Polish in-country, I had the tools to trade Lao for English lessons with Lao acquaintances, the Lao Ag staff and with Boun Suey."

E.J. Johnson was teaching agriculture at the local teacher's college just west of the house. "He and I decided that to make a difference, we needed to know about what was most important to the Lao people, and it was obvious that much centered on rice. So we set out to learn. Our success led to a greater acceptance for me at the Lao Ag office, and then the Ag Chief asked for my help in extension and research. In the last six months of my tour, he even asked me to instruct his agents in how to safely use insecticides and teach basic insect pest control methods."

RICE CULTIVATION

Bordsen believes that, "the most important step occurred when E.J. and I decided to learn more about rice cultivation. The question was, how could we achieve this? It so happened that a diversion dam and a main irrigation ditch with some short feeder stubs had previously been constructed and never used. One of the areas potentially served was just north of our house. At the same time, a flood around Vientiane had wiped out rice fields, so Taiwan donated a variety of rice seed. As the flood waters receded, the Taiwan rice seed enabled the flood-affected farmers to plant fields in the hope of getting some kind of harvest."

The USAID Agricultural Attaché in Pakse sent over two kilograms of rice seed so Johnson and Bordsen could conduct their rice-growing education during the dry season, with the help of diverted water running down the nearby irrigation canal.

"E.J., Boun Suey and I persuaded a local farmer whose paddies were closest to the canal to rent us four paddies for our trial.

At that time, the concept of 'rented land' was unknown to him, so he 'sold' us the land for that period of time at the price he would have received had he really sold that property! The cost was low for us, and it included the farmer's service of plowing and harrowing the paddies once the irrigation water had flooded them. He also prepared a small traditional seedbed as a backup for our use of a Philippine growing method, where seeds were covered by a layer of banana leaves and were flooded that way. That seedbed worked fine and produced a lot of short seedlings.

"We planted a control paddy with no fertilizer, the one closest to the water supply, and then three paddies with different rates of fertilization. Except for the help I mentioned, E.J., Boun Suey and I did all the rest: fertilization before and after harrowing, weeding, and then we took shifts during daylight hours to fend off livestock that were attracted to something green in the dry season. When the seeds started to fill, we had to rig and man lines of string and pebbles in tin cans to scare away the birds."

The Head of Extension wanted Bordsen to assist with demonstration projects, using an improved variety of rice that would respond well to artificial fertilizer, so the group planted a number of paddies during the rainy season in the fields of different farmers in the province. These successfully demonstrated much better yield, but this improved rice grew shorter than local varieties, and it was not the sticky rice that Lao people ate. It did, however, add another variety that a farmer could plant in addition to his other choices, and then could sell for much needed cash.

At the time he volunteered, Bordsen had in mind that IVS might be a stepping stone to a career in Foreign Service.

"But after I had been in Laos awhile, I began to see that the very negative Ugly American was still overly prevalent in American foreign aid. Of all the AID employees I met at that time, only one person was adequately proficient in speaking and understanding the Lao language! And most of them had attitudes of superiority over Lao people, which I found disappointing."

TED AND SOU OLBRICH, IVS LAOS, 1967-1971

Soumountha was a "poor little rich girl," widowed at nineteen from a forty-three-year-old army colonel, and left with an infant son. Her husband had only been dead a few days, when she was forced to go to work.

Sou's father had been killed and family gossip had it that it had been by his brother, who in the mid-1960s was Police General of Laos. Sou's uncle never wanted much to do with her and put her in a Catholic boarding school when she was four.

Sou was well-cared for financially but cut off from family. She did well in school and wanted to become a doctor. There were no medical schools in Laos in 1966, so she accepted an offer for a full scholarship to study medicine in the Soviet Union.

This was a huge embarrassment to her uncle, a flag-waving member of the rightwing political faction who hated communists. He had spies watching and when Sou went to market one day, they swept in with a helicopter and snatched her away.

Her uncle landed Sou at one of his many mansions. She was seated at a round table across from an army colonel more than twice her age and was told. "You two are getting married!" Sou glared at the colonel and said, "I hate you!" He muttered in response, "I hate you back!"

They were given a large cement home with servants, and one morning after their son Sinphanya (Tony) was born, Sou found her husband in bed with her cousin. She kicked them both out of the house.

A few days later, she returned from market to find her maid crying. "Your husband was here and took your son!" Sou grabbed his service 45 cal. pistol out of the closet and caught him ascending the ramp to the plane to Luang Prabang. She chambered a round and put the muzzle against his forehead, "Give him back or I'll blow your brains out!"

Sou retrieved Tony. Her husband took off for Luang Prabang and was killed two days later by friendly fire. Sou suddenly found herself cut off from both sides of the family. Her side was convinced she was a "No good Commie!" and the husband's side was angry because she would not relinquish the baby.

She moved into a one-room storefront, got a job with the U.S. Embassy at the IVS office doing translation from French to Lao for $16 per month, and another night job with a French newspaper for $30 per month writing stories at night. Her mother came in from the country to care for Tony.

On August 3, 1968, *Ted Olbrich* walked into her office, reporting as a new Agricultural Volunteer. Ted was an Illinois farm boy with a fresh degree in Agronomy from Iowa State University. He had not fared well in the draft lottery, and as the president of the Iowa State Chapter of Intervarsity Christian Fellowship, didn't relish the idea of killing Vietnamese. He settled on applying for a 1-A-O draft status, which in the spring of 1968, virtually guaranteed he'd be a Marine Corp Medic. Just a few weeks before graduation, he was walking the halls of the Agronomy Building when he noticed a hand written notice on the bulletin board; "Interviewing today for Agronomist to Work in War Zone, Offers Draft Exemption."

Within two months of graduation Ted was in Laos. The first day on the job he walked into the IVS office, and as he says, "I laid eyes on the most beautiful woman I had ever seen!" Soumountha was sitting at the back desk, working as a secretary for the IVS administrator.

After language training in Vang Vieng, he was turned loose in Borikhan Province 110 kilometers east of Vientiane. Paksane, the capital of the province, was Soumountha's hometown.

"At that time there were probably fewer than fifty of us working in the Forward Areas Program," Ted recalled. He worked the east part of the province, and *Dennis Mummert* worked the west.

Things did not go well in Borikhan. In January of 1969 a French priest was ambushed and killed in Paksane, and a month later, several of the bridges between Paksane and Vientiane were blown up.

In March, the military set up checkpoints throughout town with new passwords issued daily, to enable movement in town at night. After a specific death threat against Ted was left at the USAID gate, he transferred to the National Ag Experiment Station near Vientiane and handled his work in Paksane through irregular air visits. The worst thing you could do in Laos at that period was be predictable.

Ted caught the eye of Dr. Jamie Bell, USAID Agriculture in Laos, who felt strongly that Laos needed trained agriculturists. He asked Ted to take two Lao Agriculture Agents to a six-month, post-graduate level training program at the International Rice Research Institute in the Philippines. All Ted had to do was "re-up" for another two years.

Since Ted stayed at the IVS Guest House during this stint, he became the unofficial tour guide for all the visiting IVSers. He knew virtually every bar, and most of the girls on the strip.

He grew so tired of going out every night that he told Dennis Mummert that he wanted to meet a nice girl and just get married. Mummert started laughing. Ted was not amused. "Damn it, Mummert! I'm serious! "

Dennis stopped laughing long enough to gasp for air and explained, "You know your problem, Olbrich? You don't know any nice girls!"

Providence was at work. Since Ted was now based in the capital city, he could swing by the office and check for mail several times a week. One day he went into the office and there was no mail; it had been about a month since he'd received anything so he took his motorcycle helmet and threw it to the floor in disgust, and uttered few choice adjectives. All the secretaries in the office were laughing at him, especially the one in the back, Soumountha.

The next time Ted returned to the office, there were two boxes waiting for him. He opened the large one first. Sou had found a box with authentic looking postage and then applying a label with Ted's address. She then filled it with the contents of all the trash cans in the office: Spent scotch tape dispensers, a broken stapler, an old pair of worn out flip-flops... Ted laughed so hard he forgot about the second box he'd put in his backpack. What really got his attention was that the beautiful Soumountha had actually taken the time to do this.

Ted opened the second box after he returned to his room. In it was an Easter card from his mother, a new shirt, and a small plastic chicken that laid a jellybean egg when you pushed down on it. Ted didn't like jellybeans.

The next day was Easter Sunday. He'd just left the commissary after having breakfast when a Jeep pulled up. It was *Al Best*, the new IVS Administrator. "Where you going? I've got to get these French documents translated right away, so I'm taking them to Soumountha's house," said Al. "Want to come along?" Ted would have killed to find out where Sou lived. "You bet!"

Sou's house was a simple, unpainted, tin roofed, one room, store-front apartment with wood panel folding doors across the front. There was a lean-to on the back for cooking and bathing, as well as a "small room" with a water-seal toilet.

Sou seemed happy to see Ted, and offered her guests tea. Al couldn't stay long; they gulped the tea and excused themselves. Ted couldn't help notice the toddler called "To-To" and surmised it was her son. He also noticed an elderly woman Sou called Mother but he did not see a husband. On his way back to the commissary he made careful note of the turns and the land-marks on the winding streets and, as casually as he could, asked, "What happened to her husband?" Al never glanced up from his focus on the road and grunted, "He was killed in the war."

Ted walked into his room at the IVS Guest House. He saw

the plastic chicken. An idea popped into his head. "I'll go back to Sou's and give it to Tony!"

That's all it took. They were together almost every evening, and every free day until Ted left for the Philippines. He departed on May 30, 1969, with the promise that if they still felt the same when he returned, they would marry.

A couple of significant things took place while Ted was gone. He walked into the classroom at 7 a.m., August 9, 1969, and was handed a single side-band message. It read: "Mummert and Stillman killed in enemy action in Borikan. More later"

"It was like I got hit by a bat. The thing that really shocked me was my own reaction. I didn't cry, fall down, cuss, or say a word."

A few days later came an offer from IVS. His program has been cancelled as too risky and he was given the option to complete the study program in The Philippines and return to the U.S., or come back to Laos for re-assignment. "If I'd quit I'd go back into the draft, and I was so in love with Sou, I was determined to go back to Laos no matter what the risk.

"I wrote Sou a letter. I asked her, 'If I become a missionary will you still marry me?' She wrote back 'Yes.'

Sometime in mid-1970, President Nixon signed an order specifying that the U.S. would not draft married men with children. "I made sure my adoption of Tony was legal, and then I quit." By early 1971, Ted and Sou were in the U.S., and Ted took a job as a sales manager for a farm supply company.

They became involved with a Methodist Church with a 'Contemporary Service' run by an airline pilot. It grew; the church split, Ted and Sou went with the Charismatics. A few years later the pastor died, the next pastor fell into a moral mess and the elders voted Ted and Sou pastors in August of 1986. In 1998 they accepted a call to be missionaries to Cambodia.

Now after 15 years in Cambodia they lead one of the fastest growing church movements in the world with 6,000 congregations and 106 church/orphan homes. They have helped raise at least 11,000 orphans. You can learn more on their website: *www.fcopi.org* ✧

TRAGEDY

Lew Sitzer was also in Laos in 1966 and 1967. His experience there ended tragically. "I was placed in a remote area, the village of Muong Phalane, very close to the demilitarized zone and within sight of the Ho Chi Minh Trail. Flares lit the night sky most evenings. A young Thai associate helped with language and work."

Their job was to build schools, medical dispensaries, dig wells and educate the locals about hygiene and malaria. "After meeting with various village chiefs, projects were started, local workers enlisted, and supplies from USAID were trucked in, mostly, cement, tin and nails. Everything else was hand fashioned."

He also began to work with the refugees driven out of the mountains by the war and in need of food and housing. "They camped near me and we created enclosed gardens and cement privies, a first in the village. The refugees generally were not welcome in the local schools, so the children came to my hut and we schooled them during the heat of the day. They taught me how to speak and I taught them how to write. We got close."

Though Sitzer survived the war, his village didn't. "It was totally leveled. I took photos and wrote up a story. The U.S. Embassy intercepted my mail and I was called up to Vientiane to meet with the U.S. Ambassador. He had my letter and photos in hand and gave me the choice of leaving Laos or returning to Muong Phalane and to help rebuild the village.

"I chose to stay and help as my country had caused this tragedy. The U.S. Air Force sent a colonel, some personnel and money. Laotian villagers were paid to dig out and expose the delayed action bombs that had not yet exploded. During that time, we all lived in the forest for two weeks, while bombs were exploded by experts. In the forest, I tried to explain how mistakes are made in wartime but I could not rid myself of responsibility for something caused by my country in a war that made no sense to the villagers or me."

After a few months of rebuilding, Sitzer's closest friend, Fred Cheydler, with whom he had trained, was assassinated nearby. Sitzer himself had been warned not to sleep in his hut and had chosen to listen to the counsel of the village. His friend Cheydler did not. The Pathet Lao came through and machine-gunned under his raised hut and killed him.

"This was the last straw," said Sitzer. "I asked for leave of a few weeks, traveled to Cambodia and made the decision not to return to my duty or contract with IVS/USAID. I began to realize the insanity of war and how great the powers we had, even back in the 60s, to destroy indiscriminately."

Alex McIntosh served in Laos from March, 1967, to February 1970. Because of the Vietnam War, he had developed an interest in Asia. In school he attended classes on the history, politics, and cultures of both East and Southeast Asia. "My goal was to graduate and not get drafted, but I felt guilty about not serving my country so I looked around for an alternative. My draft board was famous for allowing young men to avoid the draft for a couple of years while they lived it up in the Peace Corps so I began applying, with the new goal of working somewhere in Southeast Asia."

THE IMPORTANCE OF CELIBACY

He was offered Nepal, but turned it down. Next were the Philippines to teach English, but, "I found this unchallenging and also wanted a country in Southeast Asia whose predominant religion was something other than Christianity. In the meantime I had stumbled onto information about IVS and applied. In March 1967, after an interview and a lecture on the importance of celibacy, I was accepted to go to Vietnam with IVS."

Two weeks before the Washington, D.C., orientation, McIntosh received a telegram informing him that too many volunteers were being sent to Vietnam that month. "I was given two choices—wait or go to Laos immediately. By this time I had passed my physical and the draft board informed me that unless I had signed with a voluntary organization before I was sent an induction letter, I would be inducted into the army. So I chose Laos."

Laos turned out to be an excellent choice. "I found a calling in life; I wanted to be good at something for the very first time."

McIntosh's IVS assignment was in construction, persuading villagers that they needed wells, schools, and markets. "I was not particularly good at getting them to see the advantages of these things, and I spent much of my time in the Muang Fuang area helping fellow IVSer *Cort Van Riper* with rice demonstrations.

"We had developed trust; unfortunately the war arrived. I was reassigned to Muang Pieng, to take over the evaluation of a leadership training program. Before Cort and I were evacuated we had played a small part in an irrigation project—a true self-help project. We were relegated to the role of paymasters, making sure the Thai irrigation engineers and their trainees were paid and that the materials destined for the project arrived at the work site undeterred. I am proud to say the dam and canals are still operating. Locals report the village that got this project got 'rich' and inhabitants from nearby villages, who wouldn't give us the time of day, wanted us to come back and do the same for them!"

McIntosh met a young Lao woman with whom he fell in love. "We got married in a traditional Lao wedding ceremony (so much for my celibacy pledge), a memory I will cherish forever." IVSers convinced him he should go to graduate school and influenced his decision to study sociology.

GREATEST IMPACT

"I claim without exaggeration that of all my experiences, the time I spent in Laos has had the greatest impact on my life. I became who I am because of it. Laos did so much for me and I did so little in return that I feel a certain amount of guilt."

Gary Alex's IVS experience in Laos started in 1968. "I was interviewed on campus and accepted for assignment to Vietnam, but then the Tet Offensive happened, and IVS decided to reduce placements in Vietnam. I received a call asking if I would take an assignment in Laos and remember answering something like, 'Yes. Where is it?'" Alex attended orientation in August, 1968, flew back to Cornell to defend his thesis, and then went for three weeks to Los Banos, Philippines, to receive training in tropical agriculture. Then it was off to Laos.

Alex had originally expressed interest in working with farmer training, thinking of extension work and the type of training classes and seminars that had been so effective in changing agriculture in his native Illinois. "I was assigned initially to teach agriculture at the Dong Dok Teacher Training School near Vientiane. On arrival in Vientiane, as I filed off the plane, someone from IVS/Laos staff shook my hand and said 'we're sending you down to Pakse next week to teach CD'. I had no idea what CD was—civil defense? Child development?"

CD was community development. "I did my best to figure out and teach community development. I had some materials from previous volunteers, but this was pretty thin. We built water seal toilets and fences, planted vegetable gardens, made compost. We also did a few other practical arts type activities and class sessions on social change, community mobilization and organization, and whatever else I could pull together. I taught through Somnhot Phomchom, an interpreter, and though this was a bit unwieldy, it actually worked better than I expected, mostly due to Somnhot's teaching and storytelling ability. We taught the same materials to several different classes with the teaching and translation going noticeably smoother by the second and third session."

FOUR YEARS IN LAOS

Alex would stay in Laos seven years, four with IVS. "At the end of my second year, I was enjoying the work and found it rewarding. I extended for a third year and then for the same reasons extended again for a fourth year. Then I decided it was enough."

In his third and fourth years, he developed lesson plans and teaching materials, taught practical courses directly, and coordinated teaching by the interpreter Somnhot and a new Lao agricultural teacher assigned to the school. "Of my three summer breaks, one year I worked with another IVS volunteer on agricultural projects in Ban Houei Kong on the Bolovens Plateau; one year I managed a paid internship program for students to work in villages and on development projects; and the third year I went on home leave." Over the four years, he also taught English in the evenings at the Lao-American Association in Pakse.

Johnny and *Linda Fink* served in Laos in 1967 and 1968. He was a forester for the U.S. Forest Service in Cokeville, Wyoming; she was a senior in Wildlife Ecology at Utah State University. "We were recently married," she remembers. "We had applied separately to IVS before Johnny was drafted as a conscientious objector. His brothers and an uncle had all been CO's. We both wanted to do something positive, rather than just protest the Vietnam War.

"We were under the auspices of USAID in Laos. Our village was Song Hong, north of Thakhet. We worked with ten recently established villages of displaced Lao having been moved down from the hills around the Ho Chi Minh trail. Johnny was supposed to help villagers build water seal toilets, which were ridiculous considering the ground water level was too high during the rainy season. Instead, he helped erect a community building and our house. We were supposed to build at the edge of the platted village so the villagers would move out to fill in between us and the town center, where they had built temporary homes. After we lived there a time with no ill effects, the villagers decided we had cleared out the bad spirits and did build new homes between the town center and our house."

EVIL SPIRITS

The Finks also convinced the villagers that the river water had evil spirits that must be boiled out lest they cause sickness. This helped stop the illnesses caused by polluted water.

Linda Fink recalls, "I was supposed to take over a handicraft project started by an earlier volunteer. That turned out to be very good and rewarding. My counterpart was a young village woman, Somphone. We traveled to nearby villages, collecting and buying handicrafts that I then sent to Vientiane to be sold. It was one of the few ways the villagers had of making money. They had been highland slash-and-burn rice farmers, and were now starting over as paddy rice farmers. Most rewarding to me is that the handicraft project, which was not just in my area, continued to some extent after IVS left Laos and is still continuing to this day, administered by Lao."

After about a year in Song Hong, Johnny Fink injured his back while working on the community building and was flown to the Philippines for surgery. Remembers Linda Fink, "Since he could no longer ride in bumpy jeeps, Johnny was terminated from IVS. After several months in Laos alone, I was given a compassionate termination to go back to the States with him."

Their return to the U.S. was a great culture shock. "There was so much abundance and so much waste," she recalls. "That's why we decided to live as simply as possible, raise our own food, and try by example to influence others. Johnny went back to work in forestry, for the Bureau of Land Management but later quit to become a handyman and roofer. I finished college and became a humor writer and dairy goat breeder. We raised two sons and now have three grandchildren. We still live on the land, raise all our own meat, vegetables and most of the fruit, and participate in the growing 'slow food' movement and community building of this century. IVS changed our lives completely. We learned we could live well on little. In Laos, like the villagers, we had no electricity or running water and managed just fine. We feel wealthy now that we have both those amenities in this country."

Now, many years later, Linda Fink concludes that, "As everyone knows by now, we should not have gone in to do USAID's bidding, but rather that of the people in the countries where we served. They knew what they needed in most cases. At the time, we did not realize that our 'peace efforts' were being used in the U.S. war effort."

SIGNS OF HOPE

Thomas Tufts did not arrive in Laos until 1968 and was already a veteran of the Peace Corps in Nigeria. His original plan was to become an IVSer in Vietnam. "When I read about IVS work in Vietnam I thought it a great opportunity to make a difference in a place that desperately needed signs of hope for the future! I remember reading some advice by Soren Kierkegaard, 'Compete by doing good.' I believed deeply that having a moral advantage was critical to resolving the issues of the war into a peaceful outcome, helping others and deepening our view of the world. My motives then were a combination of humanism informed by my mainline Christian perspective, and patriotism informed by skepticism about the redemptive value of violence."

During his training, Tufts learned there was a dire need for volunteers in Laos. "I was told it was very different from Vietnam and the work less politicized. In my mind those words translated into, 'It'll be easier to focus on agriculture and rural development without having to surmount as many bureaucratic obstacles.'"

After classes at the University of the Philippines School of Agriculture and hands-on training at the International Rice Research Institute, his IVS group set off for language courses in Laos. "I had to stay in Vientiane longer than most of the volunteers after training to await an assignment, as several tentative posts were overrun by hostile forces or deemed unsafe. I finally went to a beautiful mountain valley in Sayaboury Province called Hong Sa that was accessible by air. It contained six villages and was watered by springs and a river.

"The military and government complex of the valley, which included the IVS quarters, had come under attack a few days before. No IVSers were injured but they had spent the night in nearby drainage ditches. All except a Canadian volunteer and a Lao staff person requested new assignments."

His time in Laos involved working with new rice strains. He helped build schools and markets, and remembers that, "For almost two great years security was good, leadership was responsible, and everyone was busy. Then one day we were told we had to leave and that a plane would come for us in the evening. Chinese Communist road construction crews had reached the Mekong River from the north. It was only a matter of time before Communist troops and weapons could reach Hong Sa and seriously challenge the Royal Lao Army contingent ensconced in a wooden fort reminiscent of the American West."

That battle was fought to a stalemate. Hong Sa did not surrender to the Communists until several years later.

STRESSFUL CONDITIONS

Larry Harms, part of a team of IVS Directors and staff tasked with evaluating the programs in Vietnam and Laos, remembers that, "the IVS volunteers were clearly operating under stressful conditions, some worse than for others. Some expressed their views calmly and others through confrontation and aggression. We heard them, questioned, and talked. Our views were taking shape, even though we were not discussing them as a team. Then an unfolding event gave me a solid, accurate view of conditions."

Harms and his team were in the highlands of Laos. Volunteers had traveled in to meet with them, and the lawn of the small hotel where they were staying was the conference room.

"Our discussions were going well. Suddenly, every volunteer jumped up and ran in different directions to get under the nearest trees. We then heard and saw an airplane. Frankly, I was confused. The volunteers came back with apologies about what had happened. It became clear their rush to the trees was for urgent, safety purposes. It was also clear to me that each had experienced something like this more than once. It shaped my recommendation as a team member. All team members reached the same position that IVS needed to lay the groundwork for termination of the programs. It was correct, and the impact on IVS as an organization was severe."

HUGS AND ORDNANCES

JANE STONE

I have procrastinated attempting to reflect on my two years in Laos (1969-1971) with IVS. One of the main reasons for this is I truly don't feel I contributed much. Since returning there recently for the first time, I was made aware of the impact on Laos from the Vietnam War, namely the leftover unexploded ordnance (UXO). My shift in perspective is the hope that my presence there at least did not do more harm than good.

Much of the time I spent being homesick and dealing with culture shock. Working alongside the six Laos home economics agents in the Pakse area, I was able to join them in conducting training of cooking and clothing in villages around Pakse. The structure of these sessions had been developed at the national level and supervised by home economists in Vientiane. I learned, from them, how to make baby food from buffalo brains, design a pattern for a blouse from scratch and navigate around the area in either my USAID-loaned Jeep, or flying to more remote areas such as Khong Island via CIA planes.

One of the home agents, Liem, died after giving birth at the local hospital while we were there. Another, Sa, lived close to us; Sa and I daily rode together from the agriculture office to her home. Many days we both would be in tears, Sa missing her husband who was in Vientiane studying to be a physician, and me, dealing with the homesickness, heat and habitat, battling swarming cockroaches in the kitchen, leaning out of the mosquito net during the night to throw shoes at the ceiling to scatter the mice or rats, eating soups with large ants as a source of protein. I will always treasure the hugs between Sa and I as we bid each other goodbye until the next day. The senior home agent was a very capable young woman named Khamchun who passed away from cancer. An IVS volunteer from Pakse said Khamchun had asked about me.

These memories tug at my heart. I hope to use them to support the continued, even escalated, work of ridding Laos of the UXOs, a responsibility of our United States government, hopefully in my lifetime. ⚬⚬

Steve Stone belonged to the Church of the Brethren, an historic peace church, which taught that all war was sin. He applied for conscientious objector status when he was in high school, then, seeking adventure, became an IVS volunteer in 1969.

"I was a teacher at the Pakse Vocational Training Center. The Center offered training in vegetables, fruits, rice, peanuts, soy beans, poultry, swine and fish. Farmers with a sixth-grade education came for six months' training and returned to their village backed with an agricultural loan. I wrote an entrance exam for the center. I taught Farm Management and Farm Economics. I taught English. I taught math so farmers could figure fertilizer rates and insecticide rates, and I helped build a library."

THREE CROPS

Stone worked with the head of the irrigation department out of the office of agriculture of southern Laos. The office supported agriculture agents on their village visits and field visitation days at the Center. "We helped prepare bulletin boards for the agricultural office. We visited dams being built and rice demonstration plots. I worked with irrigation associations. The irrigation canals had to be free of debris from the Mekong River to the rice paddy so farmers could grow three crops of rice a year instead of one. We were not highly successful in persuading farmers to work on the canals; the head of the agriculture office shut off the canal water until the farmers got out and worked on the canal."

Stone was not reticent to show his Brethren roots. "It was somewhat possible to maintain a peace witness. We could make observations and expound a peace philosophy through monthly newsletters. We were threatened with having our visas revoked when we proposed a peace demonstration at the American and Russian embassies at the same time. We printed a letter in the Boston Globe. We wore armbands as a sign of protest in the American community. The Laotian People referred to us as peace people."

The rural community development work he did had an impact on three villages, Ban Ke, Ban Cang, and Ban Aheck. Through publications, Filipino understanding of Asian agriculture, the research of the International Rice Research Institute, and the use of modern agricultural techniques, "We were able to improve the farming techniques of farmers surrounding Pakse. These accomplishments were recognized at graduation ceremonies." Farmers and fellow instructors showed their gratitude through cooperation and on a trip to Bangkok with a Laotian teacher and the Filipino director of the school.

"There were three primary impacts on my life work. I was exposed to hundreds of people who were Buddhist and saw scores of Buddhist temples in Laos, Vietnam and Thailand. I am committed to a god who transcends Christianity. I am a firm believer in religious freedom and am dedicated to the protection of religious minorities."

Stone translated his rural community development experience, "To a theology of agricultural missions. Churches should be committed to agriculture ministries, health ministries, digging for clean drinking water and education. Pakse vocational training center is an excellent model for enriching agriculture. Models of agricultural training and production can either be secular or mission oriented."

ORGANIZATIONAL PRINCIPLES

Back home in Indiana, "My respect for community development found a place in urban housing. I helped manage 200 family and a hundred elderly apartments in a community of 40,000. I opened a five-story senior apartment building. I was a liaison between a community of 80,000 and a consortium of ten cities. I marketed independent living units for a senior citizen complex. I wrote a low-income housing proposal to remodel older homes. The same organizational principles that apply to maintenance of irrigation canals can be applied to helping people house themselves and govern their neighborhoods. The community organizer can be a change agent enabling low-income people to create culture and find productive employment. Common effort to meet basic human needs demands cooperative action and sound principles of community development."

Deeply affected by his Buddhist surroundings was *Lawrence Olsen*, the third son in a family with five boys and one girl, who grew up on a small diversified family farm west of Pasco, Washington.

Family, farm life, farm work, school, 4-H, and church provided the structural pillars of his formative years. "We each contributed to farm and family life according to our abilities and received food, shelter, clothing, medicine, instruction, punishment, and moral support according to our needs. We never questioned parental authority, or the parental right to tell us what to do. Our parents always worked three times longer and harder for the family than any of us.

"My goals in life were simple: go to college, travel, buy some property for a nest, and raise a family. As a high school senior with those broad life goals, and since I enjoyed both school and farm, I decided to major in Agricultural Education. I enrolled in my parents' alma-mater, Washington State University, with that intention, but the threat of being drafted was very real, so I joined the U.S. Marine Corps Platoon Leader Class (PLC)."

The PLC granted Olsen leave to travel abroad and he was accepted for volunteer positions with both IVS and the Peace

Corps. "I chose IVS in Laos over a Peace Corps assignment in Kenya because IVS was smaller and less bureaucratic and because I wanted to know more about both Buddhism and the Vietnam War."

Following a six-week orientation and Lao language course in Washington, D.C., with additional orientation in Vientiane, Olsen joined forces with other IVSers to develop a community garden and other on-going agriculture and construction projects. In November, 1965, he received an honorable discharge from the U.S. Marine Corps.

From January, 1966, to September, 1967, he was Chief Field Agricultural Advisor in Khong Sedone. He worked with Lao government agriculture and veterinary extension agents, USAID Community Development Advisors, other IVS volunteers, and IVS and USAID Lao national employees on agriculture, construction and home economics projects. He also spent a vacation as a Buddhist monk in Wat Triphum in Khong Sedone. In February, 1966, he was ordered to report for a pre-induction draft physical. He failed the physical due to a minor case of hepatitis, then passed it a month later and applied for and received 1-A-O draft status. But the Selective Service System wanted him. In late 1967, Olsen received a draft notice along with a reversion to 1-A status. In March, 1968, he returned to the U.S. and then went back to Laos as a delinquent draftee.

He had become Team Leader of the Rural Development Team in Khong Sedone. "I coordinated the work of up to sixteen Lao nationals building toilets, wells, schools and dispensaries; hog distribution and husbandry; vegetable seed distribution and organizing community and kitchen gardens. We encouraged double cropping of rice; fish farming; home economics to include weaving, nutrition, child care and sanitation."

From March 1968 to September 1970, he occasionally executed projects for IVS, "With a Lao salary of $16 a month under my Lao name, Thit Li, which I had earned by being a monk. We developed a handbook of Lao customs and culture and did orientation for new volunteers. I also taught English, built furniture, refurbished and managed an apartment complex, assisted with a commercial rice farm development venture and researched and developed an *Economic Survey of Laos* for the Japanese government.

"Several rural development IVSers were killed in those years. I went back to the U.S. in late 1970, following the drowning death of my sister and pursued a Master's in Education degree at Rutgers University." In 1971, the U.S. Military Draft order was rescinded.

CONTRACT VOIDED

He returned to Laos in October 1973 as Program Officer in Vientiane, and then helped close the IVS office when the Lao government collapsed and the IVS-USAID contract was voided. By October, 1975, he was the last IVS staffer in Laos. He crossed the Mekhong River to Thailand when his visa expired later that month.

"Early on," Olsen now says, "I came to realize that the cross-cultural volunteer experience had much more to offer me than I could possibly offer the people I had volunteered to help. That realization afforded me a phenomenal level of acceptance and integration into the lives and culture of my colleagues and my families. My Lao assistant and I hit it off like brothers at first meeting. I became a fixture and a curiosity, a man with a beard, riding a bicycle, and carrying a violin. I learned to listen. I learned better ways of interacting with others, and I gained a measure of humility.

"Much of the richness of IVS came from the level of respon-sibility we were given along with the freedom to try, to fail, and try again. I like solving problems and inventing things. I made a soil steamer out of an empty oil drum. I made a foot-powered washing machine. I made kerosene can ovens and baked bread and cakes. All involved trial and error and imperfections. None were widely adopted by the Lao."

THREE YEARS, THREE COUNTRIES

RON PULCINI*

CAMBODIA

The waiting and uncertainty was dulling our enthusiasm. This was back when the word "mercurial" got lodged in my vocabulary, from *Time* magazine's description of Cambodia's Chief of State, Prince Norodom Sihanouk. But, geeze, who could blame him for being so damned capricious? Early in November, Vietnamese leader Ngo Dinh Diem and his brother were dispatched in a so-called "revolution". Not long after, JFK was assassinated, then in early December Marshall Sarit, dictator of Thailand, passed away. More rumors were being milled throughout the area than rice. Sihanouk reportedly stayed in safe houses all over the country. The pitch of his squeaky voice ramped up over the radio every day, reminiscent of a man overboard yelling, "Help, help, SHARKS!" By December the dozen or so volunteers had been ordered back from their towns and villages, turning the IVS House on Trasak Paem Street into an uncommon youth hostel. For entertainment there were the government-orchestrated demonstrations of a few hundred people sauntering down the middle of some street protesting America's presence, especially that of the CIA. "*Teu Petaya!*" (Go Home!) resounded around the domed morning market.

Just before Christmas, IVS/Cambodia went into diaspora. After studying Khmer and teaching English as a Second Language methods for three months, we were outta there. Most of the ESL team went to Laos, a few to Vietnam. Maybe ten or more people elected to return to the states.

VIETNAM

The IVS House at Tan Son Nhut was colonial cool. Large porches surrounded the main buildings nested in an eccentric array of flame trees on a large parcel of land; an experi-

*Pulcini served in Cambodia (1963), Vietnam (1964-65) and Laos (1965-70).

mental garden lay behind the outbuildings and most of the vehicles had "Co Quan Chi Ngyuen Quoc Te" (International Voluntary Services) stenciled on them and not "USOM" or "USAID." The American and Vietnamese staff greeted us warmly. The Chief-of-Party spoke the language (I think he liked to quote Vietnam's epic poem *Kim Van Kieu*.) Emphasis was on the Vietnamese ministries, not who was who in "The Mission", as the U.S. embassy and subservient agencies were referred to. A few days later we were singing Christmas carols around the bonfire in the chilled air of Dalat, the camaraderie authentic, the "old timers" teasing one another in Vietnamese, their self-deprecating humor like bowlers on a Friday night.

The Republic of Vietnam was obviously on a war footing. From the windows above the men's urinals you could see an ARVN camp across the street from IVS House, with soldiers walking about nonchalantly lugging outsized, WW II-era rifles and with hand grenades askew. Coincidentally, this was the camp where, a decade earlier, Cambodian troop contingents in the French Expeditionary Forces were billeted. And the number of Americans in green fatigues was growing. Our first assignment was the National College of Agriculture in Bao Loc. Sociologically, Lam Dong province was beyond the Vietnamese "pale". Radé and Koho tribal people, their women bare-breasted, walked the red dirt streets; few owned bicycles, much less cars or trucks. They came to the market, woven baskets on their backs, straps across their foreheads, to trade handicrafts for food; Tieng Viet was their second language. Only recently had their own languages been transliterated into a phonic (Romanized) alphabet by the Summer Institute of Linguistics, the Bible being their first publication. The French tea plantation owners in the area didn't hire them and Vietnamese government types, especially ARVN, seemed to relish relocating these tribal people from one far hillside to another, whole villages set up behind moats of pungee sticks.

The so-called "agriculture college" was all form and no substance. The Vietnamese instructors would take off for days or weeks at a time. The students hated the place, too. Although the campus had been completed a few years earlier, the jungle was already moving in. Depending on what they'd been fed in the school cafeteria, the students were either sick or miserable, but always grumpy. Discipline was impossible; English was not French, and the center of their universe, Saigon, was five hours away by bus. Our stucco, modern-looking faculty house had never been lived in. After a few weeks, we discovered that the septic tank was missing and the gray and dark water was being deposited right outside the bathroom window. At least the climate was pleasant. Unlike The Delta, you had to do more than wake up in the mornings to sweat. A row of the campus houses along the road to Saigon had been taken over by a small MAC-V (Military Advisory Command-Vietnam) contingent. Bob Knoernschild, ex-IVSer, newly hired by USOM, and *Steve Szadek*, IVS, lived in a similar house further north near the front gate. The soldiers would invite us over for drinks from time to time; the sergeant-in-charge-of-paper-work, a Pole from Chicago, gave me WW II movie déja-vu: A non-com in need of another snafu, his complaints about the army and his divorces made me think he'd read too many Leon Uris paperbacks.

Steve got me involved in a project building a dorm for the tribal people in a nearby school. He taught me to mix ten or fifteen percent cement with clay. We worked alongside some shy Montagnard guys and made hundreds of light brown bricks. A few weeks into that, our "summer project" (1964) allowed us to travel around the country singing folk songs in orphanages and Hoi Viet-My's (Vietnamese-American Associations).

One evening in Hue we joined a group of Vietnamese teachers for dinner at a "restaurant" set up in front of a house. Just as the food was served, machine gun fire erupted about 300 yards away under the Voice of America's powerful relay towers. Everyone froze, that is, until a grenade exploded; we flew outta there like pigeons in St. Mark's—my wife June and I on the IVS Lambretta scooter, the teachers in cars, and on bicycles. We met a few blocks away and realized the shooting had stopped, so we went back and finished our dinners! Hey, the Viet Cong wouldn't target IVSers, right? We were teachers! We came in peace! A year later, *Pete Hunting* was killed by the Viet Cong after returning for a second tour in the Delta. Naiveté was no longer a hedge against the increasing violence. It wasn't long before our positions as ESL teachers in the high schools fell victim not only to the historical enmity between Buddhists and Catholics, but the increasing antagonism the Central Vietnamese people had for the American presence; graffiti in English on a wall at the University of Hue demanded: "Vietnam for Vietnamese to Solve." Again, our lives were put on hold. Again, more rumors flew around than bats taking off from Ankor Wat at sunset. Student strikes popped up everywhere. I also taught English at the Hoi Viet My, up the street from the American consulate. We were warned that a large demonstration would march past the building in early January 1965. USIS officer William Stubbs said it'd be okay if I hung out with him upstairs, above the Abraham Lincoln library. A crowd of about 3,000 marched toward us and stopped to shout slogans in front of the library. When a bunch of them suddenly dashed into the building, Stubbs and I jumped out a rear window into a rice paddy and walked back to his house (where I was introduced to Chivas Regal). The demonstrators piled some books outside and set them afire.

In March 1965, U.S. jets flew in low over the city headed for North Vietnam. Minutes later, a slew of South Vietnam's prop planes followed. IVS wives were ordered evacuated to either Bangkok or Hong Kong along with the U.S. Mission wives, but single female IVSers could stay! A photo of June appeared in *Time* magazine on her way to HK with USAID, CIA, military and diplomatic corps wives. IVS said we could return stateside, but then I had six months left of alternative service to do. Soon after, on the one trip I took to Hong Kong to see June, we bumped into fellow IVSers who'd served in Cambodia! *Phil Bueschler* took us to the U.S. Consulate where we called IVS/Laos and a

couple of days later were offered positions if we agreed
to stay a full year and not expect Lao language training.

LAOS

Vientiane, Laos, reminded me of (old) Tijuana; a squalid
town in need of a giant Dustbuster. Unlike Vietnam, IVSers
were allowed to use the American Community Association
facilities, a bar-cafe, a small commissary and a pool; IVSers
were paid in dollars. A farmer named *Chet Brown* was the
Chief of Party: "There are things you need to know and things
you shouldn't know," he said. We would hear that from
every USAID field director when they explained the Forward
Area Program, basically another "win the hearts and minds"
scheme perfect for young, raw IVSers. The problem was that
most of the places the embassy, military and USAID jointly
selected were places considered "iffy," or villages retaken
from the Pathet Lao.   June and I were assigned to Thakhet
where we'd put together a plan to live in Nong Bok, a village about an hour's drive south. I'd be doing community
development and June, family hygiene. Our supervisor on the
ground was *Val Petersen*, one of the nicest, most considerate
guys I ever had the pleasure of working with. An ex-IVSer
with USAID, he spoke and read Laotian well and knew the
territory.   The USAID office/warehouse in Thakhet had a
single side band radio, a table sized thing that needed alternate
current; check-ins were required morning and night.Val and
I, and my new assistant Houmphanh drove back and forth
to Nong Bok in a converted weapons carrier hauling this
and that to set up the new two-story house Val and USAID
had rented. Weeks later, the big stuff came on a river boat
from Vientiane which lost its propeller and drifted past our
makeshift landing area on the Mekong. The crew threw a
rope downstream and we dragged it back. We hired a bunch
of villagers to carry a desk, generator, tools, and drums of
gasoline, a fat-tire bicycle, beds, a kerosene refrigerator and
kitchen supplies over rice paddy dikes to the village a mile
inland. Some weeks later, as I was about to get settled in the
house (Sept '65), June confirmed that she was pregnant. IVS

couples were not allowed to have children in-country. Our original two-year contract was up anyway and my "civilian discharge" from Selective Service came soon after. ⊗

Inspiration for *June Ellen Davisson Pulcini* to become a volunteer came from her Church of the Brethren heritage. She served as a Summer Service volunteer in La Verne College, at a Brethren Volunteer Workcamp in Austria in 1961, then married Ron Pulcini, also a Brethren. "Ron committed to two years voluntary service as a conscientious objector and applied to Brethren Voluntary Services and IVS for alternative service.

"After a year teaching seventh grade English and history in Glendora, CA, and a summer volunteering in Washington State, we went to IVS orientation in Washington, D.C., to join a team of ten English teachers going to Cambodia. That was fifty years ago."

FRIENDSHIPS

There were new people, new experiences and knowledge. "During our orientation, our trip through Tokyo and Hong Kong, then upon arrival in Cambodia, we established friendships with team members that remain today. We made friends in Phnom Penh immediately, often thanks to Ron's talent and our singing to his guitar playing."

They trained to teach English as a Second Language, and Pulcini remembers that, "Until our arrival, only French and Russian teachers were living in the Provinces. We would be the first Americans. Prince Sihanouk saw that Cambodia needed English to communicate with Asians from countries other than those in Southeast Asia." The volunteers were welcomed as honored guests at a Cambodian Water Festival, where white suits were required for the men, since they were seated in the Queen's Barge with all the dignitaries. "We encountered our first anti-American experience on a trip by boat to a silk village. Following a rousing radio speech by Prince Sihanouk, we were detained in the village by the police who said we were spies. We were released to take the boat back to Phnom Penh."

CAMBODIA

Uncertainty followed the first trip to their assignment in Siem Reap. "Our group of ten ESL teachers visited most of the sites of our assignments around the country. We drove to Siem Reap, stopped at the school where we would teach, and saw the house that would become our home. We returned to Phnom Penh and learned that President Kennedy had been assassinated. Then Prince Sihanouk decreed that American aid was no longer welcome in Cambodia. We substituted for other teachers as they left."

They went to Dalat in Vietnam for Christmas. "Then our English team was reassigned; some went to Laos, others to Vietnam. We stayed in Vietnam and taught English at the Agricultural College in Bao Loc, which was built by a University of Michigan team that provided an English-language library. We were on campus with other IVS volunteers doing rural development, as well as with a Military Advisory Group team. We lived in Bao Loc until going to Japan for leave in August and going to a Brethren-led conference, 'Conflict and Reconciliation in Asia,' which was attended by students from eleven Asian countries. We represented Cambodia as the only ones who had lived there!"

Returning to Vietnam, Pulcini learned that she and her husband were to be reassigned to Hue. "We lived in housing outside the secure zone of Hue. I taught at Nguyen Tri Phoung Boys High School with a wonderful Vietnamese teacher, Kim Chi, who became a life-long friend."

DEMONSTRATIONS

There had been demonstrations that resulted in women being housed in protected areas, and demonstrators burned the USIS library. Later, when the bombing began, dependents were ordered to leave the next morning taking only a few essentials. "Mine included the sixteen-string Vietnamese musical instrument I was learning to play! The flight was from the Citadel to Danang with the dependent women and children from Hue.

"I was flown to Hong Kong with other women and children. Ron had to find other volunteer work to complete his two years, so following a meeting with IVS/Cambodia friends, we found a position on the Lao Rural Development team. After three months in Hong Kong, we moved to Laos. We were sent to Thakhet to open a forward area site in Nom Bok and traveled by dirt road, boat and helicopter. The area was Vietnamese-speaking, and, we were told, bordered a route for Vietnamese going to Thailand. There would be a radio and an airstrip, we were to see Lao and Thai, and Americans might come there. We would be given information on a 'need to know' basis. Each of us had an interpreter and I learned a lesson from the one assigned to me who purchased a gold chain with her first paycheck. I gently scolded her, but now I understand her wisdom, and wish I had learned then that buying gold was the only secure way to save money!"

During this transition, Pulcini lived in Thakhet. On a visit to Vientiane, she learned she was pregnant. "IVS could no longer allow us to move to Nom Bok, despite my best efforts to persuade them that a child would make me a better teacher of good nutrition."

AMERICAN FIELD SERVICE

Their USAID/Education director in Cambodia was now in Laos and hired Ron Pulcini on a contract basis to teach English language at Dong Dok and work on writing ESL materials. "When we came to Laos we agreed to extend our tour another year and we would have taught on the Education team except that IVS was contracted to work with USAID, and Ron had an individual contract with USAID. In time, this would be motivation for me to be involved on the IVS Board.

"Due to our IVS experiences, after the contract with USAID ended Ron went to work with USIS at the Lao-American

Association. I became the coordinator for American Field Service in Laos."

The Pulcinis returned to the U.S. in 1970 and settled in Hermosa Beach, CA. They separated and both re-married.

SERVICE WITH THE BOARD

"One day Nicholas Katzenbach (former Attorney General and Under Secretary of State during the Lyndon Johnson presidency) visited Hermosa Beach. He was looking for women and former volunteers to be on the IVS Board," Pulcini said. She accepted the challenge and became an active board member. "I was substitute teaching at the time and attended meetings four or five times a year as Vice Chairman of the Board and serving on the Executive Committee."

Now, she writes, "The impact of IVS is everywhere. It has been the model for countless NGOs doing education and development work in host countries. I have been involved with several of these, serving on their boards or as advisor, including, among others, East Meets West Foundation, Global Village Foundation, Lao Humanitarian Foundation, Mettha Karuna Foundation (Cambodia), and the Cambodian Students of America's Cambodian American National Development Organization. Numerous IVS Board and staff have also contributed to and are still involved in sustainable development and education programs."

Nancy Felthousen Ridenour recalls, "My first interest in going overseas developed as a teenager, when I heard of Peace Corps work in Asia. It seemed like a great adventure and a way to give back to the human community. I was introduced to IVS as a college student and the potential for travel, adventure, and service appealed to me. Although there were rumblings of war in the area, I still joined and went to Laos in 1965.

"I was assigned by the Chief of Party to be a home economist in Vang Vieng, Laos, and landed there in 1965. It was a gorgeous place with river and mountains, but the assignment was vague and not well directed by my superiors in USAID. I worked with the local women, focusing on maternal and child care and sewing projects."

Ridenour believes her biggest impact was working in Muong Phieng after marrying former volunteer *George Ridenour*, and helping him with projects. "I was no longer an IVS volunteer because the Chief of Party did not think a volunteer should be married to a USAID employee. Fortunately, some of the rules and regulations eased over the years."

While in Muong Phieng she established a Lao newspaper and information project. "We built large bulletin boards for each of the villages in the cluster to post photos of self-help projects taking place in the villages. This was to increase villager awareness of potential improvements in their lives. We all had a mobile library to take books to the villages. I worked with the Lao USAID assistants to develop and produce a cluster newsletter. This again was to increase awareness by the villagers about how to increase their own self-help projects. I think this was a very popular project, but have no idea whether or not it continued after we left the cluster.

"The years in Laos and travel to and from the States had a huge impact upon my taste in food, aesthetics, and the desire for travel. Despite the traumas of the war and concern for safety, I found the experience very educational and sensitizing. I was able to use much of what I learned and saw in my teaching, which brought a dimension of relevance to the students. I do think, though, that the Chief of Party at the time was very short-sighted in his decision to terminate my contract. I also do not think I was well trained for working as a home economist in Vang Vieng or about the politics of the area."

"WE WANT TO BUILD; THEY WANT TO DESTROY"

JAMES MALIA

Excerpted from *Southeast Review of Asian Studies / Vol XX [1998], 89-100.*).

Sometime early in 1970, I was meeting with my contact at the Royal Lao Government's Ministry of the Plan and Cooperation to discuss implementing a closer working

relationship between his ministry and IVS in Laos. Toward
the close of the meeting, he made the above statement to
express the frustration and helplessness he felt in trying to do
work in competition with a war that was consuming more
and more of Laos. The "we" were the various agencies and
programs within the Royal Lao Government (RLG) who
were responsible for the economic and social development
of Laos. The "they" were the military, Lao and American,
who were responsible for defending Laos and for defeat-
ing the Pathet Lao insurgents and the North Vietnamese
invaders. The objectives of the two groups were mutually
exclusive—building vs. destroying. And when they clashed,
as frequently they did, destruction won out. When development and destruction went head to head, development was a
secondary priority.

Advocates of development within the RLG were in a dilemma. Committed to building, they were forced to endure a
climate of destruction. What could they do? In reality, they
had few, if any, alternatives. And so they muddled along as
best they could. This same dilemma confronted IVS. As an
organization and as individuals, we had come to help the
people of Laos improve the quality of their lives and build
a better future. But we too were caught up in the chaos
and insecurity generated by the war. And our options were
limited. We could compromise our ideals and keep working, abandon projects before they were completed, or return
home before the end of our tours. Like others, we continued
to muddle along as best we could in an ever-deteriorating
situation.

It should be said that IVS was not the only non-governmental
organization in Laos at that time whose developmental efforts were frustrated by intensifying hostilities. Our close ties
with the American presence in Laos, however, exacerbated
our dilemma.

I served in Laos as a member of the IVS team from the early
fall of 1967 until the end of 1971, some fifty-one months
in all. My first assignment was to help train RLG forestry
personnel in forest inventory methods. After about a year, I

was asked to join the IVS/Laos staff and served for the next
year-and-a-half as an assistant director of the Laos team.

I had volunteered in Laos to do good works, to see some of
the world, and to learn what I could. As a practical matter, I
also was completing my alternative service as a conscientious
objector. I went to Laos excited and optimistic about what I
would be doing. In retrospect, I also was naïve.

MY EXPERIENCE

I went to Laos as a volunteer. My expectation was that I
would live close to the Lao people and learn about their
way of life. I wanted to live simply and outside my normal
cultural patterns. I wanted to learn about myself, my own
culture, and the culture of Laos.

When I arrived in 1967, the American presence in Laos
and the amenities offered to us were overwhelming. The
American homes, offices, and supporting infrastructure
stood in stark contrast to how the Lao people went about
their daily lives. Americans had access to an endless bounty
of supplies and equipment. We had our own land and air
transportation systems. At the commissary, we purchased
the same groceries and household items we did back in the
States. And many Americans lived in housing compounds
that looked like displaced suburban communities. Visually,
the impression was that America was in charge.

There was a large number of Americans who were involved
in a variety of developmental efforts. Many of these personnel were genuinely interested in the development of Laos and
worked hard to be successful. They were working, however,
within the framework of the military effort in Laos to gen-
erate support for overall U.S. and Royal Lao Government
objectives. Thus, there were a large number of American
military personnel also present in Laos, but their visibility
and activity were much less obvious.

The situation changed significantly during the time I was
in Laos. The war expanded, and American involvement
increased. And there were increasing doubts and criticisms
about America's war in Southeast Asia. Significant change

for IVS was precipitated when volunteers began to be killed—four Americans and two Lao assistants within a two-and-a-half year period. Despite all intentions to the contrary, IVS was identified with one side in a civil war. To those on the other side, we were part of the enemy and clearly marked by our white skin and round eyes. When shots were fired, IVSers were fair game. And since we were in the rural areas, where the war primarily was being contested, we were highly vulnerable.

We knew we were at risk, but for me and for the volunteers who worked in the rural areas, the war was not a daily presence in our lives. It was something, however, that always lingered in the back of our minds. We would hear and read reports about the progress of military activity. We would see the soldiers, the military vehicles, and the refugees. And, occasionally, we would see someone who had been killed. And there were security precautions that governed our lives.

Having to be overly concerned about security and personal safety clashed with my sense of what the volunteer way of life meant. I wanted to see new things, meet new people, and have new experiences. I was fortunate; during the first years of my tour, travel was less restricted, and I was able to see much more of Laos than volunteers who came later. When I left Laos, secure areas had been reduced to the major population areas—land-locked islands accessible only by air.

The war became more real for me in the spring of 1969. I had set up the training site for volunteers in Vang Vieng, a small provincial capital some sixty miles north of Vientiane, in the foothills of the mountains that covered northern Laos. The rains were late that year, so it was still the dry season— the time when military activity was greatest. As part of their training, the new volunteers were thoroughly briefed on what to do in case of an attack.

One morning two or three weeks into the training, the volunteers were attending language class, and I was meeting at the USAID compound with USAID officials in Vang Vieng and other IVS staff who had come up to observe training. Our meeting suddenly was interrupted by the cry that the airport was under attack. We went out into the compound where we heard shelling and saw that most employees now carried weapons and were hastily setting up a defense around the compound. I took a Jeep to get to the IVS house to bring the new volunteers back to a safer area. When I arrived at the house, the volunteers had followed directions exactly as they had been instructed—they were packed and ready to go. We made it to a safe area and waited to see what would happen next.

In time, the firing stopped, and we eventually found out that it had been a false alarm. Someone had panicked and started firing, which started everyone else firing. We finally were able to relax, but the experience brought home to the new volunteers the reality of life in Laos. (Shortly before this incident, we had received word that one IVS volunteer, *Chandler Edwards*, had been killed in an ambush in southern Laos.) The new recruits were scared, but in the days ahead we went on with the training schedule, and life returned to normal. Security around Vang Vieng continued to deteriorate, however, and we were soon restricted to the town.

The events of the several weeks we were in Vang Vieng were considered more or less normal. War and the issues of security were real. We had come a bit closer to them than had others, but we were not deterred. Our focus remained on our work and on how we were there to help build something for the Lao people. Chandler's death had given us all pause to think about what we must do to better ensure our safety in carrying out this work, but it did not have a lasting impact. It would take the deaths of two more IVSers, some three months later, to finally force the organization to confront the reality of what it meant to work in Laos in the midst of a civil war.

My most enduring memory of the years I spent in Laos is of having to bring two IVSers, two of my friends, back to Vientiane in body bags. *Art Stillman* and *Dennis Mummert* were killed in an ambush on August 5, 1969. That experience is as real for me today as if it happened yesterday. Their deaths were even more significant for me because I had planned to visit Dennis but acceded to Art's request to go in my place. Dennis was in Ban Thouei, a somewhat isolated station (north and east of Vientiane along the Mekong) where security was tight. Thus, staff tried to visit him as often as possible. Art had been in the Vientiane office for several weeks while I was in the Philippines coordinating training for another group of new volunteers. Now he wanted to get out of the office and spend a few days in the country. Art suggested he take the trip and that I stay in Vientiane to get caught up on my office work.

Another simple request continued the chain of events that would eventually lead to the death of four people. Two Lao veterinary agents needed a ride to a village to inoculate cattle against a disease that was spreading through the area. They did not have gas for their Jeep and asked Dennis if he would give them a ride. Ordinarily such a trip would be made by boat, but the motor on the USAID boat was broken. And so the trip was made by Jeep along a road where Americans were not supposed to travel. Someone in the village tipped off an ambush team that the four of them would be returning to Ban Thouei later in the afternoon. Art, Dennis, and the two Lao veterinary agents were killed.

Later, we were able to learn that Dennis had been the prime target. His job was to help villagers increase their rice production through the use of modern technologies—new varieties, fertilizers, and pump irrigation. Some villagers did not want to make these changes and were upset with Dennis because he was promoting them. If he could be eliminated, they apparently reasoned, life would return to normal. Art and the veterinarian agents were merely in the wrong place at the wrong time. The deaths of Art and Dennis set in motion a process of change in IVS that had been long overdue. What that change eventually would be and how it would get worked out was at first uncertain.

Despite all that had happened, we still felt a strong obligation to what IVS was all about and to the commitments we had made, regardless of how they might be perceived by the Lao recipients. It was our belief—based on feedback from local officials, Lao counterparts, and villagers—that we were doing some good for some people. In the big picture, IVS may have been wasting its time. In the little picture, however, in the day-to-day events that formed each volunteer's life, relationships were built and assistance was rendered. It would have been very difficult to just walk away from those commitments and experiences.

Feelings ran high as IVS/Laos volunteers and staff gathered in Vientiane during the middle of August to talk about what was happening to IVS and what the future should be. Two issues were paramount—security and involvement with the American development and military effort in Laos. In a series of lengthy, cathartic meetings, we decided that volunteers no longer should live or work in a situation where they had to be unduly concerned about their personal security or where they were exposed to an abnormal amount of danger. We also concluded that IVSers no longer should work with those programs in which they were the sole American representative of USAID. On both the security and work situation issues, we were trying to articulate a presence that was more compatible with our collective vision of a private, volunteer organization—rendering assistance in a culturally sensitive, politically neutral manner.

Volunteers also discussed a third issue. Many of those present believed that because IVS was strongly allied with one side in a civil war, we were in violation of our claim as a non-political organization. These volunteers proposed that IVS acknowledge this fact and leave Laos. The issue was hotly debated, but we developed no strong consensus on how to resolve it.

The IVS Board of Directors would make the final decision about the future of IVS in Laos. We proposed two alternatives for the Board's consideration: That within a specific period of time, phase IVS out of Laos, or that IVS remain in Laos, but that it make changes to better insure the safety of the volunteers, to work in closer cooperation with the Royal Lao Government, and to decrease our involvement with USAID.

The IVS/Laos staff moved ahead on the security issue without waiting for final approval from the IVS Board. By January of the following year, volunteers were no longer stationed in an area where guards, bunkers, barbed wire, or a personal weapon was needed to ensure security. In addition, volunteers were removed from areas where freedom of movement during the day or night was not possible. Finally, IVSers no longer worked where they were the sole American representative. As a practical matter, our work now was confined to the secure provincial capitals and their immediate surrounding areas.

It had taken a long time to educate the Board members. They believed very strongly that, if our intentions were pure and if we worked hard, we would be successful and recognized for our good deeds. The reality in Laos was much different. We were in the midst of a civil war.

One final confrontation was needed. USAID reacted negatively to our removal of volunteers from the rural areas. To their way of thinking, the non-education side of IVS was no longer needed, and the USAID/Laos Director moved to terminate the program. I believed that there was still a role for non-education volunteers in Laos and that we should be given the opportunity to develop and implement that role. I also believed that, whether we liked it or not, IVS was a highly political organization and that we could use our political power to some advantage. It was my belief that IVS was critical to the public image of care and concern for the Lao people that the U.S. was trying to maintain; losing IVS could well raise questions about the extent of U.S. concern. Also, if IVS was to leave Laos or radically change how it functioned in the country, I wanted it to be on our terms, not on terms dictated by USAID. Hence, I was willing to resort to political means to keep control of the organization even though we espoused a non-political presence. I brought my concerns to our contacts within the political section of the U.S. Embassy. They readily agreed and through the ambassador applied pressure in Laos as well as in Washington, D.C., for USAID to retain a strong and diverse IVS presence in Laos.

WHY WE STAYED

The war was making it more and more difficult to live and
work in Laos. Volunteers were well aware that the price for
traveling outside a secure area could be their lives, yet very
few actually left before completing their tours. Those already
in the country were knowledgeable about the possibilities
and limitations of working in Laos. To the extent possible,
we tried to convey this reality to new volunteers before they
were fully committed to coming. Few, if any, were deterred.
New volunteers continued to arrive on schedule, and most
stayed until the end of their contracts.

Our desire to help the people of Laos build a better life
for themselves through educational, agricultural, and community development assistance ultimately was not what kept
us in the country. I believe that what sustained us—what ultimately kept us in Laos for as long as any of us stayed—was
that being in Laos at that time was an adventure. It was an
exotic, interesting place. There was an element of danger and
uncertainty in the air that focused the mind and heightened
the sensations we experienced. Our day-to-day life was in
sharp contrast to what we might be doing back in the States,
and for that reason all the more appealing. Laos was different. We stayed in large part, I think, to immerse ourselves in
that difference and to learn from it for whatever might come
next. We knew that our time in Laos was temporary. If we
could do a little good in the process, if we could help build
something for the future, so much the better.

FINAL THOUGHTS

Did IVS make any significant contributions to the long-
term development of Laos? It is hard to say. Our primary
contribution was at the human level. We worked to impart
knowledge, skills, and an awareness of alternatives. How
many of those we assisted were still alive at the end of the
war, how many chose to stay in Laos, and how many were
able to work with the new government, is unknown. Hopefully there were some. IVS did what it could. Structurally
it was an integral part of the American effort. Despite its
efforts to forge greater independence and autonomy, it could

not deny what it was—an American volunteer organization rendering assistance to one side in the midst of a civil war. In such a situation, it pays to be careful. One must know the limitations of the situation and abide by them. And one must hope that what is built in some way will be there when the guns are finally silent.

IVS, along with much of the other Western development effort, left Laos when the country fell to the Pathet Lao in 1975.

IVS claimed to be a private, voluntary organization that provided developmental assistance in a politically neutral manner. Because IVS compromised its claim to neutrality in Laos by working closely with one side of a civil war, a number of volunteers believed that IVS should leave Laos on principle. I disagreed. Individuals always had the opportunity to leave and to take a stand on principle in their own way. At that time, I believed that the organization should remain as a vehicle for volunteers to learn and to contribute as best they could.

The seeds of the ultimate demise of IVS in Laos were sown at its inception. Like any classic tragedy, only time was needed to work through to its inevitable conclusion. Early leaders in Laos and Washington, D.C., put on blinders and ignored the military and political ramifications of volunteer work in Laos. Our good intentions and perceived good works were not sufficient to hold us aloof from the turmoil that was Laos in the late 1960s and early 1970s. The time to have left would have been early on, but we were hopeful and it was an adventure. And so we stayed on. At the end it was too late. We stayed to contribute and to learn until it was no longer possible. It seems only right to have done so. ⚜

IV. LIBERIA • JORDAN • ALGERIA • SYRIA • SUDAN

A RECAP OF IVS'S SECOND DECADE would show that two programs, one in Cambodia, the other in Liberia, were terminated during 1963. In Vietnam, several of the small projects were not sustainable or work was completed, and the pullout from that country took place in 1971. At the end of 1972, seventy volunteers remained in Laos, Algeria, Sudan, Libya, Zaire, Morocco, and Yemen.

Although the bulk of IVS work in its second decade was in Asia, several other events worthy of note took place between 1963 and 1973.

EDUCATORS IN LIBERIA

The American public was excited over the fledgling Peace Corps, remembers *A. W. Krueger,* and at the same time, IVS had signed a new contract to provide a team of educators in Liberia. These would teach English as a Second Language and other subjects at high school and college levels.

A. W. KRUEGER IN LIBERIA 1961-62

In 1961, after two years in the army (which never sent me more than two hundred miles from home) and three years of teaching vocational agriculture, I decided to see more of the world. I signed up with IVS for what was supposed to be a teacher training project in rural elementary schools in Liberia, West Africa. Arriving late in the year, I served temporarily as Agricultural Advisor at an agricultural and industrial high school. Just after year's end, I took over as one of two assistant chiefs-of-party, providing personal support for about a dozen men teaching in remote villages.

In December, serious problems arose. The renowned and ubiquitous Peace Corps reared its ugly head and displaced us. Our contract was to end in April, far short of a full tour in my case, and I wasn't ready to go home. I wrote to IVS and managed to transfer to IVS/Vietnam with the understanding that I would stay for a full year.

After language study I was assigned to a crop experiment station about forty miles from Saigon. New varieties were experimented with and, if promising, seeds or cuttings were shipped to various villages. Wild hogs were devastating the plot work and making them useless for research purposes, so a hog-proof fence was deemed necessary. The fence materials were on hand when I arrived and it fell to me, along with my interpreter, my driver, and a small crew of laborers, to get the job done. And we did, though the year was half-gone when we finished. I also worked on getting the first large-scale seed drying house in the nation built and running.

I like to think my experiences overseas made me a bit more realistic than the average fellow about trying to work in developing countries.

It was a little over three years after arriving home from Vietnam that I motored down to San Luis Obispo, California, from Lovelock, Nevada. I joined about fifteen other newly hired Soil Conservation Service (SCS) employees from all over the West for orientation. "Not bad," I replied to my supervisor when asked what I thought of the two week session. "And by the way," he added, "every one of you, if you remain with SCS, will have a chance to work overseas. Don't hesitate to accept, you'll love every minute of it! You can throw away the rule book and there's just no limit to what you can accomplish!" I didn't see how the rest of the group reacted, as I was staring straight ahead, frozen stiff in pure astonishment! At the coffee break, I confronted him.

"Did I hear you right, and did you really mean what you said?"

"Yes, I did," he answered.

"Well, I spent twenty-six months in two different underdeveloped nations, and I see it a little differently."

A lively discussion followed. I cautioned that an overseas assignment, while a great experience, should be undertaken with accurate expectations. Loving every minute of it and unlimited accomplishments were certainly not among them!

I mention this anecdote because I feel it parallels one of IVS's glaring failures in my time. Someone should have emphasized how slowly things work in underdeveloped nations. Change takes place over generations, not months or even years. We volunteers should have been cautioned and conditioned not to expect things to look much different when we left than when we arrived. We spanned the oceans wearing rose-colored glasses, expecting to be plugged into successful, ongoing activities, usually returning home with an entertaining series of 35mm slides and an underlying layer of disillusionment.

So what are the hard lessons I came home with and helped shape the rest of my life?

- Graft and corruption here at home are mild compared to what is found in many Third World nations. The U.S. government put up money for twenty-five modern school buildings to be constructed in rural Liberia. President Tubman (a twenty-year incumbent and one of the wealthiest men in Africa) made a visit to the U.S. during my tour. He told President Kennedy the schools were up and running, and he probably thought they were. Actually, none of them had been much more than half-completed by the contractors. They "ate the money," as the Liberian saying goes. A few eventually became operational only after construction was completed by IVS men.

- The teacher training project never got underway. Our men were used only as teachers, never given the time to help Liberian teachers obtain advanced training, as we had been recruited to do. This development contributed to low morale, as we knew we were merely free teachers for the Liberian government even though qualified Liberian teachers were available.

- During the colonial period in other African nations, pretty good civil services were created, health care was established, roads were paved, industries brought in. Free public education was sometimes established. Liberia, never a colony, was rampant with "ignorance, poverty, and disease" as their own Secretary of Education frankly stated.

- Ruling classes in underdeveloped nations think nothing

of treating their minorities worse than we ever thought of treating ours. Our race riots of the '60s made headlines around the world and we were sometimes asked about them by Vietnamese co-workers. We would reply that we didn't like it, but it wasn't as broad and consistent as their treatment of their own minorities. Usually this would silence them, but one expressed what most of them were thinking: "Oh, no, that is entirely different. It's a proven fact they are inferior to us!" Liberia differed only in that the ruling class (Americo-Liberians) was in the minority. Our city councils, boards of commissioners, school boards, grand juries, legislative watchdog committees, courts, auditors, etc. seem pretty mundane and sometimes superfluous. But they tend to keep government employees in line. The latter know their performance is periodically evaluated by higher authority responsible to voters, and they are usually under direct public scrutiny as well. This is not the case when it comes to the clandestine bureaucracy of our foreign service. The few individuals who want to work and accomplish something create a lot of problems for themselves. And the sedentary majority was embarrassed and resentful when host country officials praised the work of IVS men and women and asked for more of them. "These are the kind of Americans we want you to send us," the Liberian Secretary of Education openly stated. "People who will go out to our villages and live with our people!"

• My overseas experiences reinforced the course I took in life. I often thought of the poverty stricken lower classes in Liberia and Vietnam and how few we reached. Many of them had intelligence and talents that could never be expressed. They never had the chance to break out of the mold, living and dying in the same villages their parents and grandparents did. They were forced by circumstances to be conformists. Too many people in developed nations *choose* to be conformists; I made sure I wasn't one of them, trying to get a lot out of life as I went along rather than waiting until retirement. ⚜

IVS and the Peace Corps finally worked out an agreement. New IVSers recruited for the team in Liberia would receive Peace Corps training together with Peace Corps recruits, and the joint group fielded in Liberia would be known as an 'IVS-Peace Corps' team. "We had several new men on the staff who liked the idea," remembers Krueger, "and I had to select a batch of applications from teachers to be given to the Peace Corps. I was somewhat reluctant to do so as most were excellent candidates.

"It was a bit confusing, and became obvious to us that IVS was simply being used as a conduit for the Peace Corps. One irate letter came in from an IVS candidate who blasted the idea! He had applied for IVS precisely because we were not the Peace Corps!

"Our disillusionment was complete when word came that recruits arriving in Liberia asked 'What is IVS?' Trained by the Peace Corps, they'd never been told that it was a joint IVS-Peace Corps team! So IVS decided to drop further joint ventures with the Peace Corps and continue as an independent contractor."

After graduating from Washington State University in Pullman, Washington, *Dewade Creveling* joined the Navy and spent his tour visiting Mediterranean countries. When his time with the Navy was up, "I started looking for work and got a phone call from *Russell Stevenson*, then director of IVS, asking me if I'd like to go to Cambodia or Jordan. I had never heard of Jordan but I knew about Cambodia where some type of war was going on, so over the phone that evening I selected **Jordan**.

"About the time I arrived in Jordan, in the spring of 1963, four other young people with IVS took up residence there. These were *Arline Cary, Carol Moore, Susan Sneed*en and *James Van Zandt*. They were going to be teachers and teachers' aides."

PAYROLL CLERK

Soon after he got to Jordan, Creveling discovered that though he had been sent there to work on agriculture, in fact he would become a payroll clerk for a self-help project that was turning a donkey path into what came to be called The Road of Peace. "A Jordanian once told me that the most important reason for building a road to a village is to connect that village to the world. Without a road, villagers continue to exist as they have for centuries, not contributing anything to the betterment of man." The road also allowed education officials to visit area schools during the rainy season from November to April.

In his two years in Jordan, Creveling got a taste of Middle Eastern hospitality. "I always took the time to have a cup of tea, Bedouin coffee or Arabic coffee with the person or persons of importance in a village, although some morning this meant up to ten cups of coffee. Thank goodness the cups were small." When not overseeing the payroll of the road-building project, Creveling organized a basketball team of American volunteers and local Arab youths. "We lost more games than we won. One game ended in a tie—the Jordanian referee didn't want there to be any losers."

Fifty years later, he best remembers, "The spreading of good will." And echoing his words were those of former IVS Director *Anne Shirk*, who said, "Sometimes development isn't about irrigation ditches or livestock projects. Sometimes it's just about making life better."

The program in the **Sudan** was closed after seventeen years due to staffing problems during the continuing civil war. The expense of operations in the country became prohibitive and remaining workers were either sent home or relocated.

In **Zimbabwe**, an agreement was reached with the government for program development, and the first staff person was sent to plan specific projects. Priority was given to the resettlement of people from over-populated and marginal tribal areas to more productive commercial farms formerly owned by colonials.

Michael Call was born in Montreal and raised in a small town not far from the Vermont border. Following graduation from the local high school, he was admitted to Middlebury College and, after graduation in 1962, went to Paris as a student in Middlebury's graduate degree program. "It was there that I first heard of IVS. A fellow program member told me about a work and travel opportunity he had been offered by IVS–in Cambodia if I recall correctly–but had decided to not accept. I was intrigued and wrote to the IVS Washington office. I was aware of a similar Canadian organization but it was still in the process of formation and so I decided to follow-up with IVS.

"I say intrigued by a possible IVS posting–but I clearly remember that this initial interest did not spring from a desire to be of service and certainly not patriotism. IVS was in my eyes a fully American organization and I was Canadian after all. Rather, at the time in Paris, I quite liked my independence, absence of work responsibilities and cross-cultural living and learning experiences, and I wanted all of that to continue. In addition I had but a very vague sense of a future work and career path and convinced myself that travel and additional time overseas would help lay a more firm foundation for that future career, whatever it might turn out to be."

UNRWA

Call remembers a brief phone conversation where it was agreed that he would meet IVS's *Russell Stevenson* in September, 1963, at U.N. headquarters in New York, as well as the local representative of the United Nations Relief and Works Agency for Palestinian Refugees (UNRWA, headquartered in Beirut). This would be a first step towards taking up an assignment as an English teacher at the UNRWA vocational and technical school (VTC) in Damascus, Syria. He also obtained a U.N. laissez-passer, "a document of which I was very proud and still have.

"I was one of, I think, the six or seven IVS team members seconded to UNRWA as English or physical education teachers, the others posted at similar schools in Lebanon, Jordan and Gaza. We spent about a week as a group in the hills above Beirut in an orientation program where we learned about UNRWA and its mission, something of the recent history and current events in the region, a cursory introduction to Arabic culture, religion and family, as well as a few words of the Arabic language. In retrospect not a very full orientation program but in my naïveté and excitement I remember thinking that I had all the knowledge and understanding I needed to get started."

SYRIA

The Damascus VTC was located beside the highway leading to the airport, on an arid and stony plain about fifteen kilometers south of the city. It was a large complex with classrooms, workshops, dining hall, dormitory buildings, offices and covered walkways. "I was in fact the only non-Palestinian living at the school, although there was a team of five or six advisors (mostly from the U.K. and in whose homes I would at times spend the weekends) who commuted to school from the city every day. Students–all male and some older than I was–spent most of their day in workshops for various electrical, automotive and mechanical trades in addition to a few hours a week of general studies that included English."

ARAB HOSPITALITY

"On a personal level I got on well with my students and was the frequent recipient of the noted Arab hospitality and gener-osity. Students with little or no visible income, often two or three pooling their coins, would insist on paying for my bus fare into the city and the movie ticket, following a treat of coffee or orange juice. My attempts to reciprocate were consistently dismissed out of hand. Visits to the homes of students located in refugee camps (semi-permanent by this time following the Arab-Israeli war) on the outskirts of Damascus included generous meals, walks in the beautifully green and fertile oasis gardens surrounding large areas of the city, and small gifts before the return bus trip to school. Our chats almost always focused on current political issues, what are Jews like, did I have any Jewish friends, the perceived injustice of the U.N. and Western support for the state of Israel, the dim chance of finding employment and securing any kind of stable economic and family life given the lack of legal status, and the many restrictions placed on Palestinians in Syria."

Call's assignment ended after about fifteen months when he contracted hepatitis A which resulted in a short Damascus hospital stay followed by a longer stay in the American University of Beirut hospital, and then a three-month convalescence with the family of a senior UNRWA officer from Mauritius high in the hills above Beirut. "I recall feeling miserable while at the same time grateful for the attentive care and hospitality. At the end of this time I was in fact physically quite fit but my morale was rock bottom and I did not feel up to resuming my teaching and living in the challenging and emotionally draining Damascus VTC environment." Call explained this in a letter to IVS in Washington and was soon offered a return ticket home or another assignment; he quickly accepted the second option.

"I can say that my inexperience, limited time in Damascus and the nature of my work as a classroom teacher resulted in there being no real impact on the school and certainly none on UNRWA and its education programming. I might have offered a slightly more human, friendly and accessible face for some of the Palestinian students and staff who I think generally viewed U.N. personnel and westerners as–if not the enemy–at least antithetical to their dreams of a return to Palestine."

RECRUITER

"As for IVS, I saw its role as essentially that of a recruiter under contract to UNRWA to which it then passed the day-to-day management and supervision of the IVS-recruited teachers. There was no formal team structure in place and I only vaguely recall a visit from an IVS Washington staff member. By far the greatest impact of Syria was on me, though one thing my fifteen months in Syria did not do was expose me to the realities of Syria itself. Although located within the political boundaries of the state of Syria, I was living and teaching almost exclusively in a Palestinian and U.N. environment and apart from short and limited excursions with students or overnight stays with expatriate advisors in Damascus, I saw little of life in Syria. What I think is more important, however, is that my assignment constituted the first steps on the road to thinking more critically about the political, economic and social issues at play in the world."

That same year, a large group of volunteers was placed in Algeria, both to assist with agricultural development and to teach in village schools. Over the next fifteen years more than a hundred volunteers were assigned to that country.

Stan Ingman had completed a BS in Botany in 1961 from Miami University in Oxford, Ohio and a MS in Rural Sociology from Ohio State University in May 1963, when the Dean of the School of Agriculture told him about IVS. "I had applied to the Peace Corps and was thinking about various options. IVS was quick to move and in the summer of 1963 I spent four weeks at the Soil and Conservation Service training center at Fort Robinson, Nebraska, for engineering training. Then I spent another four weeks studying French in Washington, D.C. By fall I was on my way to Paris and on to Algiers, Algeria. I believe we had eleven in our initial group."

Ingman, *Phil Goodrich*, *Tom Gist*, and *Bill Folkerts* were assigned to Tlemcen, in western Algeria. "Basically, we tried to put refugees from the Algerian war for independence from France back to work. Projects included small dams, tree planting, picking up rocks in farm fields, repair of irrigation ditches, terraces, and erosion control. In one mountain location," Ingman remembers, "we were told we were repairing irrigation ditches built by the Roman Empire." We had some 3,000 men working on projects in our area of western Algeria. Payment for the labor was a bag of wheat, tins of cooking oil, and some cash. The payment was roughly the equivalent of $1.80 per day."

THREE SITES

The team's major accomplishment was putting 9,000 men back to work in three sites across northern **Algeria**. The program in

Algeria was much like the U.S. Works Progress Administration during the Depression in the 1920s and 1930s. In fact, Ingman recalls, "When I went to a local hardware to buy some pick handles, one had WPA stamped on it, likely from the WPA program in USA.

"The impact of our project was limited—other than we got a lot of workers doing manual labor for which they got paid. Our Algerian Forest Guard colleagues did not believe in asking locals what we should do, and often, they told us we could do whatever we wanted to do on some other people's land, without local permission. This was not good community development practice. I'd like to return to the Tlemcen area and see if any of our planted trees are growing or the dams and terraces are still functioning."

Jill Chamberlain was originally slated to go to Vietnam, but because of the conflict there, she instead went to Algeria. "My assignment was to be a nurse in an orphanage for boys in Tefeschoun, not far from Algiers. On my arrival in Algiers, there had been a coup d'état. It was the first time I had been close to an army tank. Fortunately, I was driven to a peaceful part of Algeria where the orphanage was located."

CHILDREN

"The most memorable aspects were caring for these children and working with such a kind and caring director who did all he could for these boys."

She took on a young woman to assist her in the infirmary after teaching her basic first aid skills. She also found a French doctor nearby who was able to immunize all of the boys.

"I tried to get appropriate help for a thirteen-year-old boy who had regressed to the infant state. The drive to the mental hospital was exhausting and useless since he was about two months too young to be admitted. I gave him a sedative on return and he slept in one of the beds in the infirmary. The next morning, he came to where I was staying, went into my little kitchenette and started eating my figs, peanut butter, bread, and other hard-to-get essentials. After two more days of figs, bread and peanut butter, he went back to be with the other boys and eating with them in the refectory. He found others who spoke his dialect. He and I could speak French at a very basic level and that helped too. He soon called me Mama."

She also got medical help for a woman who experienced spousal abuse and was working at the orphanage.

"This volunteer experience has shown me the harshness of life for many children and adults in the world. After IVS, in the same year, I continued my volunteer work in an Algerian village with a European group (*Service Civile International*) from September to June 1965. This affirmed my view that basic health programs such as clean drinking water and immunization are essential everywhere."

Philip Goodrich also served in Algeria from 1963 to 1965. "I grew up on a seventy-five-acre fruit farm in western New York State on the southern shore of Lake Ontario. My family often vacationed in Canada, and I fondly remember attending the Canadian National Exhibition in Toronto. We hosted Cornell University students doing their required farm practicum, as well as several Scandinavian agriculture students who lived in our home for six to twelve months, working and learning American ways of fruit growing."

Goodrich entered Cornell University in 1958 to study Agricultural Engineering where he met students from across the U.S. and other countries. Some of his friends joined IVS and the Peace Corps after graduation. "The summer after my junior year, I chose to work in Sierra Leone, Africa, on a student project sponsored by Operation Crossroads Africa. We built a lorry park in a small town called Magburaka. We visited Liberia, Guinea, and Senegal before returning to the US.

"At Cornell, I had taken a class in international development taught by Professor John Mellor who was on the IVS Board at that time. Don Luce came to campus and spoke to the class. Don also tried to recruit me to go to Southeast Asia like my friends but I wanted to work in Africa and declined. I also turned down a Peace Corps position in Guinea and returned home to work on the farm."

THE ALGERIA TEAM

Then Goodrich received a letter from IVS offering him a position on the Algeria team. "I was elated and soon was off to Washington, D.C., for training. I joined IVS because I wanted to help others better their lives using my engineering training and my farm background. I am sure there was a sense of adventure and longing for travel as well.

"French language training started at 9 a.m. on July 29, 1963, in Washington, D.C., at the Foreign Languages Services. On August 26, we went to Fort Robinson, Nebraska, for Soil Conservation Service training. We arrived in Algeria on September 22, 1963."

Goodrich's IVS team was stationed in Tlemcen near the border with Morocco. This walled town was at the base of the Atlas Mountains and had been a resort town during the French era. They lived in an apartment in a group of buildings called the City of Cherries (*Citée des Cerises*). "Our projects were in the mountains northwest of Tlemcen. Each of the three IVS locations (Tlemcen, Orleansville, Tizi Ouzou) had one or two large Ford stake-body trucks for transporting tools and wheat. USAID provided each of us with an International Scout four-wheel drive vehicle. We also shared a Ford half-ton pickup. The local prefecture administration assisted us in finding housing, finding a place to store our equipment and to house our project vehicles, paying the cash from the Algerian government and smoothing out problems if they arose."

PICKS AND SHOVELS

Goodrich designed soil conservation measures for implementation by workers using picks and shovels. His team employed previously unemployed men on the projects near the villages where they lived. The village elders were consulted about what was going to be done and decided where the IVS team was to work.

"We worked with the *Bureau de l'eau et des forêts* (water and forests). They provided a supervisor who spoke French, as well as Arabic, for each individual project near a village. They directed what the workers did and how they did it after we explained how to do the work and in most cases placed survey markers for the work to be done."

The U.S. Soil Conservation Service advisors furnished leadership for the three individual locations and specific guidance for the overall projects. USAID provided the wheat and oil that was half the pay for the workers. "The other half was supposed to be dinars paid by the Algerian government and for the most part was paid, but usually late so the workers were behind all the time. Our daily regimen was to visit one of the worksites each of us supervised. Usually that involved driving for at least an hour out to the site, evaluating what was being done, laying out and surveying more work, having tea with the workers and driving the narrow mountain roads back to town."

Goodrich saw progress when, "the workers' homes were being improved and their clothing was less tattered. Some workers were able to buy a donkey to transport materials to the land they were farming or to pull a wooden plow. The most satisfying situation was when we saw farmers in a neighboring location employ some of the changes we had introduced."

LESS EROSION

"We provided work for a lot of people in a meaningful way. They were paid for their work and improved themselves and their villages. The hillsides gained trees and were having less erosion. Farmland was returned to productivity. We did some extension teaching by using good practices that the farmers could implement on farms beyond our project area."

In the spring of 1965, Goodrich was asked by IVS Washington to return to the U.S. and recruit/interview students at a number of universities. "There were no returned volunteers with

Algerian experience, and we needed more volunteers. The timing made this a challenging and stressful task; since it was close to the end of the school year there were demonstrations against the Vietnam War on many campuses. I did meet a significant number of students who volunteered for IVS.

"When I was planning the recruiting trip back to the states, I traveled from Algiers to Paris, to New York and to Washington, D.C. When I arrived in Washington, walking down the street I met a Palestinian student whom I had roomed with in the IVS house in Algiers. What are the odds of that?"

When Goodrich returned to the U.S. from Algeria, he got married and began graduate school at Purdue University, then moved to the University of Minnesota and retired in 2008 after thirty-eight years as an engineering professor. "I've used my IVS experience in my teaching, research and extension positions.

"I remain amazed and appreciative that IVS gave young men and women the opportunity to take on responsibility that would not have been possible in the U.S. I was a young engineer, fresh out of college. I was responsible for designing projects that employed about 500 men each day. We had to manage the projects, take care of logistics, do the surveying, do quality control and also transport the wheat and oil that was used to pay the workers. That experience profoundly influenced my professional career."

Tom Gist served in Tlemcen as well. A born agriculturist from Tulare County, California, he learned about IVS when a former volunteer visited Fresno State University where Gist was getting his BS in Mechanized Agriculture, with a minor in engineering. "My faculty advisor introduced us and I eventually applied to IVS. Just before graduating, I was offered an assignment in Cambodia and Vietnam, but I turned down the offer because of the location.

"Several months after graduation, *Gordon Brockmueller*, who was with USAID/IVS, interviewed me in San Francisco for future IVS possible assignments. He mentioned that the following Monday, a group was to start training to go to Algeria for a soil and water conservation work development program. Within two weeks, I was in Washington, D.C., to join the group for the last few weeks of language classes and then on to Fort Robinson, Nebraska, for a month of concentrated soil and water conservation training, which was exactly what I was interested in."

He arrived in Algiers on September 22, 1963, where he spent a number of weeks before being sent to his duty station. The U.S. Department of Agriculture (USDA) Soil Conservation Service had assigned highly experienced senior specialists as team project leaders for each of the three IVS locations, and two engineers, a plant materials specialist and two agronomists were shared among the three locations. "Our team project leader and his wife were based in Tlemcen. He was the Assistant State Conservationist from Virginia, and they became almost like second parents to me, even long after I returned from Algeria.

"We each had multiple projects, some with as many as 500 workers and others with less than twenty-five. In some of the local and poorer villages we did some independent work such as supplying bags of cement to repair and put a roof on a two-room school."

It wasn't all work. "Fun activities included going to the Mediterranean for beach time, playing a little tennis on old clay courts, and sightseeing. I played on the local basketball team and a Frenchman and I were the only non-Algerians. The team was in a league that traveled to play in other towns. Outdoor courts were the norm but in Oran, the court was in a large and very impressive indoor gymnasium. One winter, we traveled for two weeks across Northern Algeria and then South into the Sahara Desert. We went to Morocco many times as well as to Malaga and Marbella in Spain, sailing on a passenger ship from Northeastern Morocco to Malaga over Friday night and sailing back Sunday night to be back at our projects by Monday noon."

COUP D'ÉTAT

One summer, when Gist went to Europe, "There was a *coup d'état* in Algeria and President Ben Bella was overthrown. Security was very tight when I landed in Oran. I had foolishly purchased some fireworks in Europe for the upcoming July 4th celebration with the Americans in Algeria. I was terrified of what was going to happen as the guards inspected my baggage. My main suitcase had the fireworks but I also had purchased a carton of Winston cigarettes for some of the Algerians I knew that smoked. The cigarettes were found first and the inspector made quite a scene. The head of security was called over, and I was sure I would be detained overnight or go to jail. We recognized each other; he was one of the basketball players from Oran that we had played against. He closed up my suitcase without further inspection and wished me well."

Gist recalls that project work at Tlemcen was fairly basic. "Picks, shovels and wheelbarrows were the primary tools on the projects. Some masonry work was done by the more skilled workers. While some of the bags of cement for the projects seemed to disappear, we knew (and the workers knew we knew) that they were put to perhaps greater use in the small villages since cement was prized for rebuilding the mud and rock shanties. Sometimes we would have 'extra' pine and fruit trees that would end up being planted and carefully maintained by workers at their homes.

"The fact the men could work, be paid for their efforts, see progress and accomplishments and benefit financially, made our involvement meaningful to them and to us. Their lives and their families were made better. Because of the employment, you would see villagers buying more bread, flour, chickens, goats, seasonings for their meals and cones of sugar for their mint teas. Eight to ten of them would occasionally cram into one old taxi to visit friends and relatives and make purchases."

Initially, villagers were skeptical of the volunteers and the projects, since, "It was hard to sell or see the value of soil conservation when you are living a subsistence type of life. Over time they welcomed us into their villages, included us in festivities and special occasions. Possibly, we had an impact as Americans by just being ourselves and appreciating the moment. I recall a villager saying he had a brother in America and when I asked where, he said Cuba."

Gist extended his IVS tour for an additional two months and wanted to stay longer but his local draft board would not extend his job deferment. He returned to the USA and, "I was more concerned about safety walking around New York City by myself than I was walking through the souks or kasbahs of Algiers."

In January he was admitted to graduate school at Fresno State and received a six-months deferment. He then served with the National Guard. There followed several years of work with the Soil Conservation Service and the Federal Land Bank Association in Sacramento. Eventually, Gist ended up in Washington, D.C., at the Farm Credit Administration, the Federal Government Regulator of the Farm Credit System.

Also spending time in Algeria was *Otis Hayes*, a volunteer stationed in Souk Ahras at a center for orphans. "The center was housed at an old French military outpost. The director had a staff of two teaching assistants, two seamstresses, and an aged gardener. I was a teacher. The center was destitute and received virtually no funding from the government. We got a little money to get some food but that was about it. There were little to no educational materials. God blessed us in the person of Dr. Richard Brace and his wife Joan, visiting professors from Northwestern University who gave us a $10,000 donation. That enabled us to start some animal husbandry projects and a vegetable garden. With guidance from other members of the IVS team and a nearby Mennonite mission, I ordered some chickens, sheep, and goats. The idea was to raise the sheep and goats for their offspring. The chickens were there for eggs and for meat."

USAID had some wheat condemned as unfit for human consumption. "After much begging, we got them to give it to our center for animal feed. With the wheat and the animals, we were finally able to do something positive which offered a great deal of hope to the seventy children aged five to eighteen years."

RABID DOG

"Sadly, I was forced to leave by the outbreak of hostilities between the Egyptians and the Israelis. I departed Algeria and took a long way home via Morocco and France. I enjoyed my IVS assignment and learned a lot from it. I sharpened my French language skills and learned basic Maghrebian Arabic. My most interesting experience is that I was bitten by a possibly rabid stray dog. I started taking rabies shots at the local hospital where they were using a Russian vaccine. I notified IVS/Algiers and they arranged for the U.S. Consul Lannon Walker to drive to Souk Ahras with flags flying from his official car. He took me back to Constantine. I stayed at his residence for the three weeks it took to complete my series of shots in the gut."

Dorothy Young worked more than six years in Algeria from 1965 to 1971. She was two years with the Quaker American Friends Service Committee as a community development volunteer in Skikda, one year as an IVS teacher of English as a Foreign Language volunteer in Batna, one year as a teacher and IVS/ Algeria Country Director in Algiers, and two years as Assistant to the Algerian Inspector of English and IVS Country Director.

SUPER-VOLUNTEERS

"The IVS program began and remained small with English teachers scattered throughout this huge country at the secondary school and some at the university level. We added two ag positions with super-volunteers *Amal Chatterjee* and *Antoine Nzima* from Angola. Some male volunteers were seeking alternative service. Some had served previously with the Peace Corps. We had two married couples. All volunteers spoke French."

Young went to Algeria immediately after completing her graduate studies on the Middle East and looked upon the experience as both a continuation of her education and an opportunity to develop her understanding of the Arab world, "Which has been my interest and passion for as long as I can remember," she said.

"The program in Algeria, unbeknownst to me, was a sort of landmark agreement in the midst of a great debate on what IVS's relationship should be to the U.S. government, especially in Southeast Asia. In the field, we had the view that IVS/Algeria was an Algerian program, paid for by the Algerians, and it was practically self-sufficient. The Algerians provided our lodging, and this often meant weeks to months *without* lodging. Algeria paid our stipend. It was generally a huge hassle—first to get paid and then to try to expatriate any savings to the US."

The Algerian Ministry of Education wanted to replace all the French *coopérants* with native English speakers and requested a minimum of fifty IVSers. IVS averaged up to fifteen volunteer teachers a year. Reception in the classroom was favorable, though classes were very overcrowded and sometimes there were no books. "*I write a letter posing as an American high school student and they write responses to him. Their letters are full and enthusiastic. Amazing what one can come up with when he lacks a text and faces the same forty kids three times a week,*" wrote Neal King. "*The students are full of tremendous amounts of energy which erupts as discipline problems,*" wrote Carol Soltysik. "*They have an unbounded energy level; they are anxious to learn at the lower levels. However raucous, they do appreciate a good teacher,*" wrote Fred Soltysik. "*They're very quick. Their enthusiasm is stimulating to me as a teacher,*" noted Warren Helman.

In addition to managing the IVS program, Young taught English, assisted the national Inspector in developing English language books for every *lycée* in the country, developed a weekly English language radio program, and helped develop training programs for Algerian English teachers.

Eldridge Cleaver

Young recalls, "One of my more interesting experiences came following a knock on the door of my little apartment in Algiers. It was American refugee Black Panther Eldridge Cleaver, the author of *Soul on Ice*, who wanted to alert me to a problem with one of our volunteers in the western part of the country. Many IVS/Algeria volunteers were attracted to the then-revolutionary political stance of the country. One, Mr. Cleaver warned, was unaware that he was getting unwanted attention from the secret police and I should get on this issue right away."

Small Teams

In 1965, a pair of teachers went to Sabah in Malaysia for two years to teach civil servants English.

In 1966, another team of teachers was assigned to the **Sudan**, beginning sixteen years of renewed IVS efforts in the southern part of that warring nation. Fewer than fifty volunteers were assigned in Sudan over the years, so each of the teams was small.

A range management program was opened in Morocco in 1967, and in 1969, an agricultural credit program began in the Congo. The first team in the Congo was evacuated during the revolution in 1970 but would return to the renamed country, Zaire, for three more years.

A two-man agricultural team was in Libya for two years beginning in 1971, and a public health and agricultural development program opened in Yemen, to which small individual teams were assigned for the next eight years.

Nine countries received IVS volunteers during this decade, and four programs, which had begun in the first decade, continued.

Harpers Ferry

In 1971 a conference was held at Harpers Ferry, West Virginia, to consider an enhanced role for IVS in the 1970s. Participants included staff, Board of Directors and Advisory Committee members as well as former volunteers.

Saul Chafkin, President of the American Technical Assistance Corporation, the consulting firm that prepared the report, *New Directions in International Voluntary Services*, suggested possible models for the future. These included the AID Model, which assumed that there was enough funding to operate effectively with AID funding, and the International Model, which recognized that, as many countries are uncomfortable dealing with United States government agencies working within their borders, IVS might become an organization with multiple sources of international funding.

The attendees asked themselves three basic questions:

1. Did volunteer work abroad (recognized as declining at the time of the meeting) have an important role in the 1970s;

2. If so, did IVS have a significant contribution to make in coming years; and

3. Should that be the case, what changes are required of IVS to make it responsive to the new era?

Two primary decisions were reached: That IVS must broaden its financial base so that fifty-one percent of its funding might be obtained from sources other than the U.S. government; and that IVS must diversify its programs in Asia, Africa, and Latin America. A third resolution was that IVS must strive to achieve multinational representation among volunteers, Board and staff.

Regarding Southeast Asia in particular, the IVS Board recognized "the problems and risks inherent in working in a country torn by civil and/or international war, particularly when the American government is involved." It then decided to reevaluate the situation in the coming year and, if the situation had not improved by then, allow programs to continue until the volunteers' contracts expired.

The minutes of the *IVS in the 1970s* meeting conclude with: "IVS consciously remains in low profile in Indochina in the hope that expanded program commensurate with the IVS model for the 1970s will be possible in the future and that, in the meantime, we can provide effective service to the Vietnamese and Lao people."

Sadly, the conclusions reached would in time prove not enough to ensure IVS' future.

Carl Jantzen and workers at the IVS center in Iraq, 1954

Carl Jantzen and Iraqi Kurds with seed cleaner in village near Sulaimaniya, Iraq, 1954

From left to right, Don Goodfellow, Carl Jantzen, Rud Ham, Jim Baile, Peter Barwick, in Iraq, 1954.

Roderick MacRae teaches arts and crafts in a teacher's college in Pakse, Laos, 1961

Howie Lewin testing a bucket pump made of bamboo, rope, and salvaged lumber, 1964

Susan Roberts with student nurses in Thakhek, Laos, 1966

Paul White, IVS volunteer, creates a rope climb for a playground project, Laos, 1966.

Frank Bewetz helps build a school in Kengkok, Laos, 1966

Robert Zigler and worker examine a sick chicken at Savannakhet Poultry Station, Laos, 1966

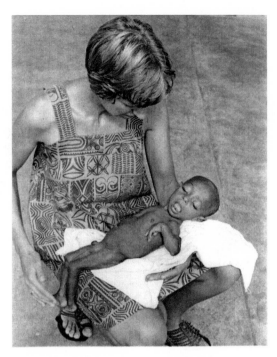

Nutritionist Marian Cast with a malnourished child in Papua
New Guinea, 1978

Hostel in Bangladesh. IVS Volunteer Caroline Corbould and coworkers, 1980

Amal Chatterjee, second from left, and Algerian workers transplant rice in Algeria, 1971

Yoshikazu Itoh and Engineer Giovani Quaglia discuss a water tank project in Yemen, 1973

Weighing supplies at the Project Development Unit, Yei, Southern Sudan, 1977

IVS Volunteer Beth Terry with Botswana basket weavers, 1980

Volunteer Vitalis Mukwewa explains organic pesticide production in Zimbabwe, 1992

Volunteer Carlos Munoz, at right, and two local farmers outside the original Cungapiti cheese factory he helped create in southern Ecuador, 1966. In 1990 the factory processed 120 liters of milk a day into cheese. This rose to 600 liters a day by 1996. The new factory processes 3000 liters of milk a day into cheese, yoghurt and caramel spread

Volunteers Eugenia DePedro and Tom Schenk teach gardeners in Ecuador, 1980

Bolivia Senor de Mayo Handcraft Office in 1993

THE THIRD DECADE
1973–1982

BANGLADESH · ALGERIA · INDONESIA · CONGO (ZAIRE) BOTSWANA · ECUADOR · BOLIVIA

BY 1973, INTERNATIONAL VOLUNTARY SERVICES was in trouble. Vietnam and Laos had drained the organization's human and financial resources, and it had become untenable to continue hosting most programs in either country. As these nations' situations deteriorated and the safety of volunteers could no longer be insured, IVS found it necessary to end its projects there or shift them over to the care of other, larger aid organizations. Then, the immediate challenge facing IVS became finding new sources of funding that would allow it to continue its work without as large a dependence on USAID grants.

At the same time, an incredible opportunity arose: That of helping a new nation, Bangladesh, establish itself in one of the poorest and most disaster-prone regions of the world.

BANGLADESH

The creation of Bangladesh was the end result of tensions between East and West Pakistan, a nation divided by vast geographic and cultural differences, as well as wildly uneven economies. East Pakistan seceded in early 1971 to form what was essentially a Bengali nation. Civil war soon erupted and within nine months, with the help of India, East Pakistan defeated West Pakistan. In 1974, Pakistan recognized the independent state of Bangladesh.

The new country was steeped in uncertainty, victim of coups and political assassinations, and its economy was in shambles as graft and corruption reigned.

At the time, *Char Cuento-Jeggle* was a graduate of the University of the Philippines and a research assistant at its Los Banos campus. After spending six years there with the Training Section and acting as liaison between IVS and the University, Cuento-Jeggle applied to work with IVS in Vietnam and Laos, just when the organization was cutting back its operations in those countries.

Then, in 1972, she received a cable from *Dick Peters*, the IVS Executive Director. The message read: "IVS planning initiative of five people in Bangladesh by July 1. Have interesting position in Dacca (now Dhaka) for you. Please confirm interest and availability. Letter follows..."

"Although I was enjoying my job," Cuento-Jeggle remembered, "Los Banos was by then too small for me. It was a cosmopolitan town with an international faculty, scientists and students, but it was also a university town with a parochial, academic focus. I needed a change. To most Filipinos, the place to seek career advancement was in North America or Western Europe. This often meant obtaining a PhD and becoming a professor, and the academic rat race was not my goal in life. I thought a country like Bangladesh, which had been devastated by floods and a war, was a place where I could work, offer my services, and thus find change. When I accepted the IVS position, my job was described as helping set up an IVS office and then looking for suitable volunteer work."

She arrived in Bangladesh in July, 1972, with only a three months contract, due to the uncertain political situation. "I had heard about the strained relationship between IVS and USAID in Laos and Vietnam. IVS was operating in those countries under a USAID contract, which set limits on its programming and personnel, and this was resented by both IVS volunteers and staff. I did not want to be a part of a similar relationship involving IVS in Bangladesh, and I was relieved to find that instead of a restrictive contract, we had a more open grant."

DOUBLE CROPPING

Bangladesh was far from an idyllic posting. The annual per capita income was only $63. Fifty-seven percent of the GNP was from agriculture, which employed eighty-five percent of the labor force. Thirty percent of rural workers were unemployed. The average land holding was two-and-a-half acres. Twenty-two million acres were under cultivation, but only one million were irrigated. The rice yield per acre was only half a ton and double cropping was practiced in only thirty percent of the cultivated area. There were seventy-five million inhabitants in a country the size of Wisconsin and the population density was 1,350 per square mile. The annual population growth was 3.1 percent, which translated to 14,000 new babies born every single day.

IVS involvement in Bangladesh began in early 1972, when the Ministry of Local Government, Rural Development, and Cooperatives requested that IVS provide mid-level technicians to five institutions. The primary purpose was to help farmers and small wage earners. The first five IVSers who came to Bangladesh were *Dick Peters, John Mellor, Warren "Bud" Day, Steve Ford* and Cuento-Jeggle. Edgar Owens, a retired USAID official who had worked in East Pakistan, came to help the group. "We drew up twenty-three volunteer job descriptions for our five counterpart Bangladesh institutions," Cuente-Jeggles said. "After six weeks of setting up IVS administrative and financial systems, all of them left the country to return to other jobs, except for me. I began working part-time at one of the five institutions, the Integrated Rural Development Program (IRDP), and I did some volunteer work as well, handling IVS affairs."

In September 1972, *Winburn Thomas* came to Bangladesh as the new IVS Director, and with his arrival, the second phase of the USAID grant for that country began. This included the placement of volunteers in Bangladesh institutions. The task proved to be difficult.

"First," said Cuento-Jeggle, "few IVS applicants were qualified for the positions required. Second, the process of getting applicants approved by the government took a long time. It was not easy adjusting to Bangladesh. The country had a conservative Islamic culture. Change occurred so slowly as to be barely noticeable. It required great patience, and the attrition rate for expatriate Private Voluntary Organization (PVO) personnel was quite high. With all this in mind, we believed that the best IVS volunteers would be mature and experienced, as opposed to those fresh from college and eager to change the world overnight. The screening of IVS applicants was quite challenging. I sat in judgment as to which applicant best fit each available job."

SUBTLE PRESSURE

By the end of 1972, there was subtle pressure from the Bangladesh government for IVS to prove itself. "IVS found itself in a Catch-22 situation. It couldn't prove itself worthy unless it had volunteers in place. But volunteer placement couldn't proceed unless the applicants were approved by bureaucrats in the various ministries and getting anything approved by the government was a major frustration."

The Bangladesh government was weak; many of its trained civil servants had either been trapped in Pakistan or killed in the recent war, and those in service were disorganized, untrained, and worried about holding on to their jobs. Junior and mid-level officials refused to make any decisions and it was said that if a junior bureaucrat made one wrong choice, he would be fired the same day. So bringing IVS volunteers into the country was a long, tedious process.

"During our first year it involved our host Ministry, the Home Ministry, and the Office of the Coordinator of External Assistance for Relief and Rehabilitation. The process was actually made even more complicated by our needing the approval of the Ministry of Foreign Affairs and the Planning Commission. Theoretically approval was easy. But correspondence was often lost, or it took four to eight weeks to travel from one office to another."

Once IVS volunteers were in the country, their visas were extended every three months, and even the extension process involved five offices. "There was an incredible amount of paperwork. Then there were the files—large green folders tied with red tape, the most disheartening symbol of Bangladesh bureaucracy. They were generally kept on open shelves but since there was always a shortage of shelf space, files ended up on the floor and stacked up high along the walls. Seeing those files was perhaps my greatest Bangladesh culture shock. There was probably a method in their filing system, but I never figured out what it was."

Red tape became the too-obvious symbol of a slow-moving bureaucracy. In late October of 1972, at the end of her three months, Cuento-Jeggle signed a longer contract and was reclassified as staff. As Program Officer, the responsibilities remained the same—basically to do whatever was needed to make IVS operational.

BOARDING HOUSES

"During this early period, the IVS office was anywhere we were living. We each moved from one boarding house to another, and we used either the slow-moving bicycle rickshaw or the faster but more dangerous motorized version. We needed an office, a staff house, and also a vehicle. With the influx of thousands of foreign aid workers and their dependents, finding housing in Dhaka was a major problem."

The first vehicle acquired was a VW microbus they dubbed the 'war victim'. It took six weeks to get permission from the appropriate ministries to buy it from the Ford Foundation. It took the Ford Foundation seven weeks to get permission to sell the vehicle, and these approvals could not be applied for simultaneously. November 1972 was memorable. Apart from

acquiring the VW, and leasing a house to serve as an office, staff
residence, and volunteer hostel, Cuento-Jeggles came down with
hepatitis.

In 1973 IVS/Bangladesh became operational as the first five
volunteers were approved by the government. *Mike* and *Susan
Carlton* arrived in January, followed by *Jon* and *Polly Griffith* and
Ian Wilkins in February. All were assigned to the Comilla institutions. (The Comilla Model was a two-part cooperative approach
to rural development. Farmers, fishermen, artisans, and special
groups such as rickshaw pullers formed their own co-ops at the
village level. These co-ops were then federated at the 'thana' level,
an administrative area of about 120 villages.) *Mildred* and *Ralph
Townsend*, and *Romana Padlan* arrived in April. Ralph Townsend
was assigned to the National Cooperative Union in Dhaka, and
the two women joined the first Comilla team.

After a year's presence in Bangladesh, Cuento-Jeggle remembers, IVS "was no longer an obscure little PVO. In fact a number
of government officials were coming to the IVS House to seek
our advice and opinions. The PVOs wanted to avoid competition
and to speak as one voice in dealing with the government when
the need arose. We helped form the Association of Voluntary
Agencies in Bangladesh. *Winburn Thomas* was one of its leaders,
and he soon became 'Dean' of the PVO community. During this
era of inter-organizational cooperation, IVS received requests for
volunteer placements from other PVOs."

THE NEXT CHAPTER

Life in Bangladesh had its interesting moments. *Benedict Tisa*,
who served there from 1974 to 1976: "In 1974 my wife Margaret,
our six-month-old daughter Antoinette, and I arrived in Dhaka,
Bangladesh. We had been Peace Corps volunteers in West Africa
and felt that we were prepared for this next chapter of our life.
We knew that times were difficult in Bangladesh, but nevertheless
felt that here we could do something that had meaning. USAID
had approached IVS to supply a volunteer who could help
with the development of educational materials and non-formal

educational methods for the government's Integrated Rural Development Program. IVS responded with me. I made my own program with other aid organizations such as CARE, the Mennonites, and Save the Children. My wife taught English at a local school. I can vividly recall our arrival at the Dhaka airport—stepping onto the rolled-up airplane stairs and being struck by the moist heat. Margaret and I looked out over the cracked tarmac at buildings streaked with mold from the humidity. We turned to each other and said almost in unison, 'I don't know if we'll be able to deal with this place.'"

As it turned out, they came to feel part of "this overpopulated little spot of land that was the wettest of the wet and the driest of the dry, a land bursting with hungry, unemployed people who would recite poetry at the slightest suggestion, and a land with a million varieties of fish, all tasting a bit like the muddy rivers where they'd been caught."

TANKS

And then there was the revolution. "At dawn on August 15, 1975, I was awakened by a sound like popping firecrackers. There were little high-pitched pops followed by short booms and then a ticking of machine guns. Just two blocks away the government had been overthrown. The President and all his family had been killed and a new government born. A tank blocked off our road and the bridge that led to the President's house. Soldiers were milling about with automatic weapons. A curfew was initiated, but no one really knew what was happening, least of all me. Starting at 8:30 a.m., there had been gunshots, large house-shaking booms, and the rumbling of tanks. Then all was quiet. The tank waiting at the end of the road turned off its engine and stood watch at the crossroads."

Tisa went out to the yard, transplanted his sweet potatoes, and put some houseplants out in the sun. The streets were empty. Radios hummed with the news, calling for all citizens to stay inside and observe martial law. The revolution had taken place only 200 yards from his front door, "but it felt like 200 years away. The sun came out and a scattered rain settled the dust stirred up by the tanks. The tank guarding the bridge to our house moved down the road, grunting and groaning under its load of armor and clinging soldiers. More pops drifted through the air, and the radio played nationalistic songs. Another tank up the road approached, chewing up the newly tarmacked road. Earlier when I went outside, this tank had looked like a national monument, all olive drab and squat with its guns poking out into the morning air. Now children were playing on its turrets. Another tank pulled into our dirt yard, turned around, and plodded up the road out of sight. Across the lake, the banks were crowded with spectators jumping and scattering with every pop and crackle of the automatic weapons, only to regroup and look on as their revolution progressed. Food merchants began to mingle with the masses. Everyone outside could look in at the revolution, but we on Road 32 in the center of the action, couldn't see anything."

A variety of IVS programs were established in Bangladesh. One, by IVS and another NGO, Friends in Village Development, involved raising ducks. Said *Jan Emmert*, an IVSer who participated in setting up the project, "It became very common in the areas suitable ecologically to see landless families herding sizable duck flocks. Duck eggs in the Sylhet area were preferred over chicken eggs and sold at a higher price." This program has survived to this day. (See Appendix III.)

William Hutchins was a twenty-three-year-old farm boy with a brand new college education in June 1975. His life plan was to return to the sort of agriculture he knew—irrigated row-crop production and pigs in Western Colorado—when he came upon a classified ad in his mother's horticultural magazine asking for horticulturists and agriculturists to volunteer for overseas work. He applied to IVS and was accepted.

The first proposed assignment was Mauritania but Hutchins' French was not fluent enough. Then, toward the end of 1976, an opening appeared in Bangladesh and within a week he was on his way. He arrived in Dhaka in time to celebrate the U.S. bicentennial birthday at the American embassy.

"My original job description was a horticulturist to continue John and Vi Peak's work in Dinajpur in the northwest part of the country. John's promotion to IVS Director in Bangladesh left open the position I filled. John and Vi were a husband and wife team; she was a nurse, he was a horticulturist whose program was a prenatal-infant health and nutrition project funded by USAID. They worked with CORR (Christian Organization for Relief and Rehabilitation) in the country. I became the horticulturist but IVS was unable to keep a nurse in Dinajpur and the program was allowed to expire."

GREEN REVOLUTION

In the meantime, Hutchins followed "my natural inclination to grow irrigated corn and wheat during the dry season. This put me in ever closer contact with the Swiss Caritas (a Swiss NGO) people who had a large agricultural project at the Rajbari Farm in Dinajpur. Their major focus was 'Green Revolution' agriculture.

"They had a four-person team of Swiss agricultural experts to implement the project, but the four and their families were unable to work smoothly together. Three were unceremoniously returned to Switzerland ten months after I arrived. Their extension expert was appointed director of the whole project and he was alone! I was there! I had the right qualifications, enjoyed Bangladesh, liked the people, by then spoke some Bengali, and my program was being de-funded. It was perfect fit!"

While still an IVS volunteer, Hutchins worked for Caritas as their farm manager during the 1977 wet season When the dry season started, he moved to the extension program and stayed until the end of his contract.

"Two of my favorite crops, corn and wheat, were then, and still are, greatly impacted by the Green Revolution. Corn was not much of a success in Bangladesh. As an animal feed for pigs in an

Islamic country it was a nonstarter, and it couldn't be used with chickens since it was too hard to keep them alive or from being stolen. It simply was not a good resource fit for the country."

Wheat however was a different matter altogether. Irrigated spring wheat grown during the dry season would do very well. The Bengalis were familiar with irrigation. "The trouble was they wished to irrigate rice during the dry season. That required a lot of pumping and fuel. Wheat had a much better ratio of fuel to food return. Bengalis were also familiar with wheat and flour. Chapattis and bread formed part of their diet and they knew milling of wheat to make flour."

The single biggest problem for wheat encountered in Dinajpur was maintaining seed viability from harvest to the next planting season. Rice was not a problem. Rice seed was held over the cool dry season and easily retained its vitality. Wheat seed, however, had to be held over the hot wet monsoon season and without help would be ruined by the next planting season.

"Caritas was working on a solution to this problem, and I was able to play a part. The project manager also knew about potatoes. There were very large refrigerated facilities for the storage of potatoes both for consumption and seed. These also worked very well to store wheat seed during the wet season.

"During the second dry season, I was to oversee as much wheat production as possible in the villages. Then, during harvest, purchase all wheat that was of a quality suitable for seed. We weighed the wheat, paid the farmers and organized transportation to the pre-cooling chambers." Caritas paid a good price for the wheat seed which generated enthusiasm for wheat cultivation the following dry season. That enthusiasm, combined with good available seed, made larger scale wheat production in the northwest part of Bangladesh possible.

STRICKEN VEHICLE

Hutchins remembers a situation that involved a broken down Jeep. A month or so after arriving in Bangladesh, he was in Dhaka for an IVS staff meeting. Later in the afternoon as the meetings were winding up for the day, one of the Jeep drivers came in to say an electrical short in a car's engine compartment had turned all of the wiring into a black, smoking, acrid smelling mess. The Jeep was miles outside Dhaka alongside the road and would be converted into spare parts as soon as the sun was down. "After talking to the driver, I thought I had a chance of driving the Jeep back under its own power. The driver and I took a bus to the stricken vehicle, where I salvaged a short strip of wire that I connected to the appropriate battery post and coil terminal. Then we asked several Bengalis standing around—there were always plenty of them watching in situations like this—to give us a good push! The Jeep started! We had no horn, lights, wind-shield wipers, dash indicators or ignition controls, but we were moving under our own power! We made it safely back to the IVS office in the gathering darkness. I could do no wrong after that, even to the extent of not submitting my monthly reports in a timely manner.

"I use this story to illustrate the necessity of knowing and understanding thoroughly whatever system an individual may be trying to exploit. Because from that familiarity a person can compromise, jerry-rig, modify, abuse, misuse and manipulate a system to achieve any number of desired outcomes."

Hutchins' contract with IVS ended during the wet season of 1978 as his life "was in the process of becoming fuller, richer and more complicated. Anna, a Swiss teacher for the Swiss families in Dinajpur, and I were to be married upon my return to the United States. She was determined that I pursue a Master's Degree, which was a difficult adjustment. Submitting to the rigors of academic discipline was not easy after two years as a very lightly supervised, free-wheeling volunteer in Dinajpur, determined to have as much fun as possible."

ALGERIA

Amal Chatterjee, an IVSer who'd served in Vietnam from 1967 to 1969, answered the call once again and in 1971 found himself in Algeria. Arriving at the Dar El Beida airport of Algiers one afternoon in September, he found the custom authorities a bit wary about the things foreigners brought into their country. "The officer wanted to charge me hefty duty on my slide projector and the camera. I managed to slip out quietly when the fellow was distracted by something or someone."

The next day Chatterjee went to see the personnel officer at the Ministry of Agriculture in Algiers. The man turned out to be less than welcoming. "He ranted that the country would soon have its own agronomists and not need any foreigners! It did not bode well for a person of my experience and education, but the mood in the country seemed to be nasty and he was simply mouthing the unofficial line.

"I began to wonder if I had made a mistake coming to Algeria. The Algerian bureaucrats did not seem to be very friendly. But the Deputy Director of the ministry was more polished. He received us warmly and said that it would be better for me to go to Tizi Ouzou in the Kabyle Mountains not too far from Algiers. He felt that the isolation in Setif, which was supposed to be my destination, would be too hard on a bachelor like me."

Tizi Ouzou is about 100 km east of Algiers and mountainous. It is a small town surrounded by hills and mountains that are always covered with snow in the winter. The southern side of the Djurdjura is where the Sahara desert begins, but the narrow land between the mountains and the coast is fertile and green. This is where winter wheat, barley, oats, corn and a variety of other crops are irrigated and grown. In fact this agricultural land covers millions of hectares and appeared more than adequate for Algeria's small population. Chatterjee began to wonder at the wisdom of being sent to Tizi Ouzou.

MORNING EXERCISE

"I liked the cold crisp mountain air and used to get up at 6 a.m., put on my shorts, tennis shoes and gloves because it was so cold in the morning, and run down four flights of stairs and down the valley where I practiced some calisthenics and other morning exercise. The Algerians watched and soon got used to this routine. Then I would buy a liter of milk, run upstairs and shower, eat a hearty breakfast and go to my office.

"I started going out with my counterpart in his tiny Renault 4 and got to know the province well in a short time, but all I saw was olives. Why did they send me here? I was a field agronomist in a mountain province. It didn't make sense."

The province was divided into districts, and each district contained state-run farms run by managers who answered to their supervisors, who in turn depended on their laborers for plowing, planting, and harvesting. "So when the agriculture office called the districts, they called the farm managers who then called the supervisors who told them that approximately so many hectares of wheat or barley were planted. The fact was, no one really knew; it was just guesswork."

This data would be meticulously compiled and sent to the Ministry every week. All the provinces in Algeria were required to do this, tying up thousands of people in useless unproductive work. What the ministry did with this massive amount of data was a mystery. "The sheer stupidity of it all appalled me," remembered Chatterjee, "but woe to you if your data were not ready when the Ministry called.

"I started to plan on how to get out of Tizi Ouzou, so I wrote a letter to the Ministry to ask for a transfer to an area where rice was grown. I had a lot of experience in rice research and could be useful to them. To my surprise they agreed and after six months in Tizi Ouzou, I was transferred to Mostaganem province in the west where a great deal of rice was grown."

Mostaganem was some 400 km west of Algiers, one of the bigger towns and on the coast. The nearest big city was Oran some eighty kilometers away.

Chatterjee requested IVS buy him a motorbike. "It was a big black and red and chrome MZ bike made in East Germany.

I loved it. I got a black leather jacket, helmet, leather gloves and goggles to go with it and would zoom past amused Algerians who told me I would fall down or catch pneumonia, and that it was not suitable for an *ingénieur*. To fight off the chill, I put thick newspaper inside my jacket, but I still could feel the cold. Once I fell off my bike on the road to Mascara because my fingers had become numb."

He remembers that, "I covered vast distances on my bike. My work at this time included rice research in the Oued Rhiou area, soybean, forage crops like trudan and fertilizer trials in Mascara and other districts. The deputy director asked if I could oversee the aerial fertilization program in the Mascara district. The vast state-owned farms of wheat and barley had to be fertilized from air using Antonov planes so I used to go very early before sunrise during the winter and supervise loading the hoppers with urea.

"The work was good and satisfying. I obtained excellent results sowing pre-germinated rice seeds using a seed drill. The fertilizer trials were also doing well."

Chatterjee's real interest was rice, so he moved to Oued Rhiou, a village a hundred kilometers east of Mostaganem where he found temporary shelter in a fertilizer storage room on a farm. The farm manager decided it was not right for an *ingénieur* to live in a storage depot and insisted Chatterjee move in with him.

The pre-germinated rice seeds came up and a mechanical weeder was used in between rows instead of herbicide. The work on soybean, forage grass and corn also progressed well. A French professor at the *Institut Technologique Agricole* of Mostaganem came to photograph the plants in the research plots to use them as teaching materials.

TIME WELL SPENT

"The work I enjoyed most was working with private farmers, most of whom, in Algeria, were doomed as the state acquired the best lands, leaving the *fellahins* the unwanted acreage for wheat, barley or other crops. I partnered with an expert who was working with the private farmers in Mascara and helping with the fertilizer trials."

Chatterjee was with farmers in Mostaganem almost eighteen months and believes his time was well spent. "I can proudly say that they all told me at one time or other they benefited from my work with them: New high-yielding crop varieties, new ways to grow them and many such things were taken up by the farmers. In some countries like Mali and Sudan I was not able to do as much as I wanted due to reasons beyond my control. I do not regret going to those countries but only the missed opportunities there."

Chatterjee was amazed by what he saw as a "colossal waste of manpower in collecting useless data. The system did not permit any deviation and initiatives were ignored. One could not go anywhere without the *ordre de mission* that had to be signed, stamped and entered in a log book."

Shortly after Chatterjee ended his years in Algeria, *Tina Martin* arrived in Medea to begin her IVS assignment there. The first few days were daunting. "I was told that Algerian men assumed any young unmarried woman who comes to Algeria was coming only because she hadn't gotten enough satisfaction back home and was after the beautiful bodies of the Algerian men. I'd heard that no woman could be taken seriously unless she was wrapped in white cloth, and with only eyes showing. Even then she wasn't taken seriously except as somebody else's property... I'd been told these things and had been advised on how to walk (like an Army sergeant), talk (seldom and little), and look (as plain and serious as possible). I gave up all my make-up, including my gorgeous green eye-shadow. Indeed life was difficult for an unmarried woman."

No Socializing

There was little or no socializing with members of the opposite sex, and friendliness was often misinterpreted. Martin knew not to smile too much or talk too readily. In a letter home, she wrote,

"My present life includes teaching eighteen hours a week. I'm also keeping a teacher's journal (which might be useful for my Master's thesis), studying Arabic with a private tutor, speaking French most the time (something I love), getting to know an Algerian family, traveling all over Algeria (tomorrow I'm off to famous Roman ruins), going to France in the summer, transferring what I can to a savings account for post-graduate work, and not being miserable. So far the Algerian people have been not only respectful, but kind and helpful. I use the little Arabic I know whenever the occasion presents itself, and sometimes when it doesn't. My repertoire takes all of twenty minutes: 'I'm a teacher and I live in Algeria. There's bread and butter on the table. I'm tired but I'm not fat. I drink coffee with sugar and milk...' Just the sort of thing to make me a brilliant conversationalist. I'm ecstatic when the Algerians even recognize that I'm speaking their language. When they understand what I'm saying, I'm absolutely floored. They seem to be impressed by my twenty minutes of Arabic, probably because most foreigners in Medea never learn any Arabic at all."

Martin taught at the Lycée Bencheneb. From her letters home: *"I'm the first to arrive at school, so I ask for the key to the teacher's room, where I take off my coat and put on a white overblouse similar to the model some teachers wear to make them look more serious than they really are. Mine has been newly mended by my students whose sewing skills are much more impressive than their occasional stabs at English. One day, when I wore a blouse they didn't like, they asked me (not in English) to wear the other one because it was much more becoming. I explained that the purpose of the blouse wasn't to be stylish but, in fact, to conceal any style I might have. They are nice girls, always ready to give you their favorite recipes and opinions, solicited or not, but determined not to speak a word of English. If you're lucky, they'll speak French, but they don't care for French either so most of the time they speak in Arabic."*

Martin discovered that one way to engage her recalcitrant

students was to ask whether they'd been to Mecca. "This is a subject the students actually like to talk about. All things related to Algeria's religion, language, independence, cuisine or history, motivate them to define and explain and describe—as if they had just gotten a national identity and wanted to put it to use."

SUDAN

AN AMERICAN WOMAN IN SUDAN

MARY L. DUNDAS

I stepped off the plane in mid-August, 1973, and walked into heat that was like an oven. I had arrived in Khartoum, Sudan, where I planned to work for IVS as coordinator of the eight IVS instructors who taught at Ahfad College. Ahfad was the first institution of higher education for women and offered a four-year degree. I had endured a long sleepless flight from Athens to Khartoum in the middle of the night when a very drunk man who sat opposite me on the plane lifted the tray table with his food and beverage on it. The food went all over the floor and almost hit me.

Although alcohol is forbidden for practicing Muslims, there were many men who were having their last drink before they returned to Sudan.

Sudan is the largest country in Africa, with Egypt on the north, the Red Sea and Ethiopia on the east, and Kenya and Uganda to the south. There are nine nations that share a border with Sudan. The White Nile flows through the southern part of the country and the Blue Nile originates in Ethiopia. The two rivers flow north to their confluence at Khartoum.

After serving in Vietnam from 1966 to 1968, I went to graduate school in Washington, D.C., to obtain a degree in education and then planned to return to Southeast Asia. When IVS suggested I go to Sudan, I had several questions, such as, "How could a Christian woman live and work in North Sudan, which is primarily Islamic in faith? Would I be treated as a woman, or as a second class citizen? Do I really want to live in a desert for two years where everything is the same tan color?" I went to Sudan because I still had the IVS spirit of helping others. John F. Kennedy's words were fresh in my mind, "Ask not what your country can do for you, but what you can do for your country."

My job as team leader for IVS was to communicate with IVS Washington every week, obtain our per diem from the Sudanese bank and distribute it to the volunteers, handle complaints and other problems, and represent IVS to the Sudanese government and the community. In addition I taught two foods and nutrition courses a semester and I served as department chair for Ahfad. I also went with IVS people to talk to post office officials when they charged an exorbitant import tax, which was added to the value of the package sent from the United States. I went with my roommate, *Penny Hogg*, to help her with this problem when she received a large package from the U.S. She wore her oldest clothes, took off her jewelry and did her best to look like an impoverished volunteer. At the end of our presentation about IVS and our work, the Sudanese official finally asked, "Well how much tax would you like to pay?" Penny replied, "About 50 cents," and he agreed. I had told my friends and family not to send me anything through international mail because packages from the U. S. were opened and frequently stolen. I found that being a foreign woman in Sudan had several advantages. I did not wear the Sudanese veil; I wore my regular clothes but not shorts. When I went to the Ministry of Health, I was greeted by the Minister, offered tea and the best chair in the office. I could talk to both Sudanese men and women by myself. In contrast, a Sudanese woman could not go alone to the market place or be alone with a man in the same room with the exception of her immediate family.

I was not prepared to handle a huge problem when our Sudanese boss fired two of the IVSers. One of the volunteers fired wanted the other six IVS teachers to resign in protest. The other fired volunteer screamed at me and I can close my eyes and still see her face and hear her words forty-one years later.

In my role as the Department Chair for the Food and Nutrition Department at Ahfad, I was responsible for the faculty and the students majoring in my discipline of nutrition. Many classrooms had no electricity, only a ceiling fan that helped circulate the air. The stoves in the food science lab frequently did not have gas, so we had no way at times to heat foods during the lab course.

As part of the nutrition curriculum, I taught a course in community nutrition. I partnered with Catholic Relief Services, which was conducting a maternal and child feeding program in Hillayt Mayo, a refugee village about five miles south of Khartoum. I had my students go once a week to help with the program and to translate the directions given by the American person who did not speak Arabic. One of my students was astonished to see the great poverty in the village and commented that she did not know that some people in Sudan lived in such squalid conditions. Many of the students at Ahfad came from wealthy homes and had not experienced poverty and food insecurity. This experiential learning helped the students to translate nutrition science learned in the classroom to real life situations.

My first trip by train was from Khartoum to Port Sudan, about 400 miles by air. The trip should have taken about fifteen hours, but after several hours of travel, the train stopped. The engine had broken down and the engineer had to send for spare parts. Although we had a fan in our first class cabin, it was hot. After two days we arrived in Port Sudan where my students participated in the United Nations-sponsored Year of the Women program. Sudanese President Nimeiry came to inspect the exhibits and shook hands with some of my students.

We endured occasional dust storms called 'haboobs' during which the visibility was twenty feet or less, similar to a snow blizzard in Minnesota. Sometimes the haboobs lasted two or three days and we would stay inside and wait it out. At the end of the haboob, a fine layer of sand covered everything in the house.

I was fortunate to have an air cooler in the house where I lived so it was fairly comfortable. We usually slept outside on the veranda where a breeze would make it a little cooler. It was mosquitos at night and flies during the day.

CARS, BUSES AND PLANES

I traveled by foot, bus, taxi, train, and airplane in Sudan and still regret not riding a camel.

My roommate and I went first to El Obeid in the middle of Sudan and then to Darfur province in the far west, winding up in El Fasher, the end of the plane route. We carried our own food and water, and Penny carried her guitar. We slept outside the hotels and I used my purse as a pillow to prevent theft.

My roommate arranged for us to travel by truck to Juba. We sat in the back of the truck with a load of tree seedlings and stopped occasionally for rest and toilet breaks behind the bushes. We arrived in Juba, the largest city in South Sudan and now the capital, at the end of three days.

The southern part of Sudan was quite different from the north. It had rain, trees, and other vegetation. There were dirt roads in the South, but they were in very poor condition and not easy to drive on. When I first went to Sudan in 1973 there was only one paved road in the entire country, which went sixty miles from Khartoum to Wad Medani, the agriculture center of the Gezira, located near the rich fertile land between the Blue and White Nile Rivers. Cotton was a crop frequently grown there for export. They also grew rice and wheat for domestic consumption. To complete our journey, Penny took the Nile steamer down the Nile River to return to Khartoum. The river route was challenging when passing through the vast marshland in the middle of Sudan where the Nile River flows. I remained behind in Juba to meet with Sudanese government officials, and I crossed the Nile in a boat where I saw hippos and crocodiles.

I met my husband-to-be at the confluence of the White and Blue Nile Rivers, which divide Khartoum to the east and

Omdurman to the west. I was waiting for friends with whom I'd go to church. When they didn't come, I met Bob who offered to take me to the Anglican Church services and then asked me for my phone number. He often drove me places in Khartoum and Omdurman since my only transportation was my feet or by taxi. I knew Bob liked me when he shared his canned bacon with me. Sudan, predominately Moslem in the north, did not have pork.

One day we went golfing. The course was sand with a small rectangular piece of grass. I had lost a contact lens the previous week and my vision was not very good. I missed the golf ball ten times before hitting it about fifteen yards. Bob soon sold his golf clubs and has never played since.

I returned to Sudan eight years later in 1983-1984 as a Fulbright Scholar studying for a doctorate in nutrition, and while I was there, civil war between the North and South started again.

I stayed at Ahfad and taught a course in nutrition but most of my time was devoted to planning my doctoral research, which involved traveling to three Sudanese villages and documenting what families were eating. The staple was sorghum grain, which in the U.S. is used to feed animals. The grain is ground into flour and used to make flat bread, porridge, and even beer in the South. I carefully recorded the sorghum food eaten as well as accompanying foods such as beans, which made the meal more nutrient-dense. I weighed and measured the children in those villages to identify malnutrition. I began my dissertation with Proverb 30:8 from the Bible, "Give me neither poverty nor riches; feed me with food convenient for me."

I was pleased to see some of my former students working in the Ministry of Health as nutritionists. I had arranged for some of our top students to attend graduate school in England and was glad they were using their education and training.

There is a Sudanese adage, which states that if one sees the sunset over the Nile River, one will return to Sudan. It has

now been thirty years since I left Sudan and perhaps someday
I will return again. ⚬❦

INDONESIA

In its third decade, IVS also went to Indonesia. *Mark Bordsen*, by
now an experienced IVS hand after his service in Laos, was near-
ing the end of his Master's degree in Community Development in
1972. He had come home to live with his parents and write his
thesis and been told about a possible assignment to Indonesia.
"I was still draft eligible, however, and I had checked with my
Selective Service Board prior to entering graduate school. The
clerk there informed me that the Board had considered my two
years as an IVS Volunteer in Laos as 'service to my country,' and
that I would not be drafted. At the time I did not want to work
in the USA, so the possibility of Indonesia was of interest.

"I had in general liked life in Laos. I liked the culture. I liked
the chance to try helping people have a better life if they chose to
do so. I liked the tropical climate; the sagebrush, ragweed, and
other plant allergies that had so affected me in Montana did not
bother me a hoot in the tropics."

BUTSI

Bordsen's IVS assignment was with BUTSI (Badan Urusan
Tenaga Kerja Sukarela Indonesia), a domestic Indonesian village
volunteer program for college graduates. It was designed to place
these youth in villages for two years where they were supposed
to promote village development. An effort was made to place
them in villages that had a different ethnicity than that of the
volunteers. After successful completion of the two-year duty,
the government gave them priority for government employment.
IVS volunteers were administratively supported via the CARE
program that was already operating there.

"After I had found and settled into a rented porch room in
a family's house, had gotten acquainted with my transportation,
a 100cc Honda motorcycle, the BUTSI supervisor and I made

rounds to the districts, sub-districts, and villages where volunteers had been placed. Every step of the way involved formal introductions and a show of a bundle of 'permissions' and an abundance of Javanese politeness. I always kept everyone informed, especially the BUTSI Supervisor. He traveled with me whenever he could, but he had responsibility for the entire province.

"IVS viewed getting a volunteer to Indonesia as a way to possibly send more IVS volunteers there. I viewed my objective as trying to help the BUTSI volunteers become more effective in the villages. To achieve IVS's goal of an expansion, I helped the volunteers achieve solid accomplishments that would demonstrate what additional IVS volunteers could do. I had been warned since the Peace Corps had departed Indonesia, that the government had not been very welcoming to the idea of foreign volunteers working in the country's villages. Perhaps I could have pushed harder for more IVS volunteer assignments, but I felt that if the Indonesian government wanted more of the kind of assistance this IVSer could supply, they would ask for it."

Bordsen's first objective was to learn Bahasa Indonesia, the national language. Fortunately, he had already learned Polish in-country, Lao in-country, and had the method and tools for knowing how best to learn yet another language. Bordsen knew the vital words to learn and made his own flash card system. But to achieve proper pronunciation, "I relied on assistance from Indonesian employees and their friends, who agreeably and laughingly corrected my attempts until I had enough ability for some basic communication."

FRUSTRATED

After making visits to the BUTSI volunteers in their villages, "I asked them how they thought they were doing. Most were pretty frustrated with the lack of progress towards modernization. Remembering my own 4-H experience with learn-by-doing projects, I recalled that demonstrations had been the successful means to get American farmers to try new varieties and farming methods. So I suggested this to the BUTSI volunteers and asked them to think about what kinds of small improvement projects might be of interest to the villagers. Soon they came back to me with ideas. Some of them, like a wet season fish pond to raise fish, took labor and the transport of fingerlings from the Surakarta fisheries office to the village. Others needed some supply of money, such as the purchase of an improved breed of rooster to mate with local hens."

Bordsen approached CARE for the funding. "It was a pitifully small amount of money for each project, but enough to show or demonstrate something. Once a villager with a fish pond harvested fish at the end of the rainy season, other villagers decided it was a good idea."

Bordsen extended his two-year volunteer commitment for another two years. He broached the idea of leasing an unused space he'd found, and building a Lao style house there. "So the lease was arranged, a contractor hired, and a simple house was built on stilts. The floor was high enough to walk under and there was space for cooking. The house had a front porch and one internal room, and it was a far better place to live and sleep than the room I previously rented."

RABBITS

There were several purposes for the house: a demonstration for a different type of home, a place for Bordsen to reside and host BUTSI volunteers, and a large lot to grow a demonstration garden as well as a place to experiment. This was where the volunteers tried raising rabbits to set up a loan program for interested villagers, where they experimented with and successfully learned how to make water seal toilets, and where they obtained and used a steel frame to make concrete rings for dug wells. The latter had been used by IVSers in Laos. A ring was set in place at the proposed site of the well, and then a hole was dug inside it and under the side of the ring, and it would slowly sink into the ground. Then another ring was set on top, and the process continued until the rings reached ground water."

With the success of some of the BUTSI demonstrations, Bordsen was invited to speak at BUTSI conferences in Bahasa Indonesia about what he had learned in the villages around Surakarta. "I was in the process of leaving for a CARE project in Sulawesi, and was being replaced by Frank Welsh. Frank later was injured in an automobile accident, and I think that abrupt event signaled the close of the IVS experience in Indonesia."

CONGO

On another continent entirely, IVS volunteers led by *Larry W. Harms* started work in 1971 in a very challenging country.

"IVS recruited an exceptional team of volunteers for the program in the Congo. We were nine. All had agricultural degrees with a variety of orientations. One was British, two were Taiwanese, and six were from diverse locations in the United States. They were individualistic, perhaps more so than most. It was a good team to work with.

"The program was shaped like many agricultural credit programs to that date. Our focus was on food production, primarily fruits and vegetables, for the urban market of Kinshasa, and a second rural area of Bamba on the northern loop of the Congo River. It took time to get things in place and operational."

TWO-YEAR PERIOD

The program was proving difficult to run. USAID, under a new Mission Director, indicated it would not continue past an allotted two-year period. The decision was sound, but it wasn't something the volunteers had ever considered.

"Like all places, the Congo had moments of interest that helped keep the IVS program in perspective. One was that the statue of Henry Morton, the famous explorer of the Congo, was torn down. His fame in the West is opposite of what it is with the Congolese. Then the name of the nation was changed to Zaire. And during one of the language training sessions for the volunteers, the instructor brought a few diamonds with him to see if any of the volunteers would like to buy some! One could read Joseph Conrad's *The Heart of Darkness* and understand how close the author was to understanding the Congo. Now, years later, the record is there."

The Congo lost a significant percentage of its human population, plus enormous amounts of elephant tusks, diamonds, and other assets during King Leopold's reign. The Belgian King, not Belgium, was the legal owner of the Congo when it was a colony.

"Our son and daughter, Peter and Anna, were born in the Congo. Peter has a Congolese birth certificate; it is about eighteen by eighteen inches square with very elaborate text. Anna was born with a heart defect and is buried there."

BOTSWANA

John Marks, a former Peace Corps volunteer in Somalia in the late 60s, returned to Africa as an IVS volunteer with his wife and son in 1980. "After the Peace Corps, I settled in an agricultural area of west-central Wisconsin where I got married and ran an old-fashioned rural general store with a gas pump in front. My wife and I had a five-year plan for the store, and when the five years were about up, one of our friends and customer introduced us to her brother who was visiting. He was working for IVS in Botswana as management advisor at an agricultural supply store and was soon to complete his assignment." Marks and his wife had attended a Peace Corps Somalia reunion in Washington in 1977 and were interested in working overseas, and "this IVS job seemed to be written for me. I applied, was interviewed by the Botswana country director who came to Minneapolis, and got the job."

The IVS program in Botswana focused on one rural development association in Molepolole, a large village. The association was part of a national movement called "brigades" that aimed to assist rural communities through a number of training and educational activities. Also undertaken were commercial activities that filled community needs and aimed to make a profit to subsidize the training units. IVS had three other volunteers working at this association, two horticulturalists and a financial advisor. "My job was at the One-Stop Service Center for Agriculture, where I advised the local manager and staff in running the business." The Center employed about a dozen local staff and had a retail store, a branch of the national agricultural marketing board that bought crops from farmers, and a training/extension unit that brought in farmers for classes.

ANCIENT WAGONS

What Marks remembers best was the great numbers of farmers at harvest time bringing in their crops, mainly sorghum, to sell. "Arriving at 8 a.m., I would see lined up in the yard dozens of carts and wagons of various types: ancient wagons with four huge wooden wheels pulled by sixteen oxen; small wooden two-wheeled carts pulled by a few oxen; rear-ends of pickup trucks pulled by donkeys."

The project filled a community need by introducing many farmers to new ideas and selling inputs at a reasonable price. Traditional traders in the village sold very few agricultural supplies at much higher prices. "I haven't been back to the site and don't know if the rural development association is still there. I think the project filled a transitional need, and guess that the commercial sector has expanded today. Many thousands of subsistence farmers became aware of new ideas for their farming and livestock rearing.

"An important factor in making my work there enjoyable and hopefully beneficial was the strong institutional support from the rural development association and its links to government, particularly the grain marketing board." This was in contrast to Marks' Peace Corps experience in Somalia, which he believed was by and large a failure due to the lack of local institutional or government linkages.

"My time at the project was two years. The fellow I trained to be the manager stayed with the job for a few years after I left, and later became the minister of agriculture."

Botswana was the first overseas experience for Marks' wife and eleven-year-old son. "They both had full and rewarding times, with many fond memories. IVS was a good family adventure. Our arrival in Botswana was timed for us to participate in a one-week 'village live-in' where volunteers from many organizations lived with average families and learned the language and culture.

"Social life in Molepolole was great, with volunteers from many countries working at the rural development association, and also with Botswanans, from the educated board of directors to our illiterate neighbors.

"We had excellent support from the IVS country director, who became a good friend. Our involvement with IVS/Washington was minimal, stopping there on the way out and on the return home."

KALAHARI GAME RESERVE

A frequent weekend activity for the Marks family was camping in the nearby Kalahari Game Reserve. "Once we were visited by a large, friendly and energetic South African who saw we were drinking wine and brought out a case of cold beer. He advised us that wine would dehydrate us and give us headaches. We chatted a bit and he invited us on a hunting trip. He was a driller on a government contract to explore for oil, and had permission to hunt meat for his workers. We rode in pick-ups through rough country with the shooters in back, not very sporting but very efficient when feeding dozens of workers." The prospector's young son was a naturalist of sorts and led the family to an encampment of Basarwa or 'Bushmen' still living a mostly traditional lifestyle. "We also got to see the wonderful Okavango Delta in northern Botswana, one of the great natural spectacles where a large river ends in an inland delta, bringing water to an otherwise dry area, resulting in huge forests, clean water, and many wild animals. Our IVS experience opened our eyes to an interesting part of the world."

After completing the two years in Botswana, Marks continued working overseas for another twenty-five years with other private organizations: Church World Service, CARE, Save the Children and USAID. Marks' son, after completing high school in Minnesota, travelled to see his mother and father in Somalia and passed through Botswana where he looked up old friends. "He's now married to a woman originally from Ethiopia," said Marks.

Another volunteer in Madagascar provided technical advice for water projects with funding from Church World Services, and the last volunteer in Zaire was completing his tour and closed the program. A married couple spent a year with Accion Cultural Popular in Colombia as teachers/administrators at farmer training institutes.

In Mauritania, a dozen volunteers overall were assigned to water resources, agriculture and public health services. Another long-term program was established in Botswana to develop subsistence and commercial horticulture and support for local rural development organizations as well as financial and agricultural resource management.

The Andes

In the Andes, skilled volunteers in agriculture, public health and community development were placed in Ecuador. The projects were focused in the highlands and the Amazon basin area among the indigenous people of the region, the most marginalized by the government. The following year similar programs were opened in Bolivia; later a crop substitution program in the coca-growing region was added. A program for vocational training instruction in health, agriculture, horticulture, and cooperative management was opened in Honduras.

IVS provided placements for Peace Corps volunteers in both Ecuador and Bolivia. In Ecuador, public health projects in the Afro-Ecuadorian area supplemented classes in nutrition by growing kitchen gardens. Recipes were exchanged which demonstrated new ways to use the fresh fruits and vegetables. Family wellness classes were also held to encourage the women to care for their children more effectively.

In the Altiplano above La Paz, a Peace Corps volunteer worker instructed a women's group knitting sweaters and shawls from alpaca and llama wool. They worked with natural dyes and experimented with methods of making the materials hold the colors. They also learned Western sizes and how to merchandize their hand work.

IVS IN THE ANDES

RICHARD POOLE

The IVS Andes program, which spanned three decades from 1973 to 2002, underwent a significant metamorphosis during its lifetime, some of it the result of tightening economic circumstances. Starting first in Ecuador in 1973 and then in Bolivia in 1977 with young American professionals, it later recognized the cultural and professional advantages of recruiting its volunteers from within the Andean region; and then finally settled for the cheaper option of recruiting volunteers in-country without any obvious diminution in levels of professionalism or commitment.

Ecuador and Bolivia were selected as the geographical locations for IVS programs, overlooking what is generally regarded as the spiritual heart and operational hub of the region, Peru. In the early days there was a certain amount of overlap between IVS and the Peace Corps both in terms of program content where emphasis was given to providing technical assistance to grassroots organizations, and also in terms of staffing with a number of PCVs joining the ranks of IVS when their original assignments ended, and vice-versa.

The Andes experience was a generally happy and relaxed affair presenting none of the threat to personal security that was an integral part of the IVS Southeast Asia experience. Although anti-American rhetoric was never far from the surface in Latin America, it seldom translated into open hostility, proof of which is that a number of American volunteers chose to remain in-country when their original assignments ended, either finding alternative employment, marrying and settling down, or pursuing post graduate courses of study which allowed them to return periodically to conduct their research.

By the time I arrived in September, 1988, both IVS Ecuador and IVS Bolivia were in good shape, recruiting 'tecnicos,' regional volunteers. However, financial constraints meant there was insufficient funding to pay the salaries of two country directors and so I was asked to take over responsibility for the two programs under the title of 'regional director'. I divided my time equally between the two countries, renting an apartment in the Ecuadorean capital Quito and travelling to Bolivia three or four times a year for periods of four to six weeks. This arrangement was made possible by the appointment of two very able administrators, *Eumelia Zarria* in Ecuador and *Jeaneth Echazu* in Bolivia, who covered admirably in my absence.

ECUADOR 1973-1997

Ecuador was the first of the two countries to get underway and it did so quite successfully, no doubt profiting at the design stage from two decades of IVS experience elsewhere in the world. Approximately fifty volunteers served during this time. Its early volunteers were technically qualified Americans assigned for two or three years to local community-based organizations with a brief to build capacity in the areas of agriculture, animal husbandry, forestry, building construction, community health, financial management, and marketing.

With the arrival of regional volunteers, which included recruitment from Chile, Peru, Colombia, and Bolivia, there came an older, more experienced crew of volunteers who saw their assignments more as a career choice than a temporary diversion, and who chose to stay for much longer periods. The outstanding Chilean veterinary doctor, *Carlos Muñoz*, for example, stayed for ten years, while the legendary Sri Lankan couple, *Su* and *Bandu Abeywickrame,* an agronomist and her mechanic-builder husband, who were recruited in-country from a church project in the Amazon region, stayed sixteen years!

In fact none of our six regionally recruited volunteers chose to resign during my eight-year tenure and it is probable they would never have left IVS at all had IVS not run out of funds and been forced to close. Their allegiance to IVS was not merely financial in its motivation—although this was no doubt an important part of it—it was also the product of a profound love for the organization and the principles it embodied. These principles were founded on a mutual respect among all members of the team and their local partners, on the one hand, and the development of program strategy that was conducted according to a process of consultation between equals, on the other.

The final phase of the Ecuador program (1990-97) involved the recruitment of national volunteers and these included an Afro-Ecuadorean woman doctor (the first to graduate in Ecuador), a female nutritionist, a livestock specialist, an economist, and a forester. Although their contributions were highly valued, the writing was now on the wall as far as IVS Ecuador was concerned and it was with great sadness that in January, 1997, all staff were let go, and the IVS program was officially closed.

All was not lost, however, because IVS Ecuador was 'spun off' in the form of a national NGO named MINGA (a Quechua word denoting a traditional system of voluntary communal labor), a fortuitous collaboration that brought together a highly respected but moribund expatriate NGO with a fledgling national NGO that was searching for identity and direction.

Although the transition was successful and MINGA continued to exist for a number of years thereby perpetuating something of the vision and values of IVS, none of the IVS volunteers chose to join the new organization. The national volunteers opted to seek employment elsewhere which they did successfully with most of them entering government service. The regional volunteers also fared reasonably well, the Chilean vet and Bolivian economist returning home to find good jobs in government; the Peruvian vet and Colombian forester joining international NGOs; and the Sri Lankan couple emigrating to Australia where they successfully began a new life and saw their two boys graduate from university.

BOLIVIA 1977-2002

The Bolivia program had two distinct phases to it: The first (1977–1992) replicated the Ecuador model by sending young qualified Americans to provide technical assistance to local community-based organizations. The volunteers later gave way to regionally recruited professionals. These numbered some twenty in all who worked in crop production and crop storage, animal husbandry, marketing and community health. The second and final phase (1992-2002) consisted of some thirty nationally recruited agronomists who made up IVS's Coca Substitution project.

The USAID-funded Coca Substitution project was a windfall for the IVS Bolivia program in the sense that news of it came from out of the blue, and our funding proposal passed effortlessly from one stage to the next of the approval process. In a matter of weeks we were given the resources to employ thirty young agronomists whose task it was to offer coca producers the opportunity to grow black pepper and palm hearts as alternatives to coca. The economics of it theoretically made sense; a hectare of coca bringing in approximately $3,000 per annum and a hectare of the alternative crops about the same. The practical difficulty lay in the fact that coca takes no effort to cultivate, growing naturally as it does on small bushes, and demanded minimal effort to harvest; in fact children can and often do the harvesting. Black pepper and palm hearts, on the other hand, are work-intensive activities both in the planting and in the harvesting. There was also the possibility that a shortage in the supply of the coca leaf would push up the price of the finished product, cocaine, and that the value of the leaf would increase accordingly making the cultivation of the leaf even more attractive to the farmers. We were aware of such issues from the outset but we persevered with the project regardless, seeing it as a lifeline that might prolong IVS Bolivia's existence, as indeed it did for a number of years.

IVS Bolivia underwent a stay of execution for a while thanks to the Coca Substitution project but eventually succumbed to a similar fate to its sister program in Ecuador. It closed its doors in 2002, only this time the closure was definitive, leaving thirty young agronomists with the unenviable task of looking for jobs in a miserably depressed economy.

In Bangladesh, Ecuador and Bolivia the programs were expanded to utilize the talents of college and technical school trained national volunteer technicians. They, in turn, worked at the village level providing training in simple health care, small business management and agricultural techniques. These three programs were to continue throughout the life of IVS. At the end of 1982 there were fifteen volunteers in the field in Bangladesh, Ecuador, Bolivia, Honduras, Sudan, Botswana, and Papua New Guinea and a Washington office staff of twelve. During this decade more than 60 percent of the volunteers were internationals following the Harpers Ferry agreement. The programs to which they were assigned were planned to provide technical expertise, both in problem-solving and working with local organizations so these new techniques could be applied to other local problems.

THE FOURTH AND FIFTH DECADES
1983–2002

ZIMBABWE • THE CARIBBEAN—ANTIGUA • DOMINICA
GRENADA • ST. KITTS/NEVIS • ST. LUCIA • ST. VINCENT—
ETHIOPIA • CAPE VERDE • MALI • THAILAND • VIETNAM
CAMBODIA • BANGLADESH • ECUADOR • BOLIVIA

IN 1983, THE IVS STAFF AND BOARD again undertook a serious review of program planning and development. The financial situation was precarious; USAID general funding was coming to an end and a matching grant request was pending. The major issue was that economies of small-scale projects with one to five volunteers in place were expensive to operate and maintain and often closed quickly. By now the IVS overall program approach was the transfer of skills by training local people to meet immediate community needs in agriculture and non-agriculture income generation, health, business management and cooperative development.

SKILLED PROFESSIONALS

It was clear that larger contingents of volunteers should be placed in fewer programs. By this time, volunteers were skilled professionals who came to projects with their families and were relatively expensive to support. It was estimated that one married volunteer in Africa cost about $40,000 per year. Fielding these skilled people in sizeable numbers would incur expenses IVS could not manage due to its limited budget.

The program in the Sudan was closed in 1983 after seventeen years due to operating expenses and staffing problems during the continuing civil war. Also during that year, agreement was reached with the government of Zimbabwe for program development and the first staff person was sent to plan specific projects. The first priority was the resettlement of people from over-populated and marginal tribal areas to more productive formerly colonial-owned commercial farms.

In 1984 IVS took a new approach opening a regional initiative in the Caribbean Basin, which assigned a multi-disciplinary team to establish a multi-national regional program. Volunteers were each assigned to a local host organization. Their task was to improve economic opportunities by building and strengthening the capabilities and skills of community-based private economic development organizations. When the project closed, all the volunteers were native to the Caribbean. This project became the first IVS venture to make the transition to an independent, indigenously managed development agency, Caribbean Advisory and Professional Services (CAPS).

At the same time, another new approach was attempted when IVS worked with Africare to locate medical staff for an Africare clinic in Ethiopia. One placement was made with the hope that IVS would gain entry into Ethiopia for more traditional IVS programs. However, funding for such expansion did not materialize.

COLLABORATION

In 1987 an IVS technical advisor was sent to Cape Verde for a year to help design and plan a new cooperative project in conjunction with the Universalist Unitarian Service Committee. A similar attempt in 1988 with a partner agency project in Mali was not implemented. However, collaboration with the Methodist Church of Zaire was very successful, and five health care professionals and construction workers spent a total of four years working with the refugee population in the western part of the country.

In 1991, IVS supported three international volunteers for Empower, an NGO in Thailand, to assist in HIV/AIDS education within the communities of sex workers in Bangkok and Chiang Mai. Two more similar agreements were reached in Vietnam and Cambodia in 1992. The first was with the Vietnamese Women's Union, a governmental organization that operates like an NGO, to provide HIV/AIDS education in clinics for commercial sex workers in Hanoi and Ho Chi Minh City, and the second with Indradevi, a Cambodian NGO, for similar work in Phnom Penh.

NATIONALS AND INTERNATIONALS

The placement of IVS volunteers with partner agencies was one of two significant changes in its role that IVS had now adopted in development. The other, and far more significant, change was recruiting and placing national volunteers in Ecuador, Bolivia, Zimbabwe, and Bangladesh. These volunteers were college and technical school graduates whose skills were not being utilized due to vast under-employment in their countries. Like the international volunteers, they were compensated at a rate far lower than a comparable job in their country and were expected to be involved on a grassroots basis in the community development projects to which they were assigned. Over the years these national volunteers became as dedicated to the spirit of IVS as any U.S. volunteer. Thus by the beginning of the 1990s, over eighty percent of IVS staff and volunteers were host country nationals or internationals.

As another decade ended, the projects in Botswana, Honduras and Zimbabwe had been closed, but the long-term programs remained in operation in Bangladesh, Ecuador and Bolivia. IVS now had twenty-two international volunteers and staff and ten national volunteers in the field with a Washington staff of nine.

THE END GAME, 1993 TO 2002

In the mid-1990s, USAID funding began to dry up. The final Cooperative Agreement with USAID had ended with IVS unable to match a significant portion of the funds available from the Agreement. A small institutional development grant from USAID, made to computerize both the Washington office and the three remaining country programs, was ninety percent matched with in-kind contributions of goods and services. USAID grants had provided funds for program development and Washington costs. Further U.S. government funding would come only as sub-grants designed to assist specific projects in the overseas programs. The financial situation was now critical. It became increasingly evident that International Voluntary Services was moving further from its roots in volunteerism and becoming a granting and placement agency.

SUPPORT FOR NATIONAL STAFF

Assigning international volunteers to national development organizations had been undertaken during the 1980s; moving into the area of HIV/AIDS within a special population was a new direction. No IVS volunteers were assigned in either Vietnam or Cambodia, but consultations by Washington staff took place on a yearly basis, and IVS provided support for national staff of other agencies. In effect, IVS became a granting organization rather than implementing grassroots development projects, which distanced it further from its original roots in volunteerism and rural development. IVS had placed public health professionals in the field since the 1950s, but they worked either in hospitals, training nurses and administrators, or in village settings training village health workers. Now, multinational and private voluntary organizations were providing medical assistance for the victims of HIV and AIDS. The IVS-sponsored program was not doing general public health programs, but was supporting AIDS and HIV education mainly with commercial sex workers in Cambodia, Thailand and Vietnam.

Unfortunately, IVS was unable to build on this partial return to Indochina or to develop broader-based, more traditional programs. Competition for funds was overwhelming. Available moneys from sources both private and public was drying up quickly, partly because of what would become known as 'aid fatigue,' and because donors could more easily justify spending funds at home rather than on overseas projects that failed to find strong political footholds.

Funding had always been a primary concern. In fact, IVS—since it was not a U.S. government agency—never managed to successfully develop a firm fiscal base as an independent entity. (In 1971 with this precarious financial picture looming, in a major meeting of the Board and advisors, IVS had planned to broaden its donor base so that more than fifty percent of its budget would be sought from donors other than USAID. It wanted to put 500 to 1,000 volunteers in the field before the end of the decade, yet a realistic approach to funding and fundraising was never developed.)

Church-funded programs were being curtailed or stopped altogether as national churches began to implement their own development work, leading to yet another major funding loss to IVS. General fundraising had dropped so significantly that IVS could not complete its final matching grant for administrative upgrading from USAID, even at the preferential twenty percent match required. Funding for the USAID education work with the Vietnamese Women's Union was being done separately from the organizational funding.

MODERATE SUCCESSES

An attempt was made to develop a project in Vietnam for preventative medicine clinics in small villages.

With many Vietnamese graduating from medical school in-country or in the region and needing jobs, this was seen as an opportunity to develop a significant return to Southeast Asia for IVS volunteers with health care experience. Meetings in Hanoi with the Ministry of Public Health indicated interest in this type of program, but the new economic realities meant the Vietnamese wanted IVS to have large sums of money committed to the planning and implementation in advance. IVS could not commit such funds, and the Vietnamese ended up relying for help on for-profit development organizations.

There were some moderate successes. The three larger programs in Bangladesh, Ecuador and Bolivia continued under the direction of national leadership using both national and regional volunteers.

In Bangladesh, a staff of senior national volunteers worked with village volunteers in many areas, including micro-credit and finance. IVS made small grants-in-aid to villagers to establish small enterprise businesses such as woodworking, weaving, metal work, concrete work, and small shops. This effort was expanded to urban Dhaka where loans were made to cyclo-drivers, enabling them to purchase their own vehicles. The national volunteers provided training in financial management, capacity building and general business acumen to the budding entrepreneurs.

Also in Bangladesh, a grant established a small revolving loan fund which would provide low interest loans of $200 to $500 for small business owners. The criteria for receiving these loans were stringent, requiring that the individual prove the ability to handle finances, operate a viable business or service, and recognize the responsibility of repaying the loan. More than fifty percent of the loans went to women, and nearly sixty-five percent of the recipients had previously received grants which gave them their initial experience in small business operations. A demonstrated skill in business was the key point in the selection process of these men and women, some of whom were functionally illiterate. Two stories give an idea of the importance of this program.

FACTORY WORK

Young Bangladeshi teenager Akter became the primary earning source for his mother and four younger siblings at age fifteen after the death of his father. He and his mother started to work in a factory. After three years in the factory at a wage of about a dollar per day, Akter began to seek funds to start a small business of his own. He joined IVS local groups and attended meetings to receive training in small business operations. Assisted by his mother and with the help of a grant of $50, combined with his own small savings, he opened a small factory producing colorful paper garlands and boxes. Later, when he was ready to expand, IVS provided him with a $400 credit from the Levi Strauss revolving loan. This expansion provided a monthly income for his family of approximately $150.

Mrs. Ano, from a poor remote area of Bangladesh, did not attend school; she married at age thirteen and within six years had four children. In common with many villagers trapped in barely subsistence lives, her family migrated to the slums of Dhaka. There she met IVS national volunteers who gave her business training that led to a conditional grant of $50, which she used to buy and sell gunnysacks.

Within three months, Mrs. Ano was earning $2 to $3 per day, or twice what her husband was able to earn as a day laborer. As she gained confidence and saw her small business thrive, she asked IVS for additional capital to expand. A loan of $200 led to increased earnings of over $100 per month, with which she could afford to make serious changes in her children's lives. The children became healthier thanks to improved diet and medical care, and began attending school. Mrs. Ano did not allow her success to go to her head; she continued to attend IVS group meetings and learned about women's rights, the role of women in society, and family planning as ways for women to become empowered in society.

Other regional initiatives met with varying success. The Caribbean project had been transitioned to an indigenous organization nearly a decade earlier.

A PLACE TO TALK

On the northern coast of Ecuador in Esmeraldas Province, a large Afro-Ecuadorian population lived in marginal circumstances due to racial tensions in the country. *Hernán Cotera*, an IVS *tecnico* (national volunteer) for several years, grew up in the Afro-Ecuadorian community of Muisne. He trained as a forester and earned both a Bachelor's and Master's degrees from Esmeraldas University. His specialty was mangrove reforestation in an area severely devastated by *El Niño*.

As part of an IVS project, Cotera trained teams of volunteers in simple methods to improve the environment of villages. Typically, a team visited a small village for several days to help clean up over-growth, dig compost pits, and tidy the village paths and banana groves. The villagers received training in organic gardening, planting vegetable gardens and enlarging banana groves. They received instructions on health and nutrition during this *minga* where the entire village came together to work for the betterment of the community. Each team of trained volunteers worked in ten communities during the year. Hernán and these volunteers, with assistance from the villagers, also raised a *Gran Palenque* or "place to talk" in a central community. This house became not only a community gathering place, but also housed the volunteers during their time in the villages.

OTHER OPTIONS

An idea that had been explored in the 1980s was reconsidered—that of entering into an alliance with a larger PVO. Encouraged by USAID, IVS entered into an alliance with Private Agencies Collaborating Together (PACT), which appeared to offer a positive direction since the two had shared resources and projects in the past. It was hoped the alliance would provide needed assistance in some joint program development and give IVS the opportunity to move back into significant development work. Unfortunately, this alliance became little more than a leasing arrangement and in little over a year was disbanded.

Another program possibility explored placing experienced, short-term, self-funded, volunteers in national NGOs and schools in countries where IVS was working.

Two professors traveled to Hanoi for six weeks to work with a Vietnamese NGO, helping rebuild university programs. Though this was certainly an interesting initiative, it did not lead to further programs. Finding placements and housing as well as providing simple orientation was time-consuming and found not worth pursuing with such a small staff.

The fact was that, by the beginning of the new century, the environment and funding availability for international private and voluntary programs had changed dramatically. Interest in overseas work had declined, and the Peace Corps offered opportunities and government program benefits to new graduates wanting overseas experience. Other options were available for tourism in well-organized groups, and these were far more appealing. Basically, there was little interest from potential volunteers and too small a staff in Washington to undertake the kind of planning or recruitment that would be required to implement the envisioned programs.

The shift away from the young volunteers who served in the first two decades sent possible candidates to the Peace Corps for placement. That government-funded agency was well-equipped to select and to place more volunteers. The decisions reached at Harpers Ferry in 1971 had changed IVS irrevocably, but the IVS administration, which had not been part of the Harpers Ferry Conference, had not recognized the changed circumstances and continued to operate with an increasingly large Washington staff but few American volunteers. While there were still volunteers in Laos until 1975, no further USAID money was in the pipeline for Southeast Asia, though there was a contract for Bangladesh. This was untenable. With no North Americans in the field, there were still eight staff people in the Washington office. This number diminished rapidly and by the end of the decade in 2000 only one paid staff person remained, assisted by contract and volunteer help.

Programs had become primarily reactive, responding to special requests from organizations and people, rather than evolving from a concrete development plan. The result was that many projects, in cooperation with national NGOs, required only one or two professional volunteers, which impaired the impact of IVS achievements. Only in Southeast Asia and Algeria were the economies of size achieved with groups of volunteers at work. The programs in Bangladesh and the Andes with volunteers working alongside national volunteers provided the broad grass-roots assistance and relationships envisioned by the founders.

The national volunteers in Bangladesh, Ecuador and Bolivia remained the core of an IVS-type program.

As the new century began, USAID policies on grants changed even more dramatically. Institutional donors preferred to fund programs in-country rather than through Washington, and the financial climate of the U.S. continued its downward spiral. IVS was in dire economic straits. The Board of Directors was faced with the decision to dissolve IVS. Although there was virtually no Washington staff, the programs in Ecuador, Bolivia and Bangladesh were still ongoing. Over the preceding fifteen years, the question of closing had often arisen, but nostalgia and a conviction that the mission of IVS was still valid, had encouraged earlier Boards to continue operations. This was no longer an option.

REALISTIC GOAL

Before IVS closed, a commitment was made to establish the remaining programs as national NGOs. This plan had been underway for several years, which made implementation a realistic goal. By 1999, Bolivia had received its national NGO status. In Ecuador plans were already in process for establishing a national NGO, Fundacion Minga/IVS, financed with a grant from the Inter-American Foundation. The nationalizing was well underway in Bangladesh, as well, and its national NGO status as IVS Bangladesh was secured. In these three countries, as had been the case in the Caribbean program over a decade earlier, the staff and volunteers were all native to their country at the time of the transition. It was with great pride that IVS was able to achieve the goal of nationalizing the programs in these countries. Over time, changes in governments in these countries affected all the national NGOs and the IVS-sponsored NGOs are now closed.

For half a century, IVS made significant contributions to an understanding of volunteerism in its deepest sense, both in the U.S. and in forty countries around the world. Crops that were introduced by IVS volunteers still flourish; teachers who were taught or trained by volunteers learned a great deal about people-to-people relationships; and national NGOs carried forward the mission and spirit of International Voluntary Services. The lessons learned and breadth of experience gained by volunteers remains incalculable.

IVSers, regardless of their time and length of service, made a difference in their world and that of tens of thousands of others on three continents. The men and women who more recently served with the organization developed an understanding and appreciation of IVS very much equal to that of any young American who set off for distant parts in the organization's early days. One and all made history, both overseas and in their own countries. And one and all exemplified the depth and very meaning of the volunteer spirit.

EPILOGUE

We give the last word to a man who was neither an IVS volunteer nor an American citizen. Richard Poole, from the United Kingdom, was IVS Andes Director from 1988 to 1996. He has spent more than thirty years working in emergency, reconstruction and development in Africa, Latin America and the Caribbean. He has worked primarily as country director with Voluntary Service Overseas of the UK, IVS, American Refugee Committee, Trocaire of Ireland, and the International Rescue Committee.

Richard Poole is the author of **The Inca Smiled:** *The Growing Pains of an Aid Worker in Ecuador;* **The Camel Strayed:** *An Aid Worker's View of Islam in the Modern World; and* **Mankind's Last Chance,** *which addresses the two primary issues of our time: the global economic crisis and the degradation of our natural environment.*

He is especially proud of the year spent playing professional football (soccer) in Ecuador as a member of the Liga Deportiva Universitaria squad, which won the national championship in 1969.

Richard is now semi-retired and lives in Colchester, UK.

RICHARD POOLE

IT IS LIKELY THAT THE VOLUNTEER MOVEMENT evolved from a missionary tradition that sought to free itself from the limitations of doctrine, and in so doing it came to reflect a trend that has gathered momentum ever since.

IVS, created in 1953, has every reason to be proud to have been at the cutting edge of this movement. Humble and unpretentious though its origins may have been, in retrospect we see now that its founding spirit was part of a much wider movement that has yet to run its course. This spirit we may loosely describe as being one of "a universal concern that recognizes no divisions in the human family."

Noble though such a vision may be, it brings with it the risk that is inherent to pioneering endeavors generally, namely, of not having a constituency to support it. This is the price IVS has had to pay throughout its existence–the price of being ahead of its time–and the realization of this risk has been the primary cause of its demise. Not having any particular political, ideological, religious or ethnic bias, and choosing to extend its recruitment to a multitude of nationalities, proved to be the organization's Achilles heel. It had not been able to muster the kind of support that such a vision required.

AUTONOMOUS DECISION-MAKING

Many other agencies have since drawn upon IVS's early inspiration to send well-meaning, energetic professionals out into the world to improve it and gain experience. The British Voluntary Service Overseas (VSO) was among the first to follow suit, forming in 1958; the Canadian volunteer agency (CUSO) formed in 1961; the Peace Corps arrived on the scene in 1962, acknowledging its debt to IVS in the process; and a plethora of other volunteer-sending agencies throughout the developed world soon followed. Many were classified as non-governmental organizations, which implied that even if they received funding from their governments in whatever measure, they were by and large autonomous in their decision-making. The primary exception to this was the Peace Corps which has been government-controlled from the outset and potentially more susceptible to political influence. By way of contrast one might consider the volunteer-sending agencies of Western Europe which have seldom if ever been subject to government scrutiny of any kind.

The Peace Corps and IVS may have shared certain similarities insofar as they both sent predominantly young Americans to developing countries on two-year assignments and paid them a basic living wage, but here the similarity ends. IVS has generally enjoyed the freedom to choose where and how it was going to operate, the prime example of which is that IVS challenged the political correctness of its day by sending volunteers to South Vietnam as agents of peace, including during the height of the Vietnam War at considerable personal risk. This fact alone is sufficient to warrant entry into the humanitarian hall of fame, reflecting as it did an independence of mind, an act of courage, and an allegiance to the human race that was all-inclusive and asked for nothing in return. A standard of selflessness was thereby set that many still try to emulate, with perhaps the French NGO, *Médecins Sans Frontières*, coming closest in more recent times.

Daunting Complexity

The mishmash of our modern world with its ever-accelerating rate of change, its daunting complexity and its catastrophic failures in the vital areas of economics and environment, makes it difficult to predict what the future holds for NGOs. Nonetheless certain trends are discernible and these may allow some room for speculation. What is certain is that the division of our planet into a developed world, on the one hand, and an underdeveloped world, on the other, no longer applies. The arrival of the BRICS countries onto the scene–Brazil, Russia, India, China and South Africa–have consigned such notions to the dustbin of history so that what we have now is a continuum from the very rich down to the very poor, which cuts through the strata of almost every country, all of which are upheld by a global economic system that few understand and no one truly controls. It is no exaggeration to say that the human race as a species has entered uncharted territory in a way and on a scale that is without precedent in human experience.

Giant economic forces backed by massive vested interests have rendered much development thinking redundant. Grassroots development, for long the mantra of NGOs, has been trampled underfoot in the stampede to exploit the earth's natural resources from the Americas to Africa to Asia, with the masses following the money wherever it goes, often at the expense of traditional values and family ties. IVS's many years of successful capacity building among the indigenous and *campesino* communities of the Andes, for example, has been all but nullified by the discovery of large deposits of oil and minerals, the easy gains of drug-trafficking, and opportunities to enter illegally into the United States. Similarly the rush to exploit oil and minerals in Central Africa has brought untold wealth to small minorities but also untold suffering to many in the form of forced labor and massive disruption in the lives of traditional farming communities.

In many instances the GDP of these nations can be said to have improved significantly as a result of such enterprises, and is often quoted by economists as an indication of successful economic development, but at what cost? Little of the wealth ever trickles down to the poorest of the poor whose wretchedness is all too plain to see on the streets and in the giant slums of the major towns and cities; these people become more desperate by the day as they are driven to ever more degrading and dishonorable strategies to survive.

MIXED BLESSING

Neither should one underestimate the impact that a revolution in communications technology is having on the lives of ordinary people. Like all technology, it is proving to be a mixed blessing. Even remote villages are now able to boast an internet café or a bar where people can communicate with the farthest corners of the earth and watch satellite television with all the latest movies, sports and world news. On the one hand, this opens up vast new horizons through the availability of distance education and a vision of other worlds that hold out the prospect of an escape from poverty, and a chance to fulfil whatever potential one may have. On the other, innocence and decades of painstaking moral education that promoted such values as patience, humility, kindness, honesty and generosity are being swept away in a tidal wave of selfish ambition. Such cultural assaults often leave the recipients restless and anxious, their appetites whetted by possibilities that cannot be met by their local environments, and so they set out *en masse* on their hazardous journeys in search of better things, on foot through the Mexican desert and in rickety boats for the island of Lampedusa.

Where, one might ask, in this maelstrom of change in which the basest of human instincts often prevail, is there a place for voluntary agencies and their goodwill ambassadors?

It seems inevitable that community development, meaning the transfer of skills and technology in a fashion that allows local communities to improve their quality of life, must take a back seat from now on. The claims of many development agencies over the years to have significantly impacted the poverty of developing nations by means of community development, have always been questionable; this impact has only ever been at the micro level and extremely limited. The classic comparison is that of China and Africa, the former having received little in the form of development assistance, is now a world power; the latter which has received countless billions of dollars in development aid has precious little to show for it. It is a fact that no robust economy anywhere in the world has ever been built on a foundation of aid alone.

The Needs of Every Home

What we know for certain is that there are sufficient resources available on planet Earth right now to satisfy everyone's needs. There is enough food to feed all of the world's seven billion inhabitants with some to spare, or at least there *would* be enough if vast tracts of prime agricultural land were not being given over to the production of biofuels. And there is enough energy in the sun, wind, rivers and seas to meet the needs of every home, factory, village and town several times over. The same may be said of the world's net wealth, which, if it were to be distributed equitably, would be sufficient to meet the basic needs of just about everyone.

The fundamental issues of today, therefore, revolve not so much around the generation of resources—although this still awaits some refinement in the energy sector-as their *distribution*, and this opens the door to the world of advocacy and ethics. It is here that NGOs will most likely find their niche.

At the heart of this debate is the realization that the global economy is interconnected right down to the very last detail, so that the mobile phone someone is using in New York is the product of the work of coltan miners in the Democratic Republic of the Congo and factory workers in Beijing, just as the clothes someone is wearing in Nairobi are the product of cotton farmers in Egypt and factory workers in Bangladesh. It is a debate that has always existed but which is becoming more urgent by the day, as a result of the growing inequality gap between those with power and those without it, and the social breakdown that has ensued. It is in essence a debate about social justice, a debate about moral values, and this brings us right back to the origins of IVS and the motivation of its founding members.

NGOs should now be shifting their focus from interaction at the grassroots level to interaction with the media at all levels, while not abandoning the dispossessed and most vulnerable altogether; to do so would deny the very reason for our existence as human beings. But their response at this basic level should be more in the form of emergency relief than as agents of social change. This will not be an easy transition; the funding relationships that currently exist between donors and NGOs are solidly based on the belief that existing social and economic development strategies actually work; most NGOs are locked into a system that obliges them to come up with tables of measurable outcomes which they must meet to receive continued funding.

Although much of this activity is fictitious in the sense that few of the stated goals and achievements are genuine, the behavior is likely to continue for a while longer for two reasons. First, because the NGOs in all likelihood will have limited options where funding is concerned; and second, because there is no alternative to the development strategies currently on the table, regardless of whether or not they work. In an easier economic climate, NGOs might have been able to look elsewhere for their funding, but today this is a luxury few can afford. The same may be said of U.S. government funding which, regardless of what one may feel about U.S. government policy, is seldom rejected on principle as some agencies have done in the past, and this despite USAID's quagmire of rules and regulations.

EXPATRIATE LIFESTYLES

Another obstacle that NGOs must contend with in their fundraising efforts relates to "donor fatigue." Members of the public have long been aware of the high overhead costs of most first-world NGOs and are understandably reluctant to see their donations going to support expatriate lifestyles; they would much rather their money go directly to the countries and the people in need. This has led to a significant increase in the number of national NGOs that are now operating-to good effect, it should be said, alongside expatriate NGOs. Although most national NGOs seem to be forever suffering from acute funding shortages and operate on a shoestring, the principle of national NGOs is basically sound, one that we might expect to see gaining in popularity in coming years.

The picture of the starving child in Africa with flies drinking from its eyes has become a cliché and many people are now asking: We have been seeing these photographs for fifty years now. When are Africans going to take responsibility for their own destiny? It is a valid question because the message that the starving child conveys is one of impotence in the face of adversity. Whereas this is often the case where medicine is concerned, when it comes to hard work and practical knowhow, Africans are a force to be reckoned with. The poster of the starving child is invariably accompanied by declarations of "desperate need" with a handful of alarming statistics tacked on, all of which are designed to arouse compassion in the viewer. This is not to say that such situations do not exist because of course they do, but it *is* to say that such images are far from the norm and represent a distortion of what is actually happening on the ground; they also do a disservice to the average African who is by nature socially responsible.

It is difficult to see how the world can possibly continue much longer the way it is going without a major restructuring of the present economic order; this inevitably means a curtailment of the excesses of capitalism and a redistribution of wealth so that extremes of wealth and poverty disappear from our midst. It is most unlikely, of course, that this will ever be accomplished by appealing to the better nature of the rich and powerful, nor will it be achieved through legislation, which has a tendency to wilt under pressure from big business. More likely, it is to come about as a panic reaction to the global collapse that will almost certainly occur at some point under the collective weight of the economic, environmental and social crises threatening our existence, crises to which we have no answer.

GREATER ROLE IN ADVOCACY

It is impossible to say how all of this will play out but it is reasonable to assume that NGOs will have a greater role in advocacy and alerting society to the many dangers that it faces. There's also the possibility that changing patterns in the global economy will create opportunities for many more people from the poorer nations to come to the more advanced countries to work and study, allowing them to repatriate their earnings and to share something of what they have learned with the folks back home. Indeed this is already happening in numbers that dwarf the volunteer contingents in the field.

In brief, the tumultuous events of our day are conspiring to make the volunteer as we have known him and her for the past sixty years redundant. And when this does finally happen, it is sure to come as a relief to the host countries, because as much as they may voice their appreciation for the help volunteers provide, there is also a sense of indignity that is seldom acknowledged for having needed volunteers in the first place.

PERSONAL REFLECTIONS

After a lifetime spent in humanitarian work in Latin America and Africa, I have come to the conclusion that the true value of the volunteer movement lies not so much in the transfer of technical knowhow, useful though this undoubtedly is, as in a deepening of understanding between diverse cultures. In other words, its true worth is neither something that can be readily quantified, nor something that can be included in a table of measurable outcomes in a funding proposal.

I look back with great fondness and appreciation on my eight years as IVS regional director in the Andes, but perhaps the fondest memory of all has nothing to do with any of our projects. I refer to the Afro-Ecuadorean community which I came to know very well during this time and to two extracurricular activities that I chose to become involved with. Arriving in Ecuador after spending seven years in Africa and three years in the Caribbean, I had developed a profound affection for African people and their culture, and I chose to share this affection with the Afro-Ecuadorean communities of the Chota and Mira river valleys of the northern sierra.

The first activity involved financing the production of a record for a group of talented young musicians, all members of a single family as it happens; the second was a project that we dreamt up amongst ourselves entitled *El Rescate de Raices Negras* or *The Rediscovery of Black Roots*. The inhabitants of these two valleys knew that they were originally from Africa but little more than this. Together we developed an awareness of their ancestral heritage and commensurate with it came a new sense of pride. Now, some sixteen years after the closure of IVS/Ecuador, I am pleased to report that the music group is still performing publicly, even though the record itself did not do too well, and the leader of The Rediscovery of Black Roots project, Barbarita Lara, has recently been elected a member of Mira district council.

None of this is ever likely to show up in any evaluation of IVS's contribution to Ecuador, yet I cannot help feeling that such matters, peripheral though they may appear, represent an important part of IVS's legacy to the region, and that this legacy is a natural extension of the priceless spirit that moved its founders to create the organization in the first place.

OUTCOMES

An appreciation of IVS has lived on in the hearts and minds of all those who were touched by the organization even when the goals of the original projects have ceased to be relevant. The cheese factory that was built as part of Carlos Muñoz's livestock improvement project in Cañar, Ecuador, is still operating successfully, but this is the only visible evidence of a project that involved hundreds of people and lasted a decade; in fact it is possibly the only visible evidence of a country program that lasted a quarter of a century. In Ecuador something of the IVS ethos may have lived on in the form of the national NGO MINGA but in Bolivia nothing remained. IVS Bolivia was established as a national NGO in 1997 but never really functioned as such. But all of this is to be expected; structures change and people move on.

What is left, therefore, are the people who worked for and with IVS who took from the organization knowledge and skills that they were able to use elsewhere, along with an assurance that there are people in the wider world who genuinely care about them, and a philosophy of life that brings us all just a little bit closer together.

In practical terms there may not be a lot to prove that we were ever around, but in the memories of the many connected with IVS, the impact has been enormous.

Appendix I

David Nuttle and the Buon Enao Strategic Hamlet Initiative in Vietnam

IVS's philosophy of non-involvement in politics or intelligence work was made clear to each and every volunteer. In Southeast Asia, however, where the intelligence agencies of a dozen nations thrived, battled and sought primacy, being uninvolved had its difficulties.

David Nuttle, who served with IVS from 1959 to 1961, remembers wanting to help shield the Montagnard tribes from the fighting that had already overtaken the country.

Nuttle's IVS experience was also foundational in providing the insights and understanding of the minority Rhade needs and aspirations.

"When I couldn't solve a problem on my own, I looked to Saigon for help. I counted on a colonel who was the hard-nosed chief of the MAAG Combined Studies Division (MAAG-CSD), which was connected with intelligence work in Vietnam. We discussed the Montagnards' problems and a variety of possible solutions."

Nuttle thought the U.S. should pressure the Government of Vietnam to provide social and economic programs that would benefit the Montagnards and make them a part of the nation. The colonel's position was that the Government of Vietnam (GVN) would never provide such assistance unless the Montagnards helped secure the Highlands from Viet Cong control. "We mutually agreed that the Montagnards would not fight for the GVN or South Vietnam per se. The Montagnards had no concept of nation or national defense, and no use for the GVN." Nuttle remembers that, "Our self-defense concept was based upon the Montagnards' obvious need to find a means of survival when caught in the middle of a war. During the French colonial administration, benevolent administrators had favored the Montagnards, providing them with education, agricultural improvement, and modern medicine. Thus, they already knew the fruits of social and economic assistance. It was a good plan, but I told the colonel that President Diem would never agree to arm the Montagnards for any reason."

AN URGENT MESSAGE

After returning to Ban Me Thuot and working ten days with the Rhade, one of the Montagnard tribes, Nuttle received an urgent message from IVS Headquarters in Saigon saying the U.S. Ambassador wanted to see him the following day. Nuttle was back in Saigon about an hour after dark, with an ulterior motive. He was seeing Bonnie, the daughter of the colonel, and hoped "to arrange a night out with her if she were home and if she had no other plans. Perhaps my luck would hold out."

The IVS Chief of party, *Gordon Brockmueller*, and the IVS staff were anxious to be updated on the security situation in Darlac Province, as well as developments at Ea Kmat Station. Nuttle told them nothing was really critical, and that security was deteriorating as it had been for months.

THE COLONEL'S DAUGHTER

Nuttle then rode his motorcycle to the colonel's house. Once there, "I immediately spotted his daughter talking with a small group of guests. I started toward her, only to be intercepted by the colonel. 'I want to talk to you,' he said.

"It sounded serious! As Bonnie turned to say hello, her father told her, 'You can have him later, but I want him now!' I was not really alarmed at this gruff statement, having gotten somewhat accustomed to the colonel's rough edges."

The colonel had been responsible for setting up a meeting with the Ambassador. "Our long conversations about the Montagnards' situation must have convinced someone that I knew a little about what was going on, and there was general agreement in the military and intelligence communities that something needed to be done."

Nuttle returned to the IVS house. "I briefed the IVS Chief at breakfast the next morning as planned then went to the Embassy.

The Ambassador started the meeting by saying that members of the Country Team wished to ask my opinion on how best to stop a possible VC takeover of the Highlands. My opinion was being solicited because of my knowledge and experience in the area. The Ambassador then brought the group up to date on the several options being considered to resolve the problem."

The most favored plan called for isolating the Montagnards from the VC or National Liberation Front (NLF). This might be accomplished by forcing the Montagnards onto types of secured reservations, thereby breaking contact with the enemy. The Ambassador said that MAAG recommended this approach because they felt that ARVN sweeps could thus be made more effective. Theoretically speaking, ARVN would establish free-fire zones and kill everything that moved outside of the reservations.

"The Ambassador then asked for my opinion. I ripped into the 'reservation plan' by focusing on all the obvious negatives. The Montagnards would resist forced relocation and would be alienated against those attempting it. If relocated, the Montagnards could and would escape any reservations by slipping away into the jungle. Living in the jungle, they would probably come under VC control." One of the military officers attending interrupted, saying that while Nuttle's arguments had some credibility, there seemed to be no other realistic alternative.

A SOLUTION

Nuttle had an opportunity to mention a solution he and the colonel had jointly conceived. Nuttle said, "If the GVN brings the Montagnards into the social and economic mainstream, there will be some motivational basis for a security program. But you should not expect the Montagnards to fight against the VC to protect Vietnam, the Vietnamese, or the GVN. The Montagnards will fight to defend family, home, and village. I believe they would indirectly support the GVN by resisting VC control, taxation, and conscription of young men. Such a program would be effective, in my opinion, if arms were provided to the

Montagnards, and if the ARVN would stop bombing and attacking Montagnard villages."

The Ambassador thanked Nuttle for his contribution but observed that the GVN would probably view arming the Montagnards as an unacceptable alternative. At this point, the Ambassador noted that Nuttle was free to leave the meeting.

EAGER TO LEARN

The month of August, 1961, passed quickly. "I spent nearly all my time at the GVN training center outside of Ban Me Thuot. The fifteen agricultural trainees learned quickly. But this was typical of the Rhade, because they were always eager to learn. As an advisor, my role was to assist in development of the training program. I would also help the instructors prepare their lessons and then observe their classes. If an instructor needed help, I would tutor him after class. The idea was to work myself out of a job as quickly as possible by upgrading the proficiency of the Rhade instructors."

Nuttle realized he and his team were trying to make quantum leaps to rapidly improve a primitive subsistence-type agricultural system. "If we could help bring it up to, say, the level of 1920s agriculture in the US, we would be happy. Of course, the Rhade would not be able to afford machines or chemical fertilizers, but there were other ways to make improvements. We placed a major emphasis on improved plant varieties, better hand tools, water conservation, natural disease control, and organic farming methods. As a result, the villagers we helped had improved both their diets and health, and a surplus of food was now being produced and stored to help overcome crop failures. Yes, it actually looked like progress was being made."

IGNORED REQUESTS

On the first of September Nuttle flew to Saigon on Air Vietnam for a quick meeting at IVS Headquarters. This was a monthly routine meeting to help coordinate plans and programs with

USOM and the GVN. He used the opportunity to see if the Vietnamese Agricultural Director, Tran Van Hieu, "had approached the Health Minister with my complaint about medical treatment for the Rhade. As I feared, Hieu had ignored my request. This was typical of some GVN officials. Their stock-in-trade was to say 'yes' to all requests and then forget about most of them. I would have to look for another solution."

He drove around Saigon in a borrowed IVS Jeep making his coordination rounds. Later, he stopped by the Colonel's and was invited to come for dinner. He took the opportunity to raise the issue of the Montagnards medical treatment problem and asked the colonel for a suggested solution. The colonel responded that he'd give the matter his consideration, since it was obviously going to further alienate the Montagnards against the GVN.

The following morning, Nuttle flew back to Ban Me Thuot, but on October 3rd, he was back in Saigon for another monthly coordination meeting where the colonel asked him to meet a friend of his. Nuttle began to suspect something was up.

"As a result of that dinner meeting, I found myself agreeing to sign a contract with the CIA, a contract to 'go forth and help the military create a pilot model of a Montagnard defended village.' In brief, the Country Team wanted to see if I could put my words into action. I immediately resigned from IVS so I could change over to my new project."

The defended village concept had just been sold to South Vietnam's President Diem. Diem agreed to "experiment" with a Montagnard-defended village as a last hope of saving the Highlands.

Nuttle believed that while the Montagnards disliked and distrusted all Vietnamese, they might agree to resist VC control if the GVN would leave them alone. The sticking point was that this would mean arming some of the Montagnards. Even so, Nuttle agreed to try to initiate a village defense experiment among the Rhade tribe of Darlac Province. He did so believing his efforts might save the Montagnards from being annihilated by opposing Vietnamese forces.

A CONTRACT WITH THE CIA

"I signed a contract with the CIA on October 4, 1961. Within a few days, a U.S. Army Special Forces medical sergeant was assigned as tactical adviser with the additional role of developing a medical civic-action program."

The province chief was briefed on the idea of village defense for the Montagnards, and gave his authorization to initiate the experiment in one Rhade village. The team studied the Rhade dilemma. Rhade villages were being attacked by ARVN and bombed by the Vietnamese air force when suspected of supporting the VC. The VC were using terrorism to extort rice, livestock and manpower from the Rhade villages. Rhade lands had been taken without compensation by the Saigon government for resettlement of refugees originally from North Vietnam.

The team decided to approach the village of Buon Enao. "I personally knew the village chief, a wise old Rhade named Y-Ju. On the first day of the team visit, the Special Forces medical sergeant was introduced as Dr. Paul. It turned out, Y-Ju's daughter, was ill. We asked Y-Ju for permission to treat her in conjunction with Buon Enao's witch doctor." Dr. Paul handed the daughter's medication to the sorcerer, thus creating a bond of friendship. The sorcerer added his own ritual chant, his stock in trade, and then gave the medication to Y-Ju's daughter. "This was the beginning of two weeks of discussions between Y-Ju, Buon Enao elders, and the team, to which was now attached another CIA Special Operations Officer."

CONCESSIONS

During the course of these discussions, the village elders were all in agreement that Rhade villages could not survive being attacked by both Viet Cong and Government of South Vietnam. They said they would resist the VC if the GVN made certain concessions. First, the ARVN and Vietnamese air force would have to stop attacking Rhade villages. Second, Rhade forced to train with or support the VC, would be given amnesty upon declaring their allegiance to the GVN. Third, medical, educational and agricultural assistance programs would have to be guaranteed to the Rhade.

If the GVN accepted these conditions, Buon Enao would act as the test village. The Rhade would meet Diem's conditions of erecting a fence around the village, complete with signs declaring their allegiance to the GVN. This would be done after training a village-defense force armed with crossbows and spears, until such time as Diem gave approval for rifles and shotguns. Underground family shelters were to be constructed to provide protection for women and children.

CROSSBOWS AND SPEARS

The tentative agreement also called for the immediate training of Rhade village medics and the building of a dispensary. The agreement was finalized and celebrated with a rice wine party, monkey meat, gong-banging and sorcerer chants for the success of the venture.

Events at Buen Enao proceeded essentially as planned; a thirty-man village defense force and four medics were trained and fences, shelters and a dispensary constructed by the villagers. A trail-watch system was established to warn of approaching VC. Signs went up on the fence. The defense force patrolled and set ambushes using crossbows and spears. Families were drilled in the use of the shelters. "Three villagers were identified as having attended VC training camps; Phu and I began a re-education program for them, and they later identified other Montagnards whom they had seen at various VC training camps."

This was the beginning of what proved to be an effective counterintelligence net. Y-Ju was asked to certify the loyalty of each villager. Each man in the defense force vouched for the loyalty of the man on his right during each inspection formation. Intelligence operations were designed to ferret out VC apparatus, actions, plans and cadres. The village defense leadership team started living at Buon Enao to boost village confidence in the experiment.

The day after the completion of the Buon Enao dispensary in mid-November 1961, a GVN inspection team arrived from Saigon and concluded that the Rhade villagers had kept their part of the bargain and approval was granted for arming the thirty village defenders of Buon Enao, and training started immediately.

AN EXPANSION

Ngo Dinh Nhu, the brother of President Diem, visited Buon Enao in mid-December 1961 and was so impressed that he authorized an expansion of the village defense concept in the Highlands, the Mekong Delta, and selected coastal areas. The chief was directed to personally oversee the expansion in Darlac province. Forty other Rhade villages within a fifteen-kilometer radius of Buon Enao would enter the program, on a voluntary basis, under essentially the same terms used for Buon Enao.

The proposed expansion went as planned but a problem surfaced. Every village had three or four villagers who were known VC supporters. Not a single village chief wanted to allow these individuals to remain in his village, while fearing the GVN would torture, jail or kill any Rhade with a VC label. No one wanted to point a finger at a fellow villager who had been forced to support the VC.

"Phu and I approached the chief and suggested he officially endorse the amnesty program proposed during inception of the Buon Enao project. Bang agreed to do so, if a re-education and resettlement effort was used to isolate the VC identified by the village chiefs. Captain Phu accepted the terms and asked for land to be used for a resettlement village. The Province Chief agreed to provide some GVN-owned land nine kilometers east of Buen Enao. A small resettlement village was started, and a major roadblock was removed. The ex-VC who became a part of this program assisted in counterintelligence efforts and actually became a major asset.

"By April 1962, the first forty-village complex had been

completed. Fourteen thousand Rhade village defenders proved they could protect their villages from frequent and heavily armed VC attack. It was clear that the VC perceived the Civilian Irregular Defense Group (CIDG) program to be a real threat. The Buon Enao complex was given authority to expand to 200 villages with a total population of 60,000."

Just prior to the proposed expansion, an official Department of Defense-Defense Intelligence Agency delegation from Washington visited Buon Enao to find out what was needed to speed up development of the CIDG program. Close air support allowed the Vietnamese forces to defend against heavy VC attacks now re-enforced by some North Vietnamese Army (NVA) components.

HEAVY VC ATTACK

But just as it appeared the project was succeeding, there were some early signs that the Buon Bnao project would fall apart. This came about after a heavy VC attack on the village of Buon Trap. At least two VC companies kept the village defenders pinned down for over forty-eight hours. A strike-force relief unit had to fight its way through a large ambush before it could relieve Buon Trap. "While all this was happening, a company of ARVN marines sat on a hill overlooking Buon Trap and lifted not one finger to help. A later investigation revealed that they were cheering for the Rhade and VC to kill each other.

"Basic distrust, dislike and suspicion continued between the Vietnamese and the Montagnards. Many Vietnamese government officials were dragging their feet to slow the implementation of economic assistance to the Rhade. Social and political isolation of all Montagnards continued despite GVN pledges to make changes. By August 1962, President Diem's brother and advisor, Ngo Dinh Nhu, ordered a thirty-day halt to the arming of Montagnards. Nhu indicated that he wanted time to conduct a review of the entire program. At the time of this review, we knew that Diem and Nhu were having ever increasing paranoia about arming their own population, a population that often resented the corruption of the GVN."

HISTORICAL ENEMIES

As a result of the review, Nhu decided that the GVN could not be secure unless the Montagnards were disarmed as soon as the local VC were defeated. "He felt the Montagnards were not to be trusted and were the historical enemies of all Vietnamese. The problem was how to disarm the Montagnards without a violent reaction. Nhu conceived a plan of declaring certain parts of each village-defense complex as being safe. Village defenders in those zones would then be required to return their weapons to the GVN. Strike force personnel in this area would be drafted for service in the ARVN. "Nhu's plan was devoid of reality, but even so, it was accepted and endorsed by members of the U.S. Country Team. The trial and error process was now being repeated once again. In this case, the opera was not over when the fat lady sang—a new fat lady came on stage, and yet another opera started."

At the same time that Nhu was making his plans, the U.S. military decided that CIDG programs were becoming too large for civilian control. ARVN was encouraged to quickly absorb the CIDG program. A plan was devised, codenamed "Operation Switchback," to transfer the support and advisory role to the Department of Defense.

DEFEAT THE VC

The focus of the U.S. effort had suddenly become how to militarily defeat the VC. The new MACV (Military Assistance Command Vietnam, the successor to MAAG) Chief supported a military takeover of the CIDG program allegedly to have a single chain of command. ARVN and the U.S. military had great difficulty in understanding the Buon Enao concept because there was no traditional military emphasis on attacking the enemy. So U.S. commanders proceeded with plans to conventionalize the war,

which Nhu favored as a means of keeping the Vietnamese population divided, disarmed, and with little means of influencing the
politics of Vietnam.

As far as the Montagnards were concerned, the GVN and
the Americans had violated the spirit and terms of their original
agreements. CIDG villages, disarmed by the GVN, were again
forced to accommodate themselves to the VC. Some CIDG strike
force personnel elected to disappear rather than be drafted into
ARVN. Other Montagnard tribesmen escaped the draft by serving as U.S. mercenaries engaged in the defense of remote and
isolated Special Forces outposts along the Ho Chi Minh Trail.
U.S. Army Special Forces understood, and performed well in the
pacification effort. But U.S. commanders effectively ordered an
end to their program as well.

Appendix II

The IVS Danang Street Boy Project

This article represents the combined efforts in Vietnam of Russ Bradford, 1966-1969; Mechell Jacob, 1967-1970; and Bill Camp, 1967-1969. The story of the boys is recounted by Bill Camp.

Bill Camp

I was a Connecticut farm boy who came to IVS/Vietnam on the agricultural team but I never worked as an aggie! At a 1967 Christmas party, I was a frustrated volunteer when I met Steve Goldberg, an antiwar protester who worked with pickpockets and shoeshine boys in DaNang, Vietnam. He seemed to accept me when I told him how I'd gotten one piaster coins from store merchants and given them to the beggars in My Tho, where I served when I was a soldier in the Army before IVS. Soon I was sent to DaNang to work with the boys. Before going his own way, Steve spent a few days teaching me where I could find blankets, food and other supplies, and suddenly in January, 1968, I was on my own in the unknown world of the pickpockets and shoeshine boys in the DaNang Street Boys' House.

Our common meeting ground was that I had nothing to lose, and neither did the boys since, by definition, theirs was a hopeless state. I did not have any goals at the beginning as I didn't understand the world these boys lived in. I had to feel my way as I went along, while learning about them and how they survived.

There was a hierarchy on the streets and it reflected the strict social and economic levels of Vietnamese society. Shoeshine boys were near the bottom, pickpockets just a step above, since the pickpockets were a little older and made more money than the shoeshiners. The pickpockets ranged in age from fifteen to seventeen years old; the shoeshine boys were much younger—some only five- or six-years-old. Both lived in a constant survival mode. The shoeshine boys needed permission from boys higher up the scale, such as those who worked in bars, to work certain sections of the street. They slept in open markets or on the street with the rats, foul odors and debris. They ate whatever they could and dressed in whatever they could find. Some of them moved up the ladder and became pickpockets who generally did not sleep in open markets, dressed better and even had homes to go to at night. A few pickpockets set up shoeshine boys in business by giving them boxes and supplies. Then they'd proceed to collect money back from them, a type of economic slavery.

Shortly after Steve Goldberg left, *Larry Peterson* came and lived in the house for some months. Together we decided to make some changes. I'd been overwhelmed with what little I understood, but went ahead with what I guessed needed to be done. The first action was to kick out the pickpockets who were using the IVS house to stash their stolen goods and not allowing the shoeshine boys into the house. We had to fight a couple of them to get them out; I had a close call when one of them, Chien, winged a brick that just missed me. Chien eventually came back to the house and behaved himself. We stopped the practice of the pickpockets setting up the younger shoeshine boys in business and then taking money from them. Most of the boys could not read or write so I started teaching them the Vietnamese version of the ABCs and some of the older boys assisted. At times I would go out on the streets and pull boys back inside the house because they were skipping their lessons. I sent some kids to typing school and others to public school, though they didn't last long there because of prejudice, no family, poor clothes and low standing. We established a schedule. The kids gambled a lot playing cards at the house. Sometimes we'd take this card money and tell them it was to buy oil for the cook stove or other necessities. We established mandatory personal hygiene. I built a compartment type of locker where the boys could stash their personal property. I kept their money in individual containers in my bedroom. No one ever tried to steal that. At times I'd go into the streets and open markets telling boys of the IVS house as a place of refuge and taking them on my Vespa directly from the streets to the IVS house. At first I was too easy, and I nearly got overwhelmed.

In order to maintain discipline, I learned to act in a way the boys understood, basically the 'rule of the streets' based on fear and respect! It was not a feel-good, lovey-dovey situation at all; I was firm, physical at times, as a father should be when necessary. I used my age to gain respect, a well-understood feature of Vietnamese culture.

Our team leader, *Rich Jones*, was of great assistance. He sent over two high school boys, Hong and Thanh, to work with me. They not only took over the educational aspects of the activities but were also very good influences on the boys. Rich actually even got IVS to pay a small salary to them. These two high school students made the biggest difference in the time I was managing the IVS house. Rich also provided much needed advice and was a good sounding board for me as well. The word spread that the IVS house was a better option than life on the streets and that I'd protect the kids.

All this occurred in I Corps, primarily DaNang, during the worst period of the war. This was warfare with B52 bombers, F15 fighter jets, tanks, flame throwers, napalm, constant troop movements and seemingly daily battles. People's lives were intertwined with the conflict and that included the shoeshine boys and pickpockets, many of whom had lost family, friends and seen war's cruelty firsthand. There was constant uncertainty that all had to adjust to. Some adjusted better than others. The 1968 Tet Offensive did not cause any more stress on the boys, all they knew was war, but it was the most difficult time for me!

The Tet Offensive brought more boys into the IVS house than I could accommodate. There was a twenty-four-hour curfew and they came to seek refuge. I obtained old gurneys from the hospitals and used them as beds. These had last been used to carry dead people and tradition called for the gurneys to be burned. I took them to the IVS house where the boys and I cleaned them as best we could. Some of the boys left the house during these trying times. I slept with a carbine, that I finally abandoned, fearful that I might shoot myself.

There were other difficulties. A plague epidemic broke out

and I got a lot of the kids vaccinated. During one mortar attack, I remember hiding in our well-built cement out-house just outside the IVS house with a bunch of the boys. That was one of several times I really thought of leaving Vietnam. *Sue Brannon*, an IVS teacher, asked me to teach school in Hoi An, a nearby small city, while she went on vacation, and there was an attack during my first night there. The war followed me to Dalat, normally a quiet place, when I went there to take a break from the IVS DaNang house. An Indian IVS agricultural volunteer and I hid underneath cement stairs in the house during a mortar attack. Once again, I thought of leaving Vietnam.

I have fond memories of rewarding times. There was an elderly Vietnamese couple who owned a small *pho* shop near the IVS house. They would also take in street boys and from what I saw, did not seek anything from them. This was unusual behavior in the status-conscious Vietnamese society. The couple would even tell me if there were Viet Cong in the area.

One boy, Thanh, was a regular live-in, along with his five-year- old brother, Tan. When their father died, Thanh asked me and *Phil Yang,* another IVS volunteer, if we'd drive our vehicle in the funeral procession. We did, and ours was the only vehicle in the funeral procession except the one carrying their father.

After IVS left Vietnam, I stayed and worked for five years in Saigon for the American Medical Association. During that time several boys followed me to Saigon. I guess they felt attached to me, and that was a good feeling. One time *Pete Stilley*, another IVS volunteer, told me of a boy who had his hand injured in an attack in the village of Nam Ho. When I approached the village on my mighty Vespa, I encountered a Marine unit and soldiers told me the area was very dangerous. He suggested I spend no more than fifteen minutes at a time there. When I entered the village there was open hostility but I found the boy anyway. It took three surgeries over a six-month period before his hand was corrected. I took him to Navy surgeons each time, stayed with him, and returned him to his village. In the same village, I was asked by some villagers, to find Hiep, a boy who had disappeared. I learned he'd been taken to a Vietnamese Catholic orphanage; I went there and talked to Sister Theresa, who verified he was there and agreed he should go home to Nam Ho. I returned him to his village—an unfriendly one—and his parents didn't invite me for tea or even thank me.

Teaching the Vietnamese version of the ABCs to the boys was my most rewarding experience.

After I left the DaNang IVS house in September 1968, *Phil Yang* remained. He turned the project over to a committee of teachers and lawyers. Unfortunately, these two groups did not work together because they were from different classes. Sadly, the project fell apart.

Over the years I have thought often of the IVS DaNang street boy project. There are questions I will never be able to answer. I am not sure that I accomplished anything. I don't know if I was a role model. I don't know if I left anything sustainable in the lives of the boys. I don't know if I made a difference.

RAISING DUCKS IN BANGLADESH, PART I

Ducks are a good and cheap source of protein in a country like Bangladesh where many people suffer from lack of protein. IVS became involved in a pilot project to promote duck-raising among local farmers, and IVSer Jim Archer, recalls the project's birth.

JIM ARCHER

WHEN I ARRIVED IN BANGLADESH IN 1973, I was without a specific job until I met Carl Ryther of the Baptist Mission at Feni, in the Noakhali district. We were both in agreement that ducks were needed in Bangladesh. There are no feeds for chicken, and flock after flock had failed, while there appeared to be abundant natural food for ducks. The government farms were still trying to raise hens for eggs, but we decided to go ahead with a duck project.

Before the duck project could start, we had to have ducks. Since I had been in Laos and Thailand, I knew we could get laying ducks in Bangkok. We decided that I would make a trip to locate good stock, prices and other supplies for raising ducklings.

I went to Thailand, at the expense of the Baptist Mission, and located duckling dealers. These men were also hatching the eggs with the rice-husk system. With the assistance of the Baptist Mission in Bangkok, we arranged shipping procedures and I took notes on the hatching system and looked over the setup they had.

The rice husk system is too complicated to describe fully here, but the main principle is the utilization of metabolic heat, produced by developing embryos, to heat fresh eggs or eggs with less developed ducklings. No electricity is required; anyone can learn the system, and only local materials are needed.

When I returned to Bangladesh, I went to Comilla, in the southeast of the country, for several months as we were to raise the young ducks in the poultry facilities that the Kotwali Thana Central Cooperative Association had laying idle. The ducklings were raised in battery brooders for a couple of weeks and then put onto the floor. We fed them damaged CSM (Corn-Soya-Milk), originally brought over as baby food and damaged in storage. We had mixed success. Some lots did well and others had a very poor survival rate. This was partly due to stress during shipping (and the fact that some ducklings were too old for shipping). Enteritis from the food we were using also took its toll.

At the beginning, I worked with employees of the KTCCA Poultry Department, who were idle since they had no poultry to work with. Later on Carl Ryther brought in a local man, Samir Barol, and this turned out to be one of the key factors in our project's success. Samir was not initially impressed with the type of work he had to do and came close to quitting on a few occasions. But, as the project developed, he became more interested until he was completely in charge by the time I left Bangladesh in 1975.

At about this time, I made an important discovery that proved to be vital to the project. I purchased some ducks in the market and they shortly fell sick and died. The symptoms matched no disease I was familiar with, so I took the remaining duck to the government's Animal Husbandry Research Laboratory in Comilla and contacted an official there who kept the duck for observation and began a series of lab tests after the duck died. He told me the duck had died of the duck plague, and gave me some literature on the disease. It turned out that this disease originated in the West Bengal area of India and had apparently spread to Bangladesh. There was a vaccine manufactured against the illness, but it was only available in India. I had meanwhile been checking around and found that the disease was causing great losses in our area, so we decided that I should travel to Calcutta to obtain the vaccine.

Upon my return, we began vaccinating the ducklings against fowl cholera and duck plague. With the ducklings growing, I moved to Feni and rented a house with an outside shed that we could convert to a hatchery. With only local materials, such as bamboo matting, rice husk, wire, burlap straw and cloth, we built our incubation room and began to experiment with the rice husk system.

We obtained eggs from a farmer who was rearing ducks in a similar manner to Vietnamese, Chinese and Taiwanese farmers. He herded his flock of about a hundred to areas where there was still ungleaned rice on the ground after the harvest. When this was exhausted, he fed the ducks on bran until the rains came again. At this time, the ducks were taken to the mud flats where they feasted on slugs and other invertebrates. In a normal year, his ducks did well and laid very well at the beginning of the rainy season and during the rice harvest.

The hatchery side began to work quite well although we never seemed to achieve the high rate of hatching obtained in Taiwan. We put this down to poor egg quality as well as lack of experience.

As the ducklings began to hatch and grow to saleable size, Carl Ryther began a system of distribution among the people in Feni. They were required to pay a basic price and then return to us a fixed number of eggs when the ducks began to lay. We would provide adequate service and vaccinations. In a few cases this worked, but it became too unwieldy to try and keep track of payments. The ducks in the Feni area generally did not do well because they caused too much damage to the rice crops and their owners would not control them.

Feed for the ducks had become a serious problem. We were raising the young on boiled rice, boiled wheat and fishmeal, and the enteritis problems had been minimized, but food for adult ducks was a constant worry. Bangladesh, with its food shortage, just has no foods that can provide calories in sufficient quantity for a duck or hen in confinement. We decided that the ducks had to be able to get their own feed by gleaning harvested fields and feeding in flooded areas.

Jim Gingerich, then the IVS Field Director in Bangladesh, and I planned some investigatory trips to other areas of Bangladesh. We found a small group of farmers in Chicknagul who had small flocks of twenty or so birds, and a young boy took them out every day to forage or glean the fields. The ducks, herded like sheep and under constant supervision, were never allowed to damage standing crops.

We talked with these men and found they were on the verge of quitting duck raising because of the constant losses from disease. We told them of our program, our ducks and our vaccines. They agreed to buy some ducks and we promised to vaccinate these for them.

In Feni, the adult ducks that Carl was keeping were suffering from the food shortage and the lack of quality feed even when we could find something. Carl decided to try to maintain a limited number of ducks in Feni, since he was established there, but IVS planned its own duck project in Sylhet. Shortly after I left Bangladesh in 1975, Samir began the new duck project in Sylhet.

RAISING DUCKS IN BANGLADESH, PART II

The project's supervisor recounts how the original effort was expanded to include a successful training center for would-be duck raisers. These edited recollections were originally published in Dialogue, IVS, *Winter/Spring 1978-79.*

FREDDIE DE PEDRO[*]

In the context of national initiatives in poultry development, IVS is seeking to stimulate interest in duck-raising among villagers in Sylhet and elsewhere, as part of an IVS-sponsored integrated rural development project now in its third year in 1978. The Government's Integrated Rural Development Program asked IVS to assist in the creation of, and provide staff for, ten regional training centers similar to the IVS center in Sylhet. Since the center began, almost 300 men and women have learned how to raise ducks through the Sylhet duck program. Many of the trainees have been women nominated by women's cooperatives. Other

---

[*]Freddie De Pedro served in Bangladesh from 1973 to 1980.

trainees have come from cooperatives within the villages covered by the IVS-sponsored village development project in Sylhet, and from other agencies in Bangladesh.

Candidates are accepted for training only if the villages or areas to which they will return are suitable for duck-raising. The trainees, whose sponsors pay 500 taka (U.S. $35) for their three-week residential courses, learn about duck raising both in the classroom and through field work with ducks in the villages where IVS is carrying on an extension program. The course covers everything from the care, feeding and housing of ducks (unhoused ducks in Bangladesh are prey to predators such as jackals and mongoose), to preventing and identifying diseases. Some useful tips are also taught—such as using hens to hatch duck eggs, since in their villages the volume of egg production is too low to make use of an incubator feasible.

The trainees are instructed by the center staff, me and three Bangladeshis. Between ten and fifteen trainees attend each three-week course and, on completion of their training, each is provided with fifty ducklings from the IVS hatchery to take home as the foundation stock for the new flock he or she hopes to develop. Trainees also receive a syringe with which to inoculate their ducks against fowl cholera and duck plague.

Those trainees who do make a go of duck raising act, in ef-fect, as extension agents for the program through demonstration: Villagers can see for themselves the benefits of duck farming and can obtain guidance and duck eggs from the trainees. And there have been some particular success stories. A man from Mymensingh district who took the IVS training course now has a thriving duck business of his own with a government contract to furnish 10,000 ducklings for the government extension program. Less spectacular, but equally rewarding, is the case of a widow with six children who is now supporting her family entirely through the sale of eggs from her duck flock.

There is no doubt that duck farming in Bangladesh makes sense agriculturally, economically, ecologically and in terms of the health benefits gained from the extra protein in people's diets from duck eggs and meat. Hopefully, rural extension programs can put the advantages of duck farming within the grasp of those village families standing to gain most from this kind of activity.

Appendix IV
WILLIE MEYERS RESIGNATION LETTER

By the summer of 1967, arguments raged regarding the roles of IVS and its volunteers in war-torn Vietnam. Willie Meyer, a Mennonite and graduate of Goshen College, sent this letter to the IVS Chief of Party in Saigon as discussion of IVS's role in Vietnam was being considered by many of the volunteers. He decided to resign from his job in Vietnam, as did three other volunteers. Another letter was written and signed by a significant number of volunteers in the country, who chose to stay and serve out their contracts. That letter was sent to the U.S. Congress.

Meyer's letter is re-printed here to illustrate the feelings many people shared during the expansion in the conflict. It must have been startling to their Vietnamese friends and colleagues to understand that Americans could make a peaceful protest to their government without any fear for their freedom.

The Board of Directors of IVS in Washington chose not to take a stand on the conflict because its charter defined it as "...non-denominational, apolitical, and free of government influence..."

Donald Luce   26 August 1967
Chief of Party   Can Tho, Vietnam
IVS, Vietnam

Dear Don:

I have worked for IVS more than four years now, three of these in Vietnam. During this time, I have developed a strong and personal attachment to the organization and to those who are responsible for its administration. During the three years in Vietnam, I have also developed a deep concern about and a better comprehension of United States policy in Vietnam and its effect on the Vietnamese people. It is the latter which summons me reluctantly to resign from IVS within three months of the date of this letter.

I could never have justified my working here in terms of the motives of the U.S. Mission, but I could and did justify working for IVS with the hope that my work would be of some benefit to a few Vietnamese people no matter what the outcome of the war was. There was always the problem that most Americans and Vietnamese considered IVS members as part of the U.S. Mission, but I considered this a necessary but not devastating misunderstanding which I tried to correct among acquaintances. However, this has continually become more of a problem and finally has become intolerable for at least three reasons:

1. The U.S. Mission has continued to develop a more rigid structure and finally placed all field operations under the United States Military Command, all of which has been destroying piece by piece the independent role and identification of IVS members.

2. This rigid structure along with United States' policy and actions in Vietnam have made it more and more difficult for IVS to serve Vietnam's needs effectively. Let me give two examples:

a. IVS members are often under pressure to assist in priority programs, which tend to be dominated by Americans, and find it more and more difficult to respond to needs as expressed by Vietnamese people they work with.

b. The effect of the massive American Presence both military and civilian and the consequent attitudes that many Vietnamese have toward Americans, make it more difficult for us to build a genuine relationship with people we wish to work with.

3. The United States' policy and actions and their consequences in Vietnam, with which we are ever more closely identified, have become so distasteful to me that I wish to be completely disassociated from them. Three major examples of this are:

a. The massive introduction of American troops and extensive bombing in the North and the South have greatly intensified the war and the suffering of the Vietnamese people. In the Mekong Delta I expect that the introduction of American troops will mean more troops from the Communist side, more fighting, more bombing, more suffering, more refugees and no improvement in the general security of the area.

b. During the three years that I've been here since June 1963, the United States has steadily increased its authoritative role in the affairs of Vietnam until today very little sovereignty remains for the Government of the Republic of Vietnam. This is a bitter thing for many Vietnamese people to accept, especially for those who are being pressured by Americans daily to do this or that. This, along with thousands of American faces also tends to confirm in the minds of many people the allegation of the NLF that the United States is just like France before it.

c. By far the most serious and intolerable action of the United States is that we have not sincerely and persistently sought to bring peace to Vietnam, but rather have brought more troops and bombs and war, and thus moved further away from the possibility of a peaceful settlement. This is completely counter to the interests and desires of the majority of the Vietnamese people.

I regret that my country, to which I owe so much, is compromising itself and its best traditions in the Vietnam Affair. The traditions and the people of the United States deserve a much better representation in the world, and I hope that someday they will have it.

To a certain extent, IVS work is part of a sugarcoating on the undesirable aspects of the American Effort in Vietnam, and I no longer wish to be used in that way or to remain silent on these important issues. I feel that IVS can still carry on some work here which is of benefit to the Vietnamese people, but for me the personal compromises which are involved in staying with IVS in Vietnam are unacceptable.

I feel strongly that developmental assistance is best carried out by truly international efforts which completely disregard the national interests of the contributing countries. I hope that I can devote many more years of my life to such efforts and to return to Vietnam in such a capacity when Vietnam has a government that is free from foreign domination and a people that is free from the ravages of war.

Respectfully submitted,

Willie Meyers
Team leader, Region IV

Appendix V
International Voluntary Services Executive Directors

John S. Noffsinger   1953 – 1961

Russell Stevenson   1961 – 1964

John Province

    November 1964 until his death in January 1965

Arthur Z. Gardiner   1965 – 1970

Richard J. Peters   1971 – 1974

Anthony Lake   1974 – 1976

John Rigby   1976 – 1980

Nan Borton   1981 – 1989

David R. Smock   1989 – 1991

Linda Worthington and Don Luce

    Co-executive Directors   1991 – 1993

Don Luce   1993 – 1996

Parker F. Hallberg   1996 – 1997

Anne Shirk   1998 – 2002

IVS FREQUENTLY ASKED QUESTIONS (FAQ)

Was IVS created so conscientious objectors could have a place to serve other than in the military?

IVS was not created as an alternative service organization, but as operations were developed, IVS did serve as alternative service for some conscientious objectors. Conversely, many volunteers had already served their military service prior to joining IVS. IVS was not created to be, nor was it, a U.S. government agency.

Were American intelligence personnel placed with IVS in Vietnam, Laos and Cambodia, during the conflict there?

IVS held a long-standing operational policy of not allowing team members to be associated with intelligence gathering responsibilities. This was enforced throughout the life of IVS.

Was IVS really the precursor to the Peace Corps?

Yes, in many ways, IVS was the precursor of and the template for the Peace Corps (PC):

- Village level projects in developing countries initiated with the assistance of young Americans were already ongoing within IVS for eight years prior to PC establishment,
- Emphasis was placed on local languages and developing relationships among IVS volunteers,
- IVS and the PC enjoyed similar levels of in-country support as well as monthly payment rate,
- Both organizations used local travel and medical support as available,
- Similar two-year tours of duty were minimally supervised by thin country staff,

At time of the PC establishment (1962) the senior consultant to Sargent Shriver, first director of the Peace Corps, was IVS Director Dr. John Noffsinger, who had long-time credentials in international development work.

How did developing countries ask for IVS help?

Different countries would have been handled in different ways, but as for Vietnam and Laos, in-country IVS assistance originated with the Ministry or agency of request, forwarded via team leadership and channeled through to IVS and USAID offices in Washington, D.C. In later years and smaller programs, IVS developed proposals for volunteer assignments and work and submitted them to USAID.

How much were volunteers paid? Were team leaders paid more?

In 1960 volunteers received $60 a month, which was deposited directly into a U.S. bank account. This was later raised to $80 a month, all in keeping with similar levels of pay for a private in the U.S. Army, according to founding IVS board member, Dr. Dale Clark. Yes, a team leader was paid more. An agricultural team leader was paid $150 a month. By the late 60s the compensation was $75 per month for living allowance plus house rental plus $75 per month repatriation allowance.

When did women begin volunteering with IVS?

Women were recruited as volunteers very early in the IVS experience, that is to say in the mid-50s. Women were on the first teams in Iraq, Laos, and Vietnam, to name a few. Martha Rupel, a nurse in Iraq who joined IVS in 1953, was the first woman IVSer. Cherie (Woodcock) Mitchell, a home economist, was the second.

Did only young people volunteer?

Young volunteers, i.e., recent college graduates were in the majority in early recruitment, but older persons were also recruited later as skill requirements began to expand. "Pop" Buell in Laos was in his late 40s, for example.

Was it suggested that IVSers bring a gun and heavy boots for the jungle?

New women members received some instructions on weapons and jungle wear in the early 60s, but this was not continued.

Did IVS ever meet the goal of less than forty-nine percent U.S. government funding?

IVS never came even close to developing support mechanisms where government funds were a minor part of the continuing budget.

How did the volunteers communicate with their friends and families when they were in the field?

Contact with family and friends back home was normally conducted via mail. Telephone and telegraph were both available but were more costly, time-consuming and quite limited.

Were there rules against fraternization with fellow volunteers? With locals?

There were no specific rules on fraternization with either team members or locals, other than with sensitivity and with respect. Rather, it was expected that new volunteers would conduct themselves on a basis of total acceptance, recognizing each new acquaintance as another addition to one's rapidly expanding circle of contacts and friends.

How were volunteers briefed prior to being sent out? Were the briefings adequate?

For the group going to Vietnam in the first teams, the briefings were scanty since Dr. Noffsinger was having health problems at that time. Later, the IVS Executive Director, Dr. Russell Stevenson, met volunteers on the West Coast for a day or two of briefing. As to adequacy, since the entire experience was totally new, the effective briefings were more likely exercises focused on creating attitude and open minds, and less on detail of the new circumstances. By the late '60s volunteers had well thought-out orientation in groups in the U.S. and in-country.

Did IVS look for specific skills when selecting volunteers?

IVS always tried to recruit for sought-after skills. Early on, IVS recruited large numbers of land-grant college graduates in support of agricultural projects. As opportunities expanded, skill sets were selected from other schools as well.

Were all volunteers U.S. citizens?

Initially, all volunteers were U.S. nationals, with an occasional exception of Canadian or English. After the Harpers Ferry gathering in 1971, a new direction of recruiting international volunteers was established.

How many volunteers were killed during the hostile actions in Vietnam, Laos and Cambodia?

A total of eleven volunteers died with nine killed during hostile actions.

In 1965, Peter M. Hunting was killed in an ambush.

In 1966, Max Sinkler was killed when his Jeep hit an Army truck.

On August 5,1966, Arthur Stillman, Dennis L. Mummert, and two Lao veterinarians were killed in an ambush.

In 1966, Michael Murphy drowned while crossing the Mekong River.

On March 25, 1967, Fred Cheydleur and his Lao assistant were assassinated.

In 1967, Martin J. Clish died when his plane crashed in Laos.

In 1967, Richard M. Sisk was killed in Phan Rang.

In 1968, David L. Gitelson was taken prisoner and shot.

On April 24, 1969, Chandler Scott Edwards and his two assistants were killed in an ambush.

On July 14, 1972, Alexander D. Shimkin was killed by a hand grenade.

Additional information on IVS volunteers killed in Southeast Asia can be found in *The IVS Experience-From Algeria to Vietnam*, edited by Stuart Rawlings.

Why did volunteers need a white suit when first departing for Vietnam?

It would be necessary for formal occasions with the expatriate community. It was worn perhaps once or twice, but generally not needed. This was a throwback to earlier colonial habits and not encouraged among later volunteers.

Were volunteers allowed to visit other countries while on vacation?

IVSers were encouraged to visit other countries during their vacation time allotments. In Vietnam, a volunteer was allotted $300 to offset costs for a month's vacation. 'Space available' on U.S. military aircraft was offered regionally in East Asia to vacationing IVSers.

How did IVS maintain housekeeping both at headquarters and with volunteers at in-country assignments?

IVS headquarters in-country and local officials would assist in securing housing for a newly placed volunteer. IVS also had a limited stock of home furnishings to be made available to new locations. Home assistance, i.e., cooking, laundry, etc., were usually arranged through local domestic contacts.

As security worsened in Vietnam during the early 1960s, how did volunteers ensure their personal safety and know where to go and not go?

IVSers probably relied most closely on local district and provincial officials for updated security information. Good working relationships were very important to assure effectiveness. And there were also American sources from its Embassy, but they were generally much less specific.

What was the protocol for working locally and how did volunteers develop relationships with local officials?

IVSers would be introduced to provincial officers of their new assignment by team leaders. Sometimes multiple visits to an IVS field location were necessary to assure good relationships with local officials.

Volunteers working in the countryside of the host country were usually in a position to become quite knowledgeable about local situations, for example, social, administrative and economic conditions. How did volunteers contribute to funneling this build-up of local familiarity into useful purposes?

Project concepts would be conceived at the village or district level and then proposals would be funneled back to provincial and national levels of the host government.

Technicians within USAID would give credence to IVS sourced concepts and observations and would be useful for planning purposes at the national level.

BIBLIOGRAPHY

BOOKS

Bonacci, Mark A. PhD. *The Legacy of Colonialism Health Care in Southeast Asia*. Washington, D.C., Asia Resource Center, 1990

Cayer, Marc. *Prisoner in Vietnam*. Washington, D.C., Asia Resource Center, 1990

Finnell, Loren. *Still a Country Boy: After Embracing the World* From Peace Corps Volunteer to Founder & CEO of the Resource Foundation, A Life of Service, Mayfair Publishing, 2011

Luce, Don and Sommer, John. *Vietnam. The Unheard Voices*, Cornell University Press, 1969

Phillips, Rufus. *Why Vietnam Matters*. Annapolis, Naval Institute Press, 2008

Poole, Richard. *The Inca Smiled*. Oxford, Oneworld Publications, 1993

Rawlings, Stuart, Editor. *The IVS Experience from Algeria to Vietnam*. Washington, D.C., IVS, 1992

Schanche, Don A. *Mister Pop, the Adventures of a Peaceful Man in a Small War*. New York, David McKay Company, Inc., 1970

Vang Pao, Gen. *The 1945-1975 War in Laos & the Plight of the Lao Refugee*. Publication date and location unknown.

Thomas, Winburn T. *The Vietnam Story of International Voluntary Services, Inc.* Washington, D.C., IVS, 1972

Weldon, Charles, MD. *Tragedy in Paradise-A Country Doctor at War in Laos*. Bangkok, Asia Books, 1999

REPORTS

(Many of the reports listed are available from the The Mennonite Church USA Archives held in Goshen, Indiana, on the Goshen College campus.)

Appleby, Gordon; Richey, John; de Yanes, Martha Cruz: *International Voluntary Services, Inc. Mid-Term Program Evaluation under Cooperative Agreement ORT-158-A-008156-00. Washington*, D.C. AED, 1991

Beery, Galen S. *A Brief History of International Voluntary Services*. Washington, D.C., IVS, 1969

Peters, Richard J. *The IVS/VN Aggie Experience in Retrospect*. Santa Fe, IVS, 2005

Reuss, Henry S. Hon. (D/Wisc.) *What a Peace Corps Man Could Do Overseas*. Washington, D.C. Congressional Record-Appendix, March 3, 1961

Rodell, Paul A. *John S. Noffsinger & the Global Impact of the Thomasite Experience*. Washington, D.C.

Shirk, Anne D. *International Voluntary Services, 1959-1998*, Presented at Portland, Oregon, during 45th anniversary Celebration. Portland, OR, 1998

Shirk, Anne D. *International Voluntary Services, 1953-2003*. Harpers Ferry, Final Report to the Board of Directors, IVS, 2003

Zigler, Robert. "An Interview with Dale D. Clark, October 14, 1998." Washington, D.C. Association for Diplomatic Studies and Training, Foreign Affairs Oral History Collection, Foreign Assistance Series, 2010

International Voluntary Services Report of 1995 Activities. Washington, D.C., IVS, 1996.

International Voluntary Services: A Strategy for the 1990s. Washington, D.C., IVS

IVS in Bangladesh. IVS, Washington, D.C., 1996.

International Voluntary Services Alumni Association Directory of Former Volunteers. IVSAA, Kennett Square, PA, 2012

NEWSPAPERS & MAGAZINES

The Grange News. "Granger Helps Refugee Arabs to Better Life." Washington, April 10, 1965

Malia, James E. "We Want to Build; They Want to Destroy." *Southeast Review of Asian Studies*, Vol. XX 89-100, 1998

NEWSLETTERS

Archer, Jim and De Pedro, Freddie. "Raising Ducks in Bangladesh, Parts I & II." *Washington. D.C. Dialogue*, IVS, Winter/Spring 1978-79.

Developments from International Voluntary Services. Various Vol. IVS, Washington, D.C.

IVS Alum Link, Newsletter of the IVS Alumni Association. Various Vols. Kennett Square, PA

Annual Reports, Vietnam, IVS

MISCELLANEOUS SOURCES

Bell, Douglas I. *Stuck in the Middle: International Voluntary Services and the Humanitarian Experience in Vietnam, 1957–1971*. http://douglasibell.com/2012/07/

IVS Authors

IVS authors have contributed a great deal to the literature of development. Among them are:

Fred Branfman
The Third Indochina War. Bertrand Russell Peace Foundation, Nottingham, UK, 1973
With Joel Martin Halpern and James A. Hafner. *The Old Man: A Biographical Account of a Lao Villager.* [Amherst]: International Area Studies Program, University of Massachusetts at Amherst, 1979
Voices from The Plain of Jars, Life Under an Air War. Harper & Row, Harper Colophon Books, 1972
Life under the Bombs. Washington, D. C., Project Air War, 1972
The Village of the Deep Pond, Ban Xa Phang Meuk, Laos. International Area Studies Programs, University of Massachusetts Amherst, 1978

Marc Cayer
Prisoner in Vietnam. Asia Resource Center, 1990

Loren Finnell
Still a Country Boy after Embracing the World. Mayhaven Publishing, Inc. 2011

Frank Huffman
Monks and Motorcycles, From Laos to London by the Seat of my Pants, 1956-1958. iUniverse, Inc. 2004

Jill Hunting
Finding Pete: Rediscovering the Brother I Lost in Vietnam. Wesleyan, 2009

Howard Lewin
Sunsets, Bulldozers, and Elephants: Twelve Years in Laos, the Stories I never Told. Hawthorne, CA 2004

Don Luce and John Sommer
Vietnam, The Unheard Voices. Cornell University Press, 1969

Harvey Neese and John O'Donnell
Prelude to Tragedy: Vietnam, 1960-1965. Naval Institute Press, 2000

Dave Nuttle
The Universal Survival Handbook. David A. Nuttle Survival Association, 1979

Richard Poole

The Inca Smiled. ONEWORLD Publications, UK, 1993).
The Camel Strayed. (Bloozoo Publications UK 1999).
The Day of the Dragon. (Bloozoo Publications, UK August 2001).
Mankind's Last Chance. (O-Books, JHP Publications, September 2013).

Stuart Rawlings

The IVS Experience—From Algeria to Vietnam. International Voluntary
Services, Inc. 1992

Don A. Schanche

Mister Pop. David McKay Company, Inc. 1970

John G. Sommer

Beyond Charity: U.S. Voluntary aid for a Changing Third World.
Overseas Development Council, 1977

Charlie Sweet, Elliott R. Morss, John K. Hatch, Donald R. Micklewait

*Strategies for Small Farmer Development - 0891580174 Empirical Study
of Rural Development Projects (Gambia, Ghana, Lesotho, Nigheria,
Bolivia, Colombia, Mexico, Paraguay, Peru: Vol. 1.* Westview Press,
1976

ACRONYMS

AFSC	American Friends Service Committee
ARVN	Army of the Republic of Vietnam
BUTSI	Badan Urusan Tenaga Kerja Sukarela Indonesia
BVS	Brethren Volunteer Service
BVSO	British Voluntary Service Overseas
CAPS	Caribbean Advisory and Professional Services
CARE	Cooperative for American Remittances to Europe
CIA	Central Intelligence Agency
CIDG	Civilian Irregular Defense Group
CO	Conscientious Objector
CRS	Catholic Relief Services
CUSO	Canadian University Services Overseas
CWS	Church World Service
ESL	English as a Second Language
FAR	Forces Armées du Royaume
FAS	Foreign Agricultural Service
FAT	Forward Area Teams
FIVDB	Friends in Village Development
GNP	Gross National Product
GVN	Government of Vietnam
ICA	International Cooperative Agreement
ICC	Commission Internationale de Contrôle
IED	Improvised Explosive Device
IFYE	International Farm Youth Exchange
IRC	International Rescue Committee
IRDP	Integrated Rural Development Program
IRRI	International Rice Research Institute
JCRR	Joint Commission on Rural Reconstruction
MAAG	Military Assistance Advisory Group
MACV	Military Assistance Command Vietnam
NEC	National Education Center
NGO	Non-government organization
NLF	National Liberation Front
NVA	North Vietnamese Army
OFDA	Office of U.S. Foreign Disaster
PACT	Private Agencies Collaborating Together

PC	Peace Corps
PCV	Peace Corps volunteer
PFP	Point Four Program
PL	Pathet Lao
PVO	Private Voluntary Organization
RLA	Royal Lao Army
RLG	Royal Lao Government
RVN	Republic of Vietnam
SCS	Soil Conservation Service
UNICEF	United Nations Children's Fund
UNRWA	United Nations Relief and Works Agency for Palestinian Refugees
USAID	United States Agency for International Development
USDA	United States Department of Agriculture
USIS	United States Information Service
USMCPLC	United States Marine Corps Platoon Leader Class
USOM	United States Operations Mission
UXO	Unexploded Ordnance
VARDA	Voluntary assistance for Rural Development Activities
VC	Viet Cong
VNCS	Vietnam Christian Services
VTC	Vocational and Technical School
YMCA	Young Men's Christian Association

Qui Nhon, 50-51

Quill, Dianna, 161, 163-164

R

Ralston, Wendell, 32-33

Rawlings, Stuart, xv, 71, 133-134

Reuss, Henry, xxi, 57, 62

Rhade 43, 47, 325-326, 328-333,

Ridenour, George 226

Ridenour, Nancy Felthousen
225-226

Rigby, John, 352

Roberts, Susan, 260

Rodell, Paul, xv, 40

Ronk, Don, 84

Ross, Charles and Louise, 80

Royal Lao Army (RLA), 33, 167,
210

Royal Lao Government (RLG),
174, 226-228, 232

Rufener, Bill, 154-155

Rupel, Martha, 28, 33-34, 354

S

Savannakhet, 37, 135, 173, 176,
182, 263

Schmidt, Don, 62, 65

Searl, Clyde, 33

Secret war, 170, 172, 176, 188,
190

Seraile, William, 137-138

Shaqlawa, 28-31

Shimkin, Alexander D., 125, 356

Shirk, Anne, xiii, xv, 241, 352

Siem Reap, 91, 223,

Sihanouk, Norodom, 36, 85, 149,
151-153, 162, 217, 222-223

Simmons, Charlie, 152

Sinkler, Max, 356

Sisk, Richard M., 356

Sitzer, Lew, 174, 203-204

Smock, David R., 352

Sneeden, Susan, 240

Soltysik, Carol and Fred, 255

Sommer, John, 80-81, 102-103,
148

Song Hong, 207-208

Steiner, Ken, 182

Stevens, Stephanie Merritt, 177,
179-180

Stevenson, Russell, 240, 242, 352

Stillman, Arthur, 202, 230, 356

Stoltzfus, Gene, 84, 148

Stone, Jane, 211

Stone, Steve, 212-213

Stung Keo, 152

Sucromo, 55

Sumner, Don, 44, 48-49

Svanoe, Vic, 124

Sweeny, Roger, 69

Szadek, Steve, 219

T

Tan Quoi, 126

Tay Ninh, 122-124, 127

Terry, Beth, 266

Tet, 77, 84, 85, 100-102, 112,
117-118, 123, 131, 133, 135,
137, 141, 143, 146, 206, 339

Thayer, Carlyle, 117

Thomas, Winburn, 271, 274

Thomasites, x, 23-24

Time, 116, 217, 220

Tisa, Benedict, 274-275

Tizi Ouzou, 248, 280-281

Tlemcen, 245-246, 248, 250-252

Townsend, Mildred and Ralph,
274

Troyer, Kristin, 173

Truman, Harry S., 24-25

Tufts, Thomas, 182, 209

U

U.S. Marine Corps (USMC),
214-215

U.S. Operations Mission (USOM),
ix, 33

ABOUT THE AUTHOR

Thierry J. Sagnier is a writer and Pushcart Prize Nominee whose works have been published in major newspapers and reviews in the United States and abroad. He is the author of *The IFO Report* (Avon Books), *Bike! Motorcycles and the People who Ride Them* (Harper & Row) and *Washington by Night* (Washingtonian Books). His short story, *Lunch with the General*, published in *Chrysalis Reader*, was nominated for a 2013 Pushcart Prize, an American literary prize that honors the best "poetry, short fiction, essays or literary whatnot published in the small presses." He is also the author of two online works published by Pigasus Books: *Thirst*, a thriller based in Washington, D.C.'s mean streets, and *Writing about People, Places and Things*, a collection of essays chronicling his thoughts on writing, family and friendships, and his bout with cancer.

He was Senior Writer with the World Bank, has traveled widely and written magazine, newspaper articles, documentary films and radio scripts about development issues. He lives in Virginia.

ABOUT NCNM Press

NCNM Press, a division of National College of Natural Medicine, publishes distinctive titles that enrich the history, clinical practice, and contemporary significance of natural medicine traditions. As well, the Press strives with its titles to recognize historical and contemporary best practices in environmental, global health, and sustainability research and history.

NCNM (National College of Natural Medicine, Portland, Oregon) was founded in 1956. It is the longest serving, accredited naturopathic college in North America and home to one of the two U.S. accredited graduate research programs in Integrative Medicine. NCNM is also home to one of North America's most unique classical Chinese medicine programs, embracing lineage and a powerful mentoring model for future practitioners. Its rare book collection on natural medicine is the largest and most complete of its kind in North America.

CPSIA information can be obtained at www.ICGtesting.com
Printed in the USA
LVOW11s1517300815

452097LV00001B/346/P